3D STUDIO MAX® 3
MEDIA ANIMATION

JOHN P. CHISMAR

New Riders

201 West 103rd Street, Indianapolis, Indiana 46290

3D Studio MAX 3 Media Animation

International Standard Book Number: 0-7357-0050-8

Library of Congress Catalog Card Number: 99-90474

Printed in the United States of America

First Printing: July, 1999

03   02   01   00   99   7   6   5   4   3   2   1

Interpretation of the printing code: The rightmost double-digit number is the year of the book's printing; the rightmost single-digit number is the number of the book's printing. For example, the printing code 99-1 shows that the first printing of the book occurred in 1999.

Trademarks

Warning and Disclaimer

Executive Editor
Steve Weiss

Acquisitions Editor
Laura Frey

Development Editor
Barb Terry

Managing Editor
Sarah Kearns

Project Editor
Caroline Wise

Copy Editor
Audra McFarland

Indexer
Craig Small

Technical Editor
Larry Minton

Software Development Specialist
Jason Haines

Cover Designer
Karen Ruggles

Interior Designer
Louisa Klucznik

Proofreader
Elise Walter

Layout Technician
Steve Balle-Gifford

Graphic Conversion Technician
Tammy Graham

Contents at a Glance

Table of Contents

Real World Case Studies

About the Author

John P. Chismar has been working in computer animation since 1991. His primary focus has been in the broadcast industry, creating 3D animation for television news. His most recent position, held since the network's inception, is with MSNBC as Senior 3D Animator. 3D Studio has been his tool of choice for 3D design and animation since the release of 2.0 DOS. Awards for John's work include the following:

- A 1998 Emmy Award for Individual Achievement in a Craft in News and Documentary Programming: Graphic Designers.
- Three Broadcast Design Association International Bronze awards in the categories of Total Package Design, Full Screen Graphic, and Promo or ID.
- *3D Design* magazine's 1998 Big Kahuna Award for Best Logo/Corporate ID.
- A 1995-96 Emmy Nomination for Outstanding Individual Achievement Graphic Artist/Animator.

Acknowledgments

I want to say "Thank you" to the following people for their advice and support:

Amy Beth Jackson: For always being there to discuss ideas and proofread chapters, and for making the authoring experience so enjoyable.

Vince Diga: For listening to my ideas and offering constructive input and organization.

Victor Newman: For offering what free time he had to design the V project.

Francine Izzo and Tsukasa Endo: For helping to create the .avi files for the real-world examples.

Christo Manco: For creating the Eyes Adobe Illustrator file for Hidden Eyes and for appearing as a criminal for the Hidden Eyes filmstrip.

Matt Wisner: For appearing as Christo's criminal counterpart on the Hidden Eyes filmstrip.

Jonathan Burleson: For generating ideas to include in the book by asking, "How did you do that?" while at work.

John "Gonzo" Gonzalez: For his theatrical lighting expertise.

Barb Terry and Laura Frey: For their hard work, help, and patience. They made writing this book a pleasure.

Larry Minton: For his careful and professional technical edit.

MSNBC and NBC: For their support and cooperation.

Discreet: For creating the greatest 3D software and for all the help they kindly provided with the software.

New Riders Publishing: For providing the opportunity to write this book. Also, a great big thanks extended to everyone who helped to make this book that much better.

John J. and Joan Chismar: For their constant encouragement. They always were there to say, "You can do anything you set your mind to." I love yas!

Tell Us What You Think!

As the reader of this book, *you* are our most important critic and commentator. We value your opinion and want to know what we're doing right, what we could do better, what areas you'd like to see us publish in, and any other words of wisdom you're willing to pass our way.

As the Executive Editor for the Graphics team at New Riders Publishing, I welcome your comments. You can fax, email, or write me directly to let me know what you did or didn't like about this book—as well as what we can do to make our books stronger.

Please note that I cannot help you with technical problems related to the topic of this book, and that due to the high volume of mail I receive, I might not be able to reply to every message.

When you write, please be sure to include this book's title and author, as well as your name and phone or fax number. I will carefully review your comments and share them with the author and editors who worked on the book. Thanks.

Fax: 317-581-4663

Email: newriders@mcp.com

Mail: Steve Weiss
Executive Editor
Professional Graphics & Web Design Group
New Riders Publishing
201 West 103rd Street
Indianapolis, IN 46290 USA

Introduction

Just a few years back, I was a young animator willing to do anything to get a job in the field of 3D animation. I worked for minimum wage, and I even worked for free—anything to get my portfolio and professional working experience started.

In my thirst for knowledge, I bought magazines, books, and training videos, hoping to get more information to develop my style and skill. It didn't take long to figure out that these materials weren't providing me with the necessary information to launch a successful career. My determination forced me to explore and experiment with the available software in an effort to re-create the beautiful animations the pros were making. After more than eight years of experimentation, wandering through the vast capabilities of 3D, I have learned a great deal about the best ways to create animations. I think it's time I share this valuable information with you.

Welcome to *3D Studio MAX 3 Media Animation,* the first book of its kind. While learning inside tricks and techniques, you will also learn how to correctly plan your projects to streamline the production process and make them "edit-friendly." You will gain insight about pre-production and post-production processes. I am going to share with you the experience I have gained, my insight into successful design in 3D, and the working style that enables me to produce high-quality animations.

What Is Media Animation?

Media animation is the rapidly growing industry that provides graphic content for television, print, Internet, and every other multimedia format imaginable. The industry demands original content under tight deadlines. In this fast-paced industry where the speed of technology pushes your skills to the edge, people working in the field need a deep understanding of the tools available to them and must know how to create cutting-edge effects on-the-fly.

Many animators in the corporate world complain that the "powers that be" think the animator clicks a "Make Animation" button and a wonderful animation manifests itself. It's true that those in management often misunderstand the term *computer animation*; they don't understand the amount work that is actually involved. Because of this misunderstanding, the animator must be prepared, must have the ability to create any type of animation or effect that is expected of him, and must be able to edit and change his work quickly.

Who Needs This Book?

Many computer graphic students learn just enough of 3D Studio MAX to make bare-bones animations and are left feeling dissatisfied with their end products. Not anymore.

This industry has many one-person graphic departments, and (believe me) I know what that's like. With no resources available to help the lonely animators, they are forced to load pre-made scenes or geometry. Not anymore.

An inexperienced animator who manages to land a job in a big-name design company has hopes of learning from the pros on the staff. Unfortunately, the pros who know the tricks don't have the time to share their expertise with new employees; they are too busy working on their projects.

In this book, however, a pro is going to take the time to share what he knows so that you can quickly create sophisticated, fascinating animations on your own.

What Does This Book Offer?

3D Studio MAX 3 Media Animation is unique because it provides 3D Studio Max animators with the working knowledge to better perform their jobs. You don't just walk blindly through steps to make prefab effects that have only a specific use. This book helps you create compelling animations with predictable rendering results, in a very short amount of production time. As you read this book, complete the exercises, and examine the sample files, you will learn how to think more creatively, plan your animations, and effectively build your projects.

The collection of sample files on the accompanying CD and the scenes you will create during the exercises are valuable reference resources. Simply refer to the samples when you later need to determine what sort of effects or moves you want to use in your animations. Then refresh your mind with the techniques you used to create them, and you're off and running. You'll probably even find yourself adding your own new discoveries and cool sample files, and you'll end up with quite a resource library as your experience and career progresses.

How Is This Book Organized?

3D Studio MAX 3 Media Animation is organized into four parts:

- Project 1: The Hidden Eyes Logo
- Project 2: Gravity Zone
- Project 3: The V
- Real-World Case Studies

This book takes readers from start to finish through three different levels of artistic direction.

Project 1, "The Hidden Eyes Logo," has a moderate level of outside artistic direction. A designer carefully designed the logo and has verbally communicated the mood and colors to be used to create the animation.

Project 2, "Gravity Zone," provides almost no outside artistic direction. The client knows what he wants to say; however, he wants us to transform his wish list into an animation. Artistic direction is in our hands.

Project 3, "The V," is entirely storyboarded in full color, providing complete outside artistic direction. It is up to us to take these still images and put them into motion.

In the section "Real World Case Studies," we take a behind the scenes look at how certain three 3D animations were created in the real world.

This book structures the projects so you are placed into the mind of an animator. Approaches to modeling, animating, effects, rendering, and compositing are described in full detail, along with choreography, composition, and color. The purpose of these projects is to help you create your own animations and to develop your own style without spending years in independent study.

What Are the Goals of the Exercises?

An essential element to getting projects completed on time and edited accurately and easily is the development of good working habits. Along with sharing technical knowledge, I've written the exercises so they expose you to the time-tested processes, which organize everything from creating geometry to final renderings. By working through the exercises, you learn these basic principles:

- *Economize.* Create your objects using only as many polygons as necessary to produce the desired rendered output. Keep your scenes uncluttered. Use lights wisely. Organize your track editor and your hierarchies.

- *Use logical naming conventions.* Give all the elements in your scene unique descriptive names so that they will be easily located for adjustments. This applies to everything from materials and modifiers to geometry, lights, and cameras.

- *Save files.* Save your work frequently, and give a file a different name each time you reach a point where enough has been changed and you are happy with the results to the point that you wouldn't want to have to redo it. Having the progression of a project at different stages is very handy when changes are necessary.

- *Test.* Create test renders frequently during setup to cut down on rework time. This also cuts down on the time it takes to locate a problem that occurs in the finalization stages of a project.
- *Identify problems.* When viewing a test render, study it carefully. Look at it frame by frame. Check the way the light hits the objects, and make sure that the motion is smooth. Look for anomalies in the output, and make sure the materials are applied correctly.

How Should You Work with the Files on the CD?

To organize your work with the exercises, I highly recommend that you create the following directory structure on your hard drive:

Example: Drive:\tut_work\

Before starting a chapter, you should create a subfolder for the chapter and a maps subfolder within that chapter folder. Then copy the CD chapter's maps folder into your new maps folder on your local drive.

Example: Drive:\tut_work\ch01\maps\

You should also create an images subfolder to render your scenes to:

Example: Drive:\tut_work\ch01\images

Throughout the book, I abbreviate the drive:\tut_work\ch01\maps directory structure as ch01\maps.

Personal Statement

In my opinion, a book of this type is way overdue. For more than two years, I wrestled with the idea of writing a book like this, but I struggled with not wanting to take time from my own explorations and a little reluctance to reveal the secrets of my expertise. I finally decided that, in this fast-paced occupation, we can't afford to spend time leafing through the same old tutorials which have been rephrased to be current. We need to share ideas and information to push 3D design further. Our combined knowledge will take the world of 3D animation to new levels. Thank you for joining me in this pursuit!

Security camera film snakes to left. Has criminals caught in act.

Film continues moving left as hidden eye logo enters from right.

Film continues moving. Logo centers in frame. Eyelids open.

Project I
The Hidden Eye Logo

Film continues moving.
Logo centered.
Eyeball scans.

designed by Vince Diga

Chapter 1

Making the Filmstrip

Over the course of the next four chapters, we will be creating a logo animation for the Hidden Eyes detective agency. The logo will be displayed over a background that consists of a filmstrip with images of criminals caught in the act.

The mood we are trying to convey with this animation is eerie and full of suspense. We want all those criminals to be shaking in their boots as they view the animation. We want the good guys to have faith in Hidden Eyes, so the animation must be solid and slick.

Creating the Filmstrip

The first step toward creating this logo animation is to create the filmstrip background. The filmstrip background is going to create the mood and environment for the logo object. The dramatically lit filmstrip object, along with the smoky dark background, will create the perfect stage for the logo.

Constructing the Filmstrip

The background is a snaking piece of film animated along a path. The filmstrip frames show different surveillance images slowly drifting along its length, and the sprocket holes will be blurred to indicate that the film is moving at a high rate of speed.

Exercise 1.1   Creating the Spline for the Filmstrip

To begin the process, we need to create a spline that will act as the path for the filmstrip object to follow. To create the path spline, we will use keyboard entry. A camera will also be created in this section.

1. Reset MAX.
2. From Create, Shapes, select Line. Then, in the Creation Method rollout, set Initial Type to **Smooth**. Maximize the Top viewport using the Min/Max Toggle.
3. Open the Keyboard Entry rollout, enter XYZ values of [**225,75,55**], and then click Add Point.

> **Note**
>
> When you click the Add Point button, a point is created. Enter the XYZ values before you click Add Point.

4. Enter the following fourteen points, remembering to click Add Point after entering each set of coordinates:

   Point 2: XYZ [**90,–15,15**]

   Point 3: XYZ [**25,–30,–10**]

   Point 4: XYZ [**25,10,20**]

   Point 5: XYZ [**80,35,10**]

   Point 6: XYZ [**55,75,5**]

   Point 7: XYZ [**15,45,–10**]

Point 8: XYZ [**–20,65,–20**]

Point 9: XYZ [**10,115,–20**]

Point 10: XYZ [**–50,150,–25**]

Point 11: XYZ [**–95,70,–20**]

Point 12: XYZ [**–20,30,–15**]

Point 13: XYZ [**–5,–20,5**]

Point 14: XYZ [**–85,–90,20**]

Point 15: XYZ [**–200,15,15**]

5. Click Finish and name this spline object **Film_Path** (see Figure 1.1).

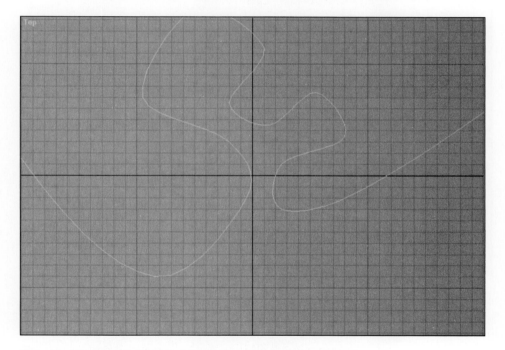

Figure 1.1   The Film_Path spline object in the maximized Top viewport.

A spline shape snakes through the maximized Top Viewport.

Exercise 1.2   Creating a Camera

Next, we will create a camera to properly view the Film_Path shape.

1. Minimize the Top viewport, activate Create, Cameras, and create a Free camera in the Front viewport.

2. Activate the Perspective viewport and press the C key to change the viewport from Perspective to Camera01 view.

3. Activate and right-click the Select and Move icon to open the Move Transform Type-In dialog box. Enter the following values in the Absolute:World field to position the camera correctly: XYZ [**–170,–155,70**].

4. Click the Select and Rotate icon. This changes the Move Transform Type-In to Rotate Transform Type-In. Enter the following values in the Absolute:World field to rotate the camera to view the spline correctly: XYZ [**65.5,–16,–30**]. Your Camera viewport should look like the one in Figure 1.2.

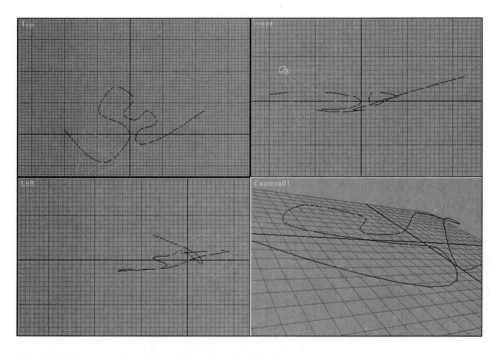

Figure 1.2   The correct position and rotation for Camera01.

5. Save your work as **ch01-01.max.**

Exercise 1.3   Creating the Filmstrip Object

Now that the path for the film exists, it's time to build the filmstrip object that will conform to this path and snake along it. The object will be a primitive box with lots of segments along its length so it will have enough faces to bend and curve along the path.

1. If you do not have ch01-01.max loaded from the previous section, load the file now.

2. In Create, Geometry, select Box. Then create a box in the Front viewport and change the box's values to the following:

> Length: **40**
>
> Width: **1**
>
> Height: **1100**
>
> Length Segs: **1**
>
> Width Segs: **1**
>
> Height Segs: **200**

This gives the geometry plenty of faces along its length to bend and curve (see Figure 1.3).

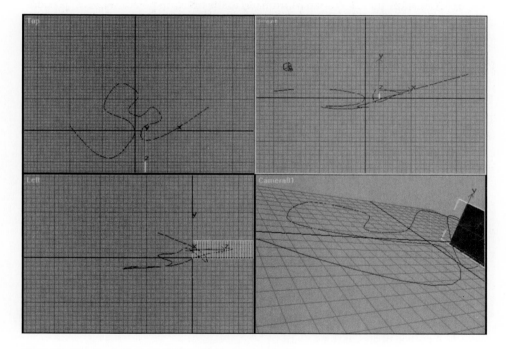

Figure 1.3   The Box object created in the Front viewport.

 Note

You will be applying a Path Deform to the box object to make the filmstrip snake through the scene. The reason you added so many Height Segs to the box in step 3 is that you will be deforming the box along its height or Z axis.

3. Name this object **Filmstrip** and save your work as **ch01-02.max**.

The filmstrip object we just created does not have sprocket holes. We can model them by using Boolean operations, or we can simply apply an opacity map to the object to simulate the sprocket holes. Using Boolean operations will add unnecessary faces to the filmstrip object, making it hard to work with in real time in the viewport. Boolean operations also affect the layout of the faces on the object, possibly opening the door for anomalies to show up when we deform the object on the path. Therefore, using an opacity map is certainly the most predictable way to create the sprocket holes. The opacity map may increase rendering time, but we know the result will be correct on the first try.

Finishing the Filmstrip Object

Before we can apply the UVW Map coordinates to the filmstrip object, we need to examine what types of texture maps are going to be applied. We will definitely need to apply UVW Map coordinates for the images on the filmstrip. We will also need to apply an opacity map to the filmstrip to cut the sprocket holes. Then we'll deform the filmstrip.

Exercise 1.4   Examining the Textures

Let's take a second to look at the textures we are going to apply to the filmstrip object. First, we'll look at SpyCam1.jpg, the image that produces the negatives on the filmstrip.

1. From Files, View, load SpyCam1.jpg from the ch01\maps directory of the accompanying CD. A portion of the file is shown in Figure 1.4.

Figure 1.4   A portion of SpyCam1.jpg.

SpyCam1.jpg is a long strip of surveillance images, in which the images travel from left to right. This means that the UVW Map gizmo on the filmstrip object must be applied so that the left and right of the image match left and right on the filmstrip (see Figure 1.5).

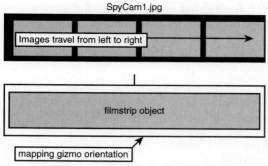

Figure 1.5   The correct UVW Map application for SpyCam1.jpg

Now let's examine the sprocket hole texture, hole.jpg.

2. From Files, select View, and choose hole.jpg, the sprocket hole image we will use to cut the sprocket holes from the filmstrip.

   Hmm. If we use the same UVW Map coordinates for hole.jpg that we used for the SpyCam1.jpg image, we will not achieve the desired result. The sprocket holes would be on the left and right of the filmstrip, not the top and bottom (see Figure 1.6).

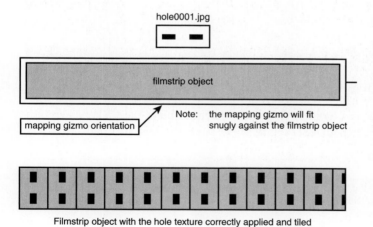

Figure 1.6   The sprocket holes are incorrect if you use the SpyCam1.jpg UVW Map coordinates for hole.jpg.

Luckily for us, we can apply up to 99 different UVW Map coordinates per element in 3D Studio MAX. We will simply apply two UVW Map modifiers, each with a unique Map Channel, which gives us two separate UVW Map coordinates on the filmstrip object to choose from. The first UVW Map modifier we apply will be for SpyCam1.jpg.

3. Load ch01-02.max, select the filmstrip object, open the Modify panel, and apply a UVW Map modifier. Click Zoom Extents All Selected.

4. In the Alignment group, choose X and click Fit. The UVW Map gizmo is now applied correctly for SpyCam1.jpg (see Figure 1.7).

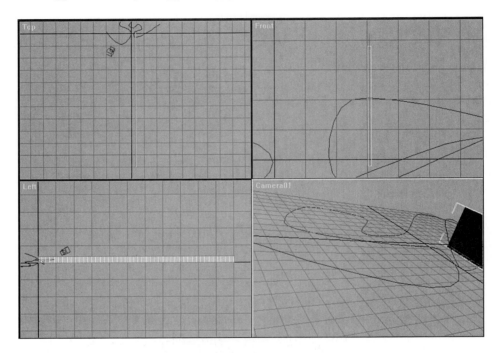

Figure 1.7   The UVW Map is in correct position for SpyCam1.jpg.

Notice that the Map Channel is 1 in the Channel group of the UVW Map modifier. We will need to remember this when we apply the SpyCam1.jpg.

Tip

Usually when I am working on a project, I keep notes on a pad of paper reminding me what UVW Map Channels I've used for what maps. This is easy to reference and keeps me from having to guess later in production.

Next we will apply the UVW Map modifier to create the mapping coordinates for the sprocket hole map.

5. From the Modify panel, apply another UVW Map modifier. In the Alignment group, choose Y and click Fit.

The UVW Map is placed correctly along the length of the filmstrip object, but in the Front viewport we can see that it is pointing up and down. It needs to point left and right.

6. Activate Sub-Object/Gizmo and Angle Snap. Rotate the Gizmo 90 degrees in the Front viewport. Then, in the Alignment group of the UVW Map modifier, click Fit. Figure 1.8 shows the result.

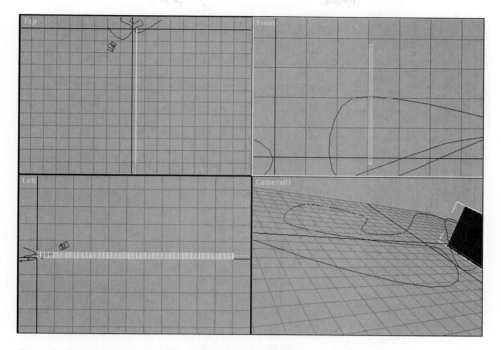

Figure 1.8 The UVW Map modifier for the sprocket hole image sequence.

The UVW Map is now in the correct position. Notice that the Map Channel is 1; it needs to be 2 to put the UVW Map coordinates on that channel.

Note

If we left the value at 1, the second UVW Map modifier's coordinates would override the previous UVW Map settings. Changing the value to 2 gives you the option of choosing the coordinates for UVW Map 1 or 2 in the Material Editor.

7. In the Channel group of the UVW Map modifier, change the Map Channel to **2**. Deactivate Sub-Object.

Exercise 1.5 Deforming the Filmstrip

The next step is to assign the filmstrip object to the spline so that it snakes the object through the scene. After we apply the deform to the filmstrip, we can add materials to the object to make the filmstrip look reel—oh, I mean real.

1. Make sure the filmstrip object is selected. Then, in the Modify panel, click More and select PathDeform from the WORLD-SPACE MODIFIERS (see Figure 1.9). Click OK to add the modifier.

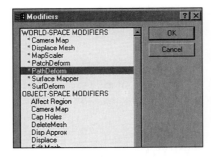

Figure 1.9   Select PathDeform from the WORLD-SPACE MODIFIERS.

2. In the Path Deform Parameters rollout, click Pick Path and click the Film_Path shape. Make sure the Path Deform Axis is set to Z and click Move to Path. The Filmstrip object should wind nicely through the camera viewport at this point (see Figure 1.10).

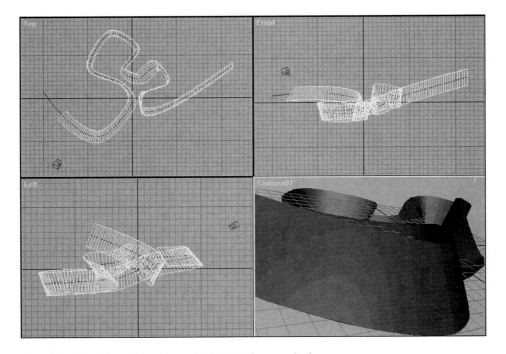

Figure 1.10   The Film_Strip object with Path Deform applied.

3. Save your work as **ch01-03.max**.

Applying the Filmstrip Material

Now that the path-deformed filmstrip has been created and the UVW Map coordinates are applied, we can begin to apply the materials. First we will apply the sprocket hole opacity map to the filmstrip. After the holes are opacity mapped, we can add the SpyCam1.jpg to the object.

Exercise 1.6   Applying the Material

It is time to apply the sprocket hole opacity map to the filmstrip object you created earlier. This will make the filmstrip object appear to have sprocket holes cut in it when the scene is rendered.

1. Load ch01-03.max, the filmstrip you created earlier.

2. Open the Material Editor, activate the first material slot, and name the material **Filmstrip**.

   Let's change the shader type and add some highlights to the material.

3. Select the Filmstrip object and click Assign Material to Selection to assign the material to the filmstrip. In the Shader rollout, choose Multi-Layer.

4. Now we will add specular highlights to the material. Enter these values:

   First Specular Layer group

   　Color: RGB (**250,250,250**)

   　Level: **100**

   　Glossiness: **65**

   Second Specular Layer group

   　Color: RGB (**80,90,180**)

   　Level: **50**

   　Glossiness: **35**

   These settings will make the filmstrip look shiny by producing sharp highlights.

5. Render frame 0 through the Camera01 viewport. It should look like Figure 1.11.

6. To make the material seem more metallic, enter a Diffuse Level of **50**. Render the Camera01 viewport again.

   Because we will be working with opacity, it would be smart to change the background color. This will help us see the effect on the material when we render the Camera01 viewport.

7. From the Rendering menu item, open the Environment dialog box (see Figure 1.12).

8. Click the Color swatch to open the Color Selector and enter RGB (**125,125,125**). Then close the Environment dialog box.

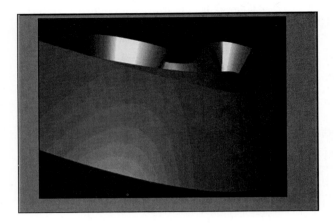

Figure 1.11   Frame 0 rendered through the Camera01 viewport.

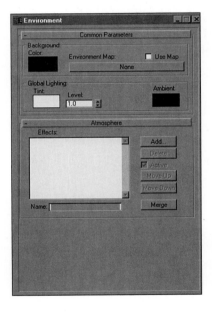

Figure 1.12   The Environment dialog box.

Exercise 1.7   Adding the Opacity Map to the Material

Next, we will add the sprocket hole opacity map to our material. Then we'll check the sprocket hole opacity map to make sure it is applied correctly.

1. In the Material Editor with the Filmstrip material active, open the Maps rollout and click the Opacity button to open the Material/Map Browser (see Figure 1.13).

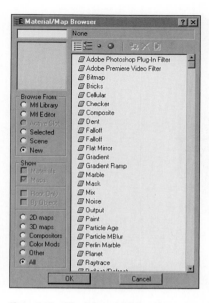

Figure 1.13   The Material/Map Browser.

2. Choose Bitmap from the Material/Map Browser and click OK to exit.

3. In the Select Bitmap Image File dialog box, navigate to ch01\maps, select hole.jpg, and click Open to close the window. In the Image File List Control dialog box, click OK to accept its default settings. Name this opacity map **Fstrip-opc**.

4. Click the Background button in the Material Editor to see a colored checkered background in the material preview.

   It seems as though we did something quite wrong and the entire material has disappeared. Actually, the opacity map that was rendered needs to be inverted (make black white and white black).

5. Open the Output rollout in the Material Editor and check Invert. Now we see the solid preview ball in the material preview. Although the holes are there, they can't be seen.

6. Render Frame 0 of the Camera01 viewport (see Figure 1.14).

   Hmmm, that's an awfully large sprocket hole in the middle of our filmstrip. Oh, wait a minute! We forgot to change the Map Channel to 2 so it is applied using the UVW Map coordinates from the second UVW Map modifier we applied to the filmstrip.

7. In the Coordinates rollout, change Map Channel to **2** and click Show Map in Viewport. Now in the shaded Camera view, the object has two stripes where the sprocket hole should be.

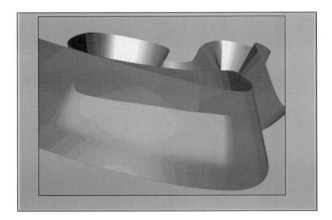

Figure 1.14 Frame 0 rendered.

The two stripes on the Film_Strip object are the two sprocket holes in the correct positions, but the holes are stretched the length of the strip. Let's add more holes.

8. In the Coordinates rollout of the Opacity Map, set the Tiling column V to **130**. This will add enough holes to the filmstrip.

9. The sprocket holes appear too close to the edges of the filmstrip. This is a simple adjustment. To adjust the spacing of the holes from the outer edge of the film, set Tiling U to **1.05**. The holes aren't so close to the edges now.

10. Now we can see the U tiling of the sprocket holes on the edge of the filmstrip, and we certainly don't want to see that. In order to hide the tiling of the map, uncheck U Tile. Now your image should look like Figure 1.15.

Figure 1.15 U Tile is unchecked.

Exercise 1.8   Animating the Sprocket Holes

The sprocket holes are not animated on the filmstrip object. The effect we want to create is that the filmstrip is moving quickly along the filmstrip path. To do so, we can animate the offset of the map. This will make the sprocket holes travel faster than the filmstrip object.

1. Advance to frame 30 and activate the Animate button. Enter a V Offset value of **.02**. Turn off the Animate button.

   Now the sprocket hole opacity map is animated to travel along the filmstrip through frames 0 through 30. We need to continue the animation of the sprocket holes beyond frame 30.

2. Open the Track View and expand the Scene Materials\Filmstrip\Maps\Opacity: Fstrip-opc\Coordinates track (see Figure 1.16).

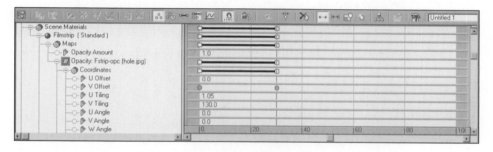

Figure 1.16   The Track View with the correct tracks expanded.

3. Select the V Offset track name and click Parameter Curve Out-of-Range types to open its dialog box. In the Param Curve Out-of-Range types dialog box, click Relative Repeat Out (as shown in Figure 1.17), and click OK to close the dialog box.

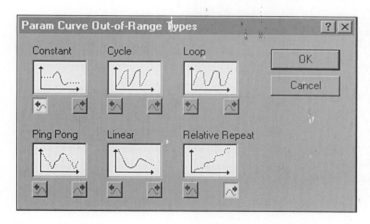

Figure 1.17   The Param Curve Out-of-Range Types dialog box with Relative Repeat Out selected.

4. Close the Track View, save your work as **ch01-04.max**, and return to frame 0.

Adding the Spy Cam Photos

Now we're ready to give this filmstrip object its pictures. For the animation, the filmstrip will have hidden camera shots of two thugs participating in an illegal after-hours business deal. Enough explanations—let's take a look at the suspects.

Exercise 1.9   Adding the Diffuse Map

We will now add SpyCam1.jpg to the Diffuse map slot to add the photos to the filmstrip.

1. With ch01-04.max still loaded, open the Material Editor and return to the parent level of the Filmstrip material.

2. In the Maps rollout, click the Diffuse Color button. Choose Bitmap from the Material/Map Browser and click OK to exit the browser. In the Select Bitmap Image File dialog box, choose SpyCam1.jpg (from the ch01\maps directory) and click Open to load the bitmap and close the dialog box. Name this map **Fstrip-dif**.

3. Render frame 0 of the Camera01 viewport (see Figure 1.18).

Figure 1.18   Camera01 viewport rendered.

The SpyCam1.jpg is applied to the filmstrip object, but two things are incorrect. The images extend past the sprocket holes, and the images are stretched along the length of the filmstrip. We need to fix those things now.

4. Click Show Map in Viewport to view SpyCam1.jpg on the filmstrip. Then, in the Coordinates rollout, change U Tiling to **2.3**. Changing the U Tiling to 2.3 makes the images less stretched along the length of the filmstrip.

Now we need to adjust the V Tiling to move the top and bottom edges away from the sprocket holes.

5. Change V Tiling to **1.4** and uncheck V Tile. We uncheck V Tile because we don't want the image to tile top to bottom. Render frame 0 from the Camera01 viewport.

The spy cam images now fit on the filmstrip nicely. However, because we unchecked V Tiling, we can now see the Diffuse color of the material in the areas of the filmstrip that SpyCam1.jpg no longer covers. To fix this, we need to change the Diffuse color of the material.

6. Click Go to Parent to return to the root of the material. In the Multi-Layer Basic Parameters rollout, change the Diffuse color to RGB (**0,0,0**). The black color matches the color of the edges of SpyCam1.jpg. Render frame 0 again to see the result, which is shown in Figure 1.19.

Figure 1.19   With the Diffuse color changed to RGB (0,0,0), the edges of the filmstrip match the color of SpyCam1.jpg.

Creating Transparency

The sprocket holes and photo images look pretty good on the filmstrip now. However, the effect of the filmstrip material would be much better if it were a little transparent. Here's the problem: An opacity map is already applied to the material. If we were to go to the parent level of the material and decrease the opacity map amount from 100 to 80, the film would not become more transparent; instead, the sprocket holes would become less transparent. That isn't the effect we want.

Exercise 1.10 Adjusting the Black

Originally, the opacity map was white sprocket holes on black. We realized this was wrong and inverted the map to correctly punch the holes in the filmstrip, so it is currently black holes on white. In order to make the film more transparent, we must somehow apply more black to the white. Although there are several ways to do so, I have chosen to use the following way because it provides versatility when adjusting the percent of black added.

1. The Material Editor should still be open. In the Maps rollout, click the Opacity button to open its settings.

2. Click the Type:Bitmap button. Then, from the Material/Map Browser dialog box, choose Mix, and click OK. In the Replace Map dialog, click Keep Old Map As Sub-Map? to keep the sprocket hole map and click OK to exit. Name this map **Fstrip-opc-mix**.

3. Drag the Black color swatch from Color #1 to Color #2 and choose Copy from the Copy or Swap Colors dialog box.

    The Mix type allows you to mix, or dissolve, between two colors or maps. The sprocket hole map is loaded in place of Color #1 and overrides the black color. Because no map is loaded for Color #2, the black color will be the other map. Now a Mix Amount needs to be added to the Mix type so we can mix between the sprocket hole IFL and the black color, adding more black to the sprocket hole map.

4. Change the Mix Amount to **30**. This adds 30% of Color #2 (the black color) over Color #1 (the sprocket hole map). You can see in the Material Editor's material preview that the material is more transparent (see Figure 1.20).

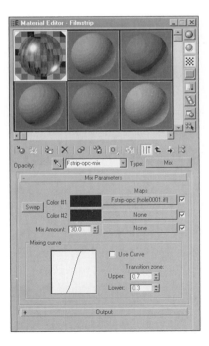

Figure 1.20 The filmstrip with a Mix applied at 30%.

5. Render frame 0 of the Camera viewport.

6. Save your work as **ch01-05.max**.

Masking the Sprocket Holes

Did I hear you say, "Hey! The sprocket holes aren't transparent where the specular high-lights are bright!"? The truth is, the sprocket holes *are* transparent. The problem is that the renderer knows there is really geometry there, and it applies the specular highlight over the sprocket holes. We need to apply the sprocket hole image sequence to the Specular Levels of the highlights to mask the sprocket holes.

Exercise 1.11   Adding a Map to Specular Layer 1

We will start by adding a map to Specular Layer 1.

1. With ch01-05.max loaded, open the Material Editor and return to the parent level of the Filmstrip material. Open the Maps rollout and click the Specular Level 1 button to open the Material/Map Browser. Browse From: Scene and select Fstrip-opc. Click OK to exit the browser, and then, at the Instance Or Copy? prompt, choose Instance and click OK.

2. Render frame 0 through the Camera01 viewport (see Figure 1.21).

Figure 1.21   The sprocket holes masked from Specular Layer 1.

Much better. The sprocket holes are now masked from Specular Layer 1. The luminance value (in percent) of the pixels in the map determines the value of the Specular Level. This means the white in the map is equal to a Level of 100, and the black in the image is equal to a Level of 0. Because the Level value was 100 before we placed the map on the material, we don't see a change in the highlight.

Exercise 1.12   Adding a Map to Specular Layer 2

This one is going to be a little tricky because its current value is 50. When we apply the map to the Specular Level, the white in the image is going to override the setting of 50 and change the level to 100, making the highlight much brighter. We will then have to fix that.

1. Click Go to Parent to return to the root of the material. In the Maps rollout, click the Specular Level 2 button to open the Material/Map Browser. Set Browse From: to Scene and choose Fstrip-opc. Click OK to close the browser. At the Instance Or Copy? prompt, choose Copy and click OK. Render frame 0 again.

   The sprocket holes are now punched through the filmstrip, but—as predicted—the highlight got brighter. We will need to apply a Mix to the map so we can add 50% black to the map and return the highlight to its original state.

2. Click the Type:Bitmap button to open the Material/Map Browser. Set Browse From: to New and choose Mix. Click OK to close the browser. In the Replace Map dialog box, choose Keep Old Map As Sub-Map? and click OK to close the dialog box. Copy Color 1 swatch to Color 2 and enter a Mix Amount of **50**. Then render frame 0 again. The highlight returns to its normal state.

3. Save your work as **ch01-06.max**.

Crash Course in Lighting

Lighting is a very critical part of the 3D animation process. However, it is often not taken seriously, and poor animation effects are the result. Why put all the work into creating great models, textures, and animation, and then forget about taking painstaking care with lighting?

Almost every 3D animator I have met, myself included, has a shortcoming in at least one aspect of the 3D animation process. For example, I have a great time building the models and applying the materials. Then, by the time it comes to lighting and animating the models, my interest in the project is not at its peak. However, it is very important to remember that work isn't always fun, and we are getting paid to create animations that represent a company, business, or television identity. Therefore, we must do our best work at *all* stages of a project.

Knowing the basic lighting principles speeds up the process of using correct lighting and helps you produce great results. The lighting for the filmstrip object is a perfect example of the basic lighting setup I use on a daily basis, which is generally the starting point for any studio lighting. It is called Three-Point Lighting.

As you could have guessed, Three-Point Lighting consists of three main lights:

- *Key light.* This is the main light, or Key light, of the scene. It should light the point of interest in the scene and is generally the brightest light. I generally place this light to the right of the scene.

- *Fill light.* This light illuminates the areas that the Key light leaves in shadow. It helps show detail in shadowed areas, and it softly lights the object. I generally place this light to the left of the scene.

- *Back light.* This is, ever so often, the forgotten light in a scene. The Back light is a light that is generally above and behind the object, and it catches the edges of objects to give them a slight halo that separates the objects from the background. This light's intensity varies in application from scene to scene. In most scenes, I have more than one Back light in order to show depth and create special effects. It's not unusual for me to have more lights behind objects than in front of them.

Three-Point Lighting allows for other lights to be added to the scene. However, these lights are more for effect than for widespread coverage of light:

- *Special light.* This light is added to a scene to cast light to a particular region or to create a certain effect.

- *Practical light.* This light emanates from actual sources in the scene, like a lamp on a table. It is casting light, but is not a primary source of light (at least in Three-Point Lighting). Practical light adds realism to a scene when it is necessary.

In Figures 1.22–1.25, I use a sphere to illustrate the types of lights involved in the Three-Point Lighting scheme.

Figure 1.22 Sphere with Three-Point Lighting applied.

Figure 1.23   Sphere with only the Key light rendered.

Figure 1.24   Sphere with only the Fill light rendered.

Figure 1.25 Sphere with only the Back light rendered.

The file from which these figures came is included on the CD-ROM in the \ch01 directory and is called 3pt-lite.max. Examine this file to better understand the location of the lights. Each light is an Omni light, and they are labeled according to function. It is important to understand the location of the lights and how they illuminate the object. There is a direct correlation between the positions of the lights, object, and camera.

If you could imagine the sphere in this scene as a chrome ball with mirror-perfect reflections, it is easy to position the lights where you want them to be. The light's position must reflect directly off the surface of the object and into the camera. In fact, when setting up raytraced reflections, I often place an Omni light in place of a reflected object I want to reflect on a raytraced object, and then I move it around to see where the highlights fall on the raytraced object. Then I place the reflected object exactly where the light is. I use this method because lights show up in MAX's real time rendering window, whereas raytraced reflections do not.

To emphasize this point, I have included another MAX file called 3pt-lite-ray.max on the CD-ROM. This file is identical to the Three-Point Lighting sphere, but the sphere in Figure 1.26 now has a raytraced reflection texture, and the lights have object labels that are reflected exactly where the lights' highlights fall.

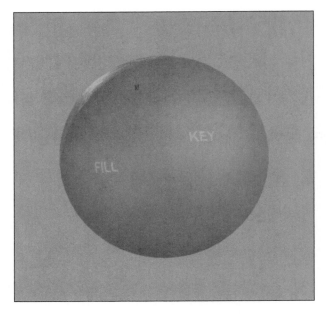

Figure 1.26   3pt-lite-ray.max scene with raytraced reflections.

It is also possible to position highlights on the objects in a scene by using the Place Highlight tool from the Align fly-out. Make sure the light you want to use to create the highlight is selected, click the Place Highlight tool, and click in the viewport on the object where you want the highlight to appear. This will move the light to the correct coordinates in the scene to create the desired highlight.

This completes your crash course in lighting. Now let's light that filmstrip.

Lighting the Filmstrip Object

To light the filmstrip object, we will use Three-Point Lighting to illuminate the filmstrip scene and will add one Special light. By the end of this section, we will have a beautifully lit scene.

Exercise 1.13   Creating the Lights

Because the Key light is the most important light in the scene, we will create it first. Then we'll create the Fill and Back lights.

1. With ch01-06.max still open, open the Create/Lights panel. Click the Omni button and click in the Top viewport to create an Omni light. Change the light's color to dark blue by using these values: RGB (**71,108,150**). Name this light **Omni-Key** to mark it as the Key light.

2. Open the Move Transform Type-In dialog box, and move the light to XYZ [**–250,–180,300**].

3. Render a frame from the Camera viewport to see the results. You should see a nice blue highlight on the foreground of the filmstrip and a few touches of blue on the film's curves in the back.

    After creating the Key light, we can create the Fill light to illuminate the areas of the filmstrip the Key light misses.

4. Create an Omni light in the Top viewport and change its color to a nice blue/teal color: RGB (**48,60,120**). Name it **Omni-Fill** and move it to XYZ [**520,–85,150**].

5. Render a frame from the Camera viewport to see the Fill light's results.

    The filmstrip is pretty evenly lit along the front of the film. The Fill light is doing its job by lighting the filmstrip just enough to make it pop off the background. Now it is time to create the Back light to add a little separation to the overlapping sections of the filmstrip.

6. Create another Omni light in the Top viewport, name it **Omni-Back,** change the color to RGB (**150,30,149**), and move it to XYZ [**240,370,240**].

7. Render a frame from the Camera viewport to see the Three-Point Lighting at work. We can see the purple highlight cast on the top edge of the film.

    Although the filmstrip looks pretty good right about now, it lacks depth. A Special light is needed to help separate the layers of film. We are going to place a Special light into the scene to illuminate some sections of the filmstrip not illuminated by the three main lights.

8. Create another Omni light in the Top viewport and change the light's color to RGB (**100,85,34**), a dark yellow color. Name it **Omni-Special** and move it to XYZ [**–195,55,–50**].

9. Render a frame from the Camera viewport to see all four lights play their parts in the scene (see Figure 1.27).

Figure 1.27   The filmstrip is rendered with Three-Point lighting and a Special light.

Exercise 1.14   Adjusting the Material

As you probably noticed, the SpyCam1.jpg is barely seen through all of our wonderful highlights. Here, we will adjust the materials to improve the look of the filmstrip.

1. Open the Material Editor and go to the root of the Filmstrip material. Change Self-Illumination to 50 to make the images shine through the highlights a bit.

2. To make the filmstrip appear darker as it overlaps, open the Extended Parameters rollout and activate Subtractive.

3. Render a frame from the Camera viewport. It's much better, isn't it? Now we can see the criminals caught in the act (see Figure 1.28).

4. Save your work as **ch01-07.max**.

Figure 1.28   The finished filmstrip with Three-Point Lighting, a Special light, and self-illuminated material.

Creating the Background

Right now we have a dramatically lit filmstrip on a gray background. It doesn't show as much depth as we would like to see, though. Wouldn't it be great if it were possible to add just a little more "punch" to the scene? Hey, the only thing that we are limited by is our imagination. We have a few tricks up our sleeves.

Exercise 1.15   Adding Depth to the Scene

To add some depth to the scene, we will add a background to separate the film from the boring gray background:

1. With ch01-07.max loaded, open the Rendering menu and select Environment to open the Environment dialog box. Click None in the Environment Map group. Set Browse From: to New, select Gradient from the list, and click OK to exit.

2. Open the Material Editor and drag the Gradient map from the Environment/Environment Map: field into the second material preview slot in the Material Editor. Choose Instance from the Instance (Copy) Map window and close the Environment dialog box.

3. Change this map's name to **Background**. Then, in the Gradient Parameters roll-out, choose Gradient Type: Radial. This changes the gradient type from a linear top-to-bottom gradient to a radial gradient that emanates from the center (see Figure 1.29). The radial gradient creates a sort of tunnel effect that gives virtually any background instant depth.

We need a nice blue/purple background for the filmstrip to live in. Because a background that is too outrageous will ruin the contrast between the logo and the background, we will keep it pretty dark. That will make the logo pop off of the background. Enter these values:

Color #1: RGB (**0,0,0**)

Color #2: RGB (**65,18,90**)

Color #3: RGB (**137,53,130**)

4. Render a frame from the Camera viewport (see Figure 1.29).

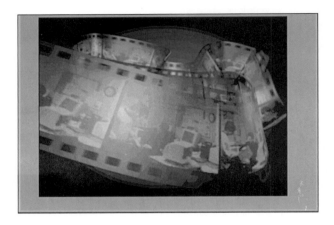

Figure 1.29   The filmstrip rendered with a radial gradient background.

Exercise 1.16   Manipulating the Background's Gradient

At this point, it is almost impossible to see the gradient behind the filmstrip. To fix that, we'll make it a little bigger. It's a cinch to adjust its size with the UV Tiling setting in the Coordinates rollout.

1. In the Coordinates rollout, change the Tiling to U: **0.6**, V: **0.6**. This removes 40% (the missing 0.4) of the outside edges of the gradient.

2. Render a frame from the Camera viewport.

   The background looks about right now, but the gradient is round and uninteresting. Let's add some noise to the gradient to loosen up its shape a bit.

3. In the Gradient Parameters, find the Noise: group and change Amount to **0.5** and Size to **5.0**. Now we have an eerie, smoke-like gradient.

   Excellent. But what is a smoke-like background without undulating smoke? No sweat, it's easy to make the gradient appear to be undulating by animating the Phase parameter of the Noise.

4. Move to frame 30 of the animation. Activate the Animate button.

5. In the Noise group of the Gradient Parameters, change Phase to **0.5.** Deactivate the Animate button. Animating the phase will create a slow undulating effect.

6. Click Make Preview in the Material Editor. Select Custom Range, enter **0 to 50,** and click OK to build the preview.

Exercise 1.17 Animating the Phase with Track View

The preview yields very nice results. The problem is that it is only animated to frame 30. There is a way to tell MAX to continue animating the phase at its current rate throughout the entire animation, but we must use the Track View to do so.

1. Click the Open Track View button on the toolbar. Expand the Environment tracks, and then expand the Environment Texture Map track. Scroll down until you can see the Noise Phase track (see Figure 1.30).

Figure 1.30 Track View displaying the Environment Texture Map tracks.

2. Select the Noise Phase track title and click the Parameter Curve Out-of-Range Types.

3. From the Param Curve Out-of-Range Types dialog box, select Relative Repeat Out. Click OK to close the dialog box.

4. In the Material Editor, create a 100-frame preview of the background gradient.

5. Save your work as **ch01-08.max.**

As you can see, the phase of the noise continues to animate even though there are no keyframes beyond frame 30. This is because we set Relative Repeat Out of the phase's animated keyframe range. In other words, clicking Relative Repeat Out tells MAX to continue animating the parameter at its current rate beyond its animated range. As a result, this parameter will animate smoothly whether the animation is 100 frames long or 10,000 frames long.

The secret to making any realistic 3D animation is the illusion of depth. We already added a background, but our animation needs even more depth. I often add a simple effect to a very plain scene to create the illusion of depth, making the scene more dramatic and believable. Let's do that in the next exercise.

Exercise 1.18   Applying Atmospheric Effect

Adding fog can create more depth in the scene. You create the effect by adding distance cue, darkening the area of the filmstrip that is toward the back of the scene.

1. With ch01-08.max loaded, open the Rendering menu and select Environment to open the Environment dialog box. In the Atmosphere rollout, click the Add button. From the Add Atmospheric Effect dialog box, choose Fog and click OK to exit.

2. Click the Fog: Color: swatch, change the color to a very dark blue using RGB (**2,4,9**), and uncheck Fog Background.

Note

The Fog Background button fogs the Environment background that we just completed in the last section. We do not want to make it any darker than it already is. With the Fog Background unchecked, the fog will only be applied to geometry.

3. In the Standard: group, check Exponential and set Near% to **0.0** and Far% to **50**.

Note

When you click the Exponential check box, the fog effect is added to the scene exponentially, making the fog much thicker as the distance from the camera increases.

Let's adjust the camera's Environment Ranges before we render a test frame.

4. Select Camera01 and click the Modify tab.

5. In the Environment Ranges group, check Show. Feel free to play with the numeric values of the Ranges and watch the planes (that represent the range) to get a better grasp of how they work. The lower the number, the closer the plane gets to the camera.

6. Set Near Range to **70** and Far Range to **370**. This adjusts the Near Range to start right before it touches the filmstrip, and the Far Range is set to extend just beyond the filmstrip. This ensures that we will have very even coverage of fog over the filmstrip.

7. Render a frame from the Camera viewport (see Figure 1.31).

8. Save your work as **ch01-09.max**.

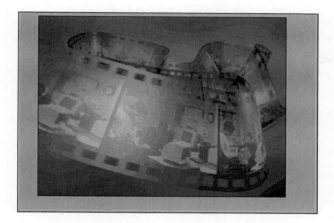

Figure 1.31   The rendered scene with fog applied. The fog is subtle but effective.

Cool. Looks pretty neat. The fog certainly added plenty of depth to the scene. However, it also added a problem. Notice that the sprocket holes in the far back of the scene got darker. This is because the holes really aren't there. Even though the geometry has an opacity map, the renderer—and more importantly, the fog—still thinks that it's solid and applies fog. There is no easy fix for this problem, but I wanted to point this problem out to you. Because everything else looks so cool with the fog applied, we are just going to leave it in. Don't worry, I won't tell anyone your secret.

Finishing the Scene

The scene is complete. The only thing left to do is to animate the camera and the scene to create the background image sequence for the Hidden Eyes animation. Because this scene is the background to the logo animation, it should be subtle and smooth.

Exercise 1.19   Adding the Finishing Touches

It is now time to animate the camera in our scene to create a very slow pan of the filmstrip.

1. Load ch01-09.max if it's not already loaded. Right-click the Play button to open the Time Configuration dialog box. Change End Time: to **210** and close the dialog box. Activate the Animate button, advance to frame 210, and select Camera01. Move the camera to XYZ [**−135,−160,75**] and rotate the camera to XYZ [**61.5,−17,−22**] as shown in Figure 1.32.

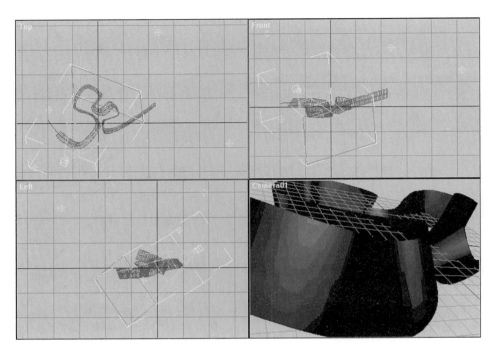

Figure 1.32   The correct position/rotation for Camera01 at frame 210.

2. Play the animation in the Camera viewport. The camera pans slowly from right to left and rotates to keep the filmstrip centered.

   Now that Camera01 is animated, we can add a little motion to the filmstrip object along its path.

3. To animate the filmstrip so the film moves along the deform path, make sure the Animate button is still on and the current frame is 210. Select the Filmstrip object.

4. Click the Modify tab and change the Path Deform group's Percent to **10**. Deactivate the Animate button.

5. Play the animation in the Camera viewport.

   Looks great! All we have to do now is set an output filename in the Render Scene dialog box, and we can render this bad boy.

6. Save your work as **ch01-10.max**.

   Now that the scene is finished, it can be rendered. We will use these rendered images as the background sequence of the logo scene.

7. Click Render Scene to open the Render Scene dialog box. Enter Output Size: **320×240**. Click the Files button and set the filename to **ch01\images\back.jpg**. Click Render to render the scene.

In Summary

This completes the first chapter. The file that you just created has a filmstrip object with texture mapped sprocket holes following a deform spline. The background is created with a radial gradient with screen coordinates. An over it all, you've added an environmental fog effect. A slow moving camera move and dramatic camera angle makes the filmstrip look larger than life. It is a beautiful background for the logo element that you will create in the next chapter.

In the next chapter, we will create the logo element that's to be rendered over the background we just created. Our client, Hidden Eyes, has a circular logo with a creepy eyeball peering from the center. The logo will surely grab people's attention.

Chapter 2

Modeling the Logo

In media animation, having a streamlined approach for working with imported Adobe Illustrator files can sometimes be critical to the success of the project. For example, a client may want an animated logo or corporate icon to represent the company.

Usually, that client will already have the logo/icon created as an Adobe Illustrator file (.ai) for print purposes. Using that .ai file can not only save you time by eliminating the need to build the splines from scratch, but it will also provide you with an accurate template for building the logo, thus preventing any problems that may occur from eyeballing.

When working in a graphics department (where speed is key), an artist working in Adobe Illustrator usually creates logo splines to then be imported into 3D Studio MAX for animation. This process has two advantages. First, it allows the artist to create an accurate representation of the logo. Second, it gives the art director an opportunity to make any changes to it before 3D object creation begins. Importing the .ai file frees up the animator to do what the animator does best: animate.

In this chapter, we work with an .ai file, comparing it with a rough representation of the logo as a reference. The reference image is not the output of the .ai file, but an artist's rendition of the main concept of the logo. A different artist placed the text, roughed out the main shapes of the logo, and then output the .ai file. It is our job to take the rough .ai file and make it resemble the artist's rendition.

Working with an Adobe Illustrator File

Before we import the Adobe Illustrator file, let's take a look at the artist's rendition (see Figure 2.1).

Figure 2.1   The artist's rendition of the logo.

The logo is pretty straightforward: a ring of text surrounded by two solid rings. The center part of the logo isn't really our concern right now. Our main interest is making sure the text is connected to the rings and looks great. The center part of the logo is going to be an eyeball looking through a circular hole, not a camera as this logo appears to represent. Isn't it great when the boss makes last-minute changes? We will have to improvise on our own to make that work.

Importing the Adobe Illustrator File

Although importing an Adobe Illustrator file is a great way to speed up the production process, you must keep a few things in mind when working with imported .ai files. One thing is that when a person is creating line art in Illustrator, he or she needs to create only one spline and assign a stroke width. In order to duplicate this effect in MAX, you must create a second spline, giving the line an "edge" on each side. We do this in the tutorial that follows.

MAX generally does a fantastic job of importing the logo splines. However, you will want to form the good working practice of reassigning vertex types for each vertex and re-adjusting the Bézier tangents. Doing so allows you to familiarize yourself with the splines and ensures optimum results when you are beveling or extruding the splines to create an object.

Exercise 2.1   Importing the File

Let's import the .ai file and see what we have to work with.

1. Reset MAX.
2. Choose File, Import, and from Files of Type, select Adobe Illustrator (*.ai). Then from the accompanying CD, open tut-work\Ch02\Adobe tut2.ai.
3. From the Shape Import window, choose Single Object and click OK. Maximize the Top viewport. The Top viewport should look like the view in Figure 2.2.
4. Choose Edit, Hold to temporarily save your work.

Note

If you make a mistake and need to undo it, choose Edit, Fetch, and the file will return to this stage.

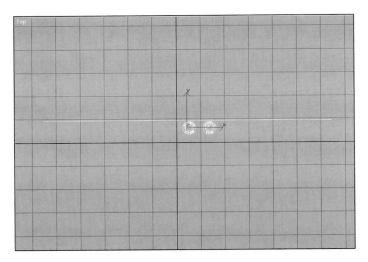

Figure 2.2   The Top viewport with tut2.ai imported.

Exercise 2.2   Cleaning Up the Spline

Yuck! Already we can tell our work is cut out for us. This file is more of a curse than a blessing. But, with a little work, it will be just fine. We have several tricks up our sleeves to make sure this comes off without a hitch the first time. For now, let's just clean this spline up a bit.

The first step toward removing the unwanted splines from the scene is to remove the long horizontal line that strikes through the scene. After the line is deleted, we will examine the two sets of logo splines and decide which one to keep.

1. With the imported shape selected, open the Modify panel and activate Spline to enter the Sub-Object Spline level.

Note

Each shape has three sub-object levels: Vertex, the individual control points of the spline; Segment, the line between two vertices; and Spline, one continuous set of vertices. Before we finish this chapter, we'll have used all three.

2. Select the long horizontal line in the Top viewport (see Figure 2.3).

3. Press the Delete key on the keyboard to remove the line, and then click the Zoom Extents button to zoom in on the two logos (see Figure 2.4).

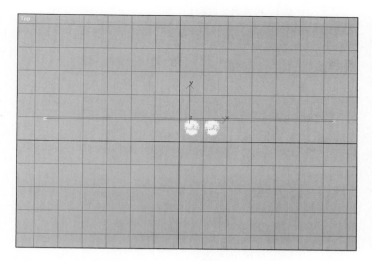

Figure 2.3   The Top viewport with the horizontal line selected.

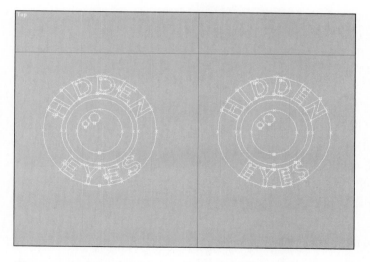

Figure 2.4   Two logo splines with the horizontal line deleted and Zoom Extents applied.

Now we can see that the file has two of the same logo. The talented artist who traced the logo for us in Adobe Illustrator was kind enough to make his own artistic interpretation and give us two fonts to choose from. A decision like this requires input from the designer, and together we decide that we are going to stick with the original font. So let's just get rid of the extra logo to avoid confusion.

4. Using Rectangular Selection Region, select the splines in the logo to the right and press the Delete key to remove the unwanted logo.

5. Click Zoom Extents to zoom in on the logo spline (see Figure 2.5).

Figure 2.5   A zoomed view of the remaining logo.

    6. Save your work as **ch02-01.max**.

So far, the work we've done has been pretty harmless. But something tells me we have a lot of work ahead.

Editing the Spline to Match the Artist's Rendition

In this section, we edit the spline to prepare it for beveling. You must keep several potential problems in mind when working with imported Illustrator files; we will examine those as we come across them. The fixes to these problems are the result of many hours of head scratching and learning the hard way. You'll learn many valuable lessons while working on this tutorial, so please take the time and pay close attention to each step.

Exercise 2.3   Matching the Shape to a Background Image

The first thing we must do is match the logo shape to the artist's rendition. We can load the artist's rendition as a background in the Top viewport and use it to align the splines.

    1. With ch02-01.max loaded, make sure the Top viewport is maximized.

    2. Using Zoom, zoom in on the shape so the top and bottom of the spline are at the edges of the viewport.

    3. Choose Views, Background Image. From the Viewport Background dialog box, click the Files button in the Background Source group and choose \ch02\images\HiddenEyes.JPG on the accompanying CD. Click OK to exit the Select Background Image dialog box. (The Viewport Background dialog box should still be open.)

4. Select the Match Bitmap radio button in the Aspect Ratio group, and click OK to exit the Viewport Background dialog box.

5. Click the Zoom Extents Selected button. The screen should look like the one in Figure 2.6.

Figure 2.6   The Top viewport with the Background Image applied.

Note

The background image was loaded into Adobe PhotoShop as a 640 × 480 image. The contrast was reduced 50 percent to remove the black and white from the image. Splines that are selected are white, so dropping the contrast makes the splines easier to view.

6. Use the Pan and Zoom tools to match the spline to the background image as closely as possible (see Figure 2.7). The center circle spline should match up to the edge of the black circle in the background image.

Note

The center circle spline should match up to the edge of the black circle in the background image.

I guess our work is cut out for us. It surely didn't take long to realize the spline isn't matching up to the background image, did it?

Figure 2.7   A first attempt at aligning the shape to the background image.

Exercise 2.4   Moving the Logo's Splines with Edit Spline

Our next task is to line up all the letters to the background image. This phase is a snap when we use the right tools—the Select and Move and Select and Rotate tools.

1. Select the spline (Shape1) and rename it **Logo-Font**.
2. In the Modify Panel, make sure Sub-Object is still on and set the sub-object level to Spline.
3. Activate Use Selection Center for both the Select and Move and Select and Rotate tools.
4. Using the Select and Move and the Select and Rotate tools, select each letter's spline and align it with the background image.

Tip

Each D in *HIDDEN* has two splines. If you select both splines of a D as you align it with its background image, the rotation is more accurate than if you rotate the splines separately.

5. Double-check that each letter matches the rotation of the letters on the background image and that the tops and bottoms of each letter are properly overlapping the black rings of the background image.

   Your Top viewport should look something like Figure 2.8. All the splines perfectly match the letters and overlap the black circles of the background image.

Note

Matching the splines to the image is a very big step in the tutorial. Try to match the background image exactly. Having perfect splines at this point will make the rest of the tutorial flow much faster.

Figure 2.8   The splines of the letters match the background image.

If you haven't noticed yet, the logo doesn't have enough ring splines to make up both the interior and exterior edges of each ring. Why not? As mentioned earlier, the artists working in Adobe Illustrator draw only one spline and "stroke" the width of the line on it. In order for us to obtain a similar effect, we must add an extra spline to provide an interior and exterior edge to the "line." If we don't, MAX uses the outermost spline as the exterior edge. MAX then uses the next inner spline as its interior edge.

Exercise 2.5   Creating More Ring Splines

To create the extra splines, we scale the existing splines while holding down the Shift key on the keyboard. What we're doing is cloning the splines; the new ones will serve as the interior and exterior edges.

1. Make sure the Sub-Object/Spline level is still active. Then click the Select and Uniform Scale tool and activate Use Selection Center.

2. Select the outermost ring and Shift+drag the spline to match the outermost edge of the large black ring.

Tip

Adding the Shift key to any transform in the Sub-Object/Spline level creates a new spline. It's a very easy way to make duplicate splines.

3. Select and drag the other inside edge splines of the two rings and create outside edge splines (see Figure 2.9).

Earlier in this tutorial, we learned that the center part of the logo was not going to be a camera, as originally portrayed by the designer, but an eyeball. Because the splines in our logo representing a camera lens are not needed, we must remove them.

Figure 2.9   The finished spline paths.

Exercise 2.6   Getting Rid of the Camera Lens

We've removed an unwanted spline before, but now we're removing several at one time.

1. Select the center circle spline and the two "highlight" circle splines shown in Figure 2.10, and press the Delete key to delete them.

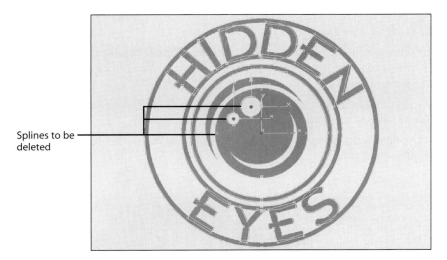

Splines to be deleted

Figure 2.10   Delete these splines.

2. Save your work as **ch02-02.max**.

Finishing the Shape

Before we dive in and finish the logo shape, let's take some time to examine some of the potential problems we need to be aware of. We will look at a few examples illustrating the best and worst ways to prepare splines for beveling. After we've explored the best way to create a beveled object, we can apply our knowledge to the logo splines we have been working so hard on.

Preparing Splines for Beveling

Beveling is a piece of cake when you begin with the correct splines. However, recognizing a good spline when you see it is not always easy. Not only that, using a Bézier vertex rather than a Bézier Corner vertex affects smoothing groups when beveling. And what do you do if you've worked your spline into a tight corner? The following sections address these issues.

Good Spline/Bad Spline

From the accompanying CD, open the file \ch02\Good-BadSpline.max. Figure 2.11 shows the file.

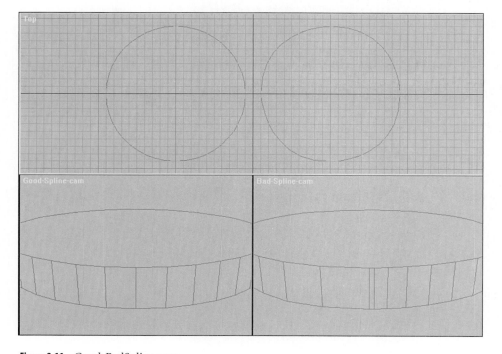

Figure 2.11   Good-BadSpline.max.

Notice the spacing of the faces on the two circle objects. The object in the Good-Spline-cam viewport has nice, evenly spaced faces, whereas the object in the Bad-Spline-cam viewport has very irregularly spaced faces. This irregularity is due to poor vertex tangent manipulation.

The tangent handles of the vertices on the "Good Circle" object are pulled evenly both in and out (symmetrically) of each vertex (see Figure 2.12). The tangent handles of the vertices of the "Bad Circle" are incorrect (see Figure 2.13). One tangent is resting on the vertex and the other tangent is over-pulled to create the curve.

Figure 2.12   The tangent handles of the Good Circle spline.

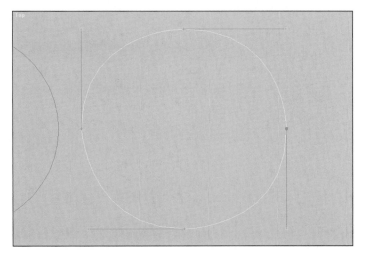

Figure 2.13   The incorrectly positioned tangent handle of the Bad Circle spline.

Note

You can access the vertices of these objects by opening the Modify panel, going to the Edit Spline modifier in the modifier stack, and entering the Sub-Object/Vertex level.

The two object shapes are virtually identical, but the tangent handles of the vertices have created uneven distribution of faces along the extruded edge. The faces bunch up as they move toward the tangent handle sitting on the vertex. This bunching up of faces is common when you import Adobe Illustrator files into MAX.

Bézier Vertex versus Bézier Corner Vertex?

From the accompanying CD, open the file \ch02\Bézier-BézierCorner.max. Figure 2.14 shows the file.

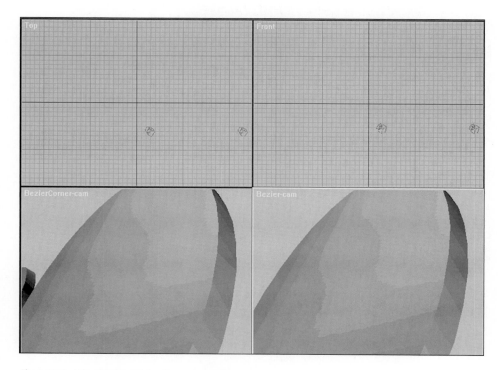

Figure 2.14   The Bézier-BézierCorner.max file.

The viewports display two extruded circle objects. They have been extruded from almost identical circle splines. The difference between them is that the extruded circle in the Bézier-cam viewport has Bézier vertices assigned, and the extruded circle in the BézierCorner-cam has Bézier Corner vertices assigned.

Although the difference is subtle, it has a huge impact during the rendering process. Look closely at the edges of the extruded circles in the shaded viewports. In the BézierCorner-cam viewport, a break in the smoothness along the extruded circle has occurred. This break occurs because the vertex type is a Bézier Corner. When MAX sees a Bézier Corner vertex, it assigns a different smoothing group to the faces coming in and going out of that vertex. To correct the problem, we must change the vertex type, which we will do in the tutorial.

Tight Corner, Big Problem

From the accompanying CD, open the file \ch02\TightCornerBevel.max. Figure 2.15 shows the file.

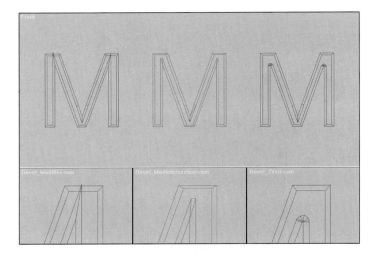

Figure 2.15   The TightCornerBevel.max file.

In the Front viewport, you see three very different letter M's. The differences are shown in the three bottom viewports. The first two M's have Bevel modifiers applied, but their Bevel settings are different. The third M has a standard Bevel modifier applied, but the spline is different.

The first two M splines have one vertex in the interior tight corner (see Figure 2.16). In the third M, two Bézier vertices were added in the tight corner and then the original corner vertex was deleted (see Figure 2.17).

When a spline is beveled, MAX tries to keep the width of the bevel an equal distance from the edges. This conformity is usually a good thing, but it's a very bad thing for those who haven't caught on to the secret of working with bevels.

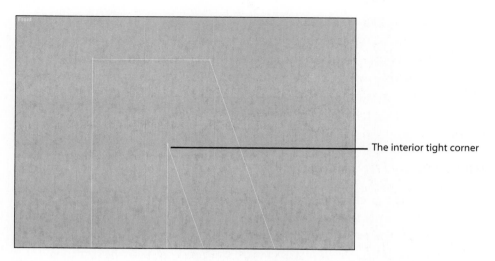

Figure 2.16   The first two M's have one vertex in the interior tight corner.

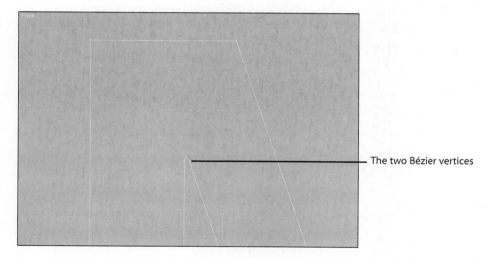

Figure 2.17   The third M has two vertices in the interior tight corner.

Here is why each bevel reacts the way it does:

> *Bevel_Modifier (left M).* This object is completely unacceptable. Because MAX has made the bevel equal from all of the sides, the interior bevel has extended past the exterior edge's bevel. The crossed faces of this object cause the front faces to disappear.

Bevel_ModIntersection (middle M). The spline of this object is identical to the Bevel_Modifier object with one small difference. The Keep Lines From Crossing feature has been activated in the Intersections group of the Bevel modifier. When this box is checked, MAX tries to keep the bevels apart by the number of units entered in the Separation field. However, this creates a very unevenly distributed bevel.

Bevel_2Vert (right M). The bevel on this one is perfect. Why? It has two Bézier vertices, as explained earlier, in the tight corner of the original spline. What this does is gives MAX a rounded path to follow, keeping the integrity of the bevel even. The two Bézier vertices in the tight corner are extremely close to each other so they appear to be only one vertex when not viewed as an extreme closeup. The vertices could be assigned Corner vertex types to make straight corners like the corner on the Bevel_ModIntersection object. The difference between making two straight corners with two vertices and using the Keep Lines From Crossing feature is that the corner with two straight corners will have an even bevel applied.

It is very important to note out that no matter which of these techniques you choose to use when beveling splines, there is still the possibility that something can go wrong (such as the crossing faces). Such problems are generally due to poor vertex type assignments and/or tangent handles.

The more you work with Spline and Bevel modifiers, the more you will learn what you can and cannot do. The guidelines in this chapter give you a solid foundation to help you understand why and how things are happening. To understand them further, you must learn by trial and error, experimenting to see what works best for you.

Exercise 2.7   Fixing the Vertices of the Logo Shape

Now that you have an understanding of working with vertices and splines for the purpose beveling, let's continue working the logo shape. The splines are exactly the shape of the desired logo. Now we must fix all of the vertices of the splines in order to ensure maximum control over the beveled object.

1. Open ch02-02.max.

   We no longer need the background image as a template, so let's turn it off.

2. Choose Views, Background Image. In the Viewport Background dialog box, click to remove the check from the box next to Display Background, and then click OK to exit the Viewport Background dialog box.

Our shape needs more segments to make it a little smoother along the rounded edges. Time to add more.

3. Select the Logo-Font shape. Then, in the Modifier panel, open the General roll-out, look for the Interpolation group, and enter Steps: **15** to add more segments. Leave Optimize turned on.

Note

Activating Optimize instructs MAX to create steps only along the spline on curved segments. When a segment is linear (a straight segment), MAX doesn't create steps.

Now it's time to sink our teeth into fixing up this logo shape. Before we move on with modifying the vertices, it would be a smart idea to make a clone of the object. We do this for two reasons. The first reason is to have a backup in case things take a turn in a bad direction; the second is that we can use it as a template for tracing. Trust me. We are going to make this shape a lot worse before it gets better.

4. From the Edit menu, click Clone. Then, from the Clone Options dialog box, select Copy and name the clone **Logo-Template**. Click OK.

   The new Logo-Template object is selected now. Let's go freeze it so we can lock it in for our template.

5. Click the Display tab and in the Freeze rollout, click Freeze Selected to freeze the shape.

Note

Freezing an object makes the object turn black in the viewport. It cannot be selected or modified until it is unfrozen (unless it's an instance of another unfrozen object).

6. We can now enter the Logo-Font's Sub-Object level and adjust all the vertices. Select the Logo-Font shape. Click the Modify tab and click the Vertex button in the Selection group to enter the Sub-Object/Vertex level. Choose Edit, Select Invert to select every vertex (see Figure 2.18).

Note

Versions of MAX previous to the 3.0 release imported splines with a Bézier vertex type applied to every vertex. The 3.0 release of MAX now imports corner vertices as corner vertices. However, Bézier corner vertices import as Bézier vertices with a tangent handle on the vertex, which is visible where a straight segment meets a curved segment (in the letter D, for example).

Figure 2.18   The logo shape with all vertices selected.

7. Now for a bold, brazen move on our parts. We are going to turn all of the vertices into Smooth vertices. It's really going to make a noticeable difference.

   With all the vertices selected, right-click one of them and change the type to Smooth (see Figure 2.19).

   Hey, I said there was going to be a noticeable difference. I didn't say it was going to look better.

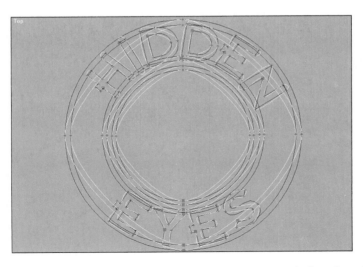

Figure 2.19   The Logo shape with a Smooth vertex type applied to all vertices.

The major reason for turning all the vertices into Smooth is that, when we turn them all back to Bézier vertex types, the tangent handles will be symmetrical from their vertices. Another reason is that using the Smooth type changes the shape so dramatically it is impossible to accidentally miss a vertex.

It is important, especially when working with imported .ai files, that you change the vertex type and change it back again. This step ensures that we familiarize ourselves with the vertices and check for any problems similar to those discussed earlier in this tutorial. When I am working with imported Illustrator files, I always change the vertices into Smooth and then back to Bézier.

Exercise 2.8   Assigning the Correct Vertex Types

Let's change the vertices back to Bézier.

1. Select all the vertices of the Logo-Font shape, right-click one, and change the type to Bézier. In Figure 2.20, notice how each vertex has even control tangents.

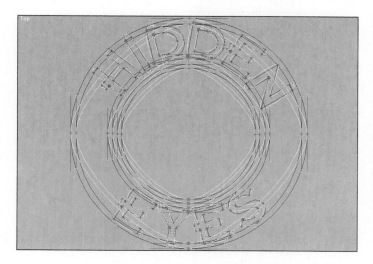

Figure 2.20   Vertices with the Bézier vertex type applied.

2. Let's get the easy, straight corner vertices out of the way right now.
   Deselect all of the vertices by clicking in the screen anywhere except on a vertex.

3. Ctrl+click all the vertices of the letters H, I, E, N of the word *HIDDEN*, and all the vertices of the letters E, Y, E of the word *EYES*. Be careful not to accidentally select any of the other vertices.

Tip

If you do accidentally select other vertices, Alt+click to deselect them.

4. Right-click on one of the selected vertices and choose the Corner vertex type. Your screen should look like Figure 2.21.

Figure 2.21   The Logo shape with the Corner vertex type applied to selected vertices.

5. Select the vertices of the two Ds in the word *HIDDEN* and change them to Corner vertex type (see Figure 2.22).

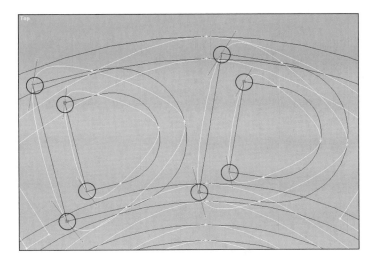

Figure 2.22   Select and change the circled vertices of the Ds to Corner vertex types.

6. Now it's time to fix the letter S in *EYES*. Remember, all the vertices are Bézier vertex types. This letter's spline has four hard corners. We don't want to apply the Corner vertex type to these vertices. Instead, we will individually change the tangents on these vertices.

Use the Select and Move tool to adjust the four vertices that create hard corners in the S spline. You must change the vertices shown as selected in Figure 2.23 into Bézier Corner types by holding down the Shift key and dragging the tangent handle to the appropriate length to create the proper curve. These four vertices remain Bézier Corner type.

Figure 2.23   The tangent handles on the circled vertices must be uneven to create the proper curve.

7. In this step, we finish the vertices of the S spline. Using the Select and Move tool, adjust the remaining vertices of the S spline to match the template. Shift+drag the tangent handles of the vertices to create the correct curvature. Remember, Shift+dragging a tangent handle changes the vertex type to Bézier Corner. You will need to right-click these vertices and return them to Bézier type when you finish. The finished spline should look like the one in Figure 2.24.

Now that you have an understanding of working with vertices, you're ready to finish the Ds in the word *HIDDEN* all by yourself.

8. Use the Select and Move tool to adjust the tangent handles of the two D's in the word *HIDDEN* (see Figure 2.25).

Now that you are a pro at working with tangent handle, it's up to you to make the circles round again. To speed up the process, we can use a trick.

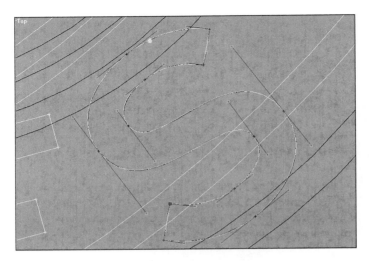

Figure 2.24   The proper tangent handles of the S spline.

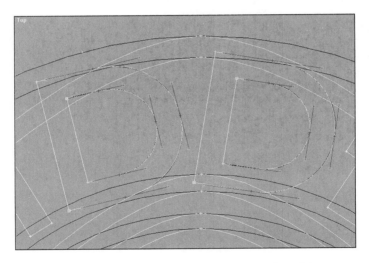

Figure 2.25   The proper placement of the tangent handles of the Ds.

9. Click Zoom Extents to view the entire logo in the Top viewport and constrain the Select and Move tool to Y. From the Sub-Object/Vertex Selection rollout, activate Lock Handles/Alike and select all the vertices of the circle splines. Click and drag one of the vertical tangent handles to adjust the contour of the circle splines, making them round again (see Figure 2.26).

Note

It is possible to make one spline round, change the Sub-Object level to Spline, select all the bad circle splines and delete them, and then use Select and Uniform Scale with the Shift key to clone the rest. Just make sure that Use Selection Center is active.

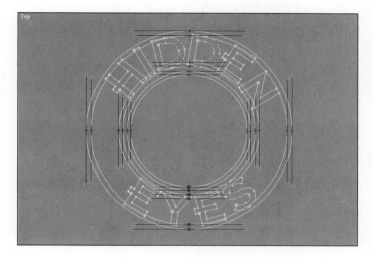

Figure 2.26   The almost finished, retouched logo shape.

10. Save your work as **ch02-03.max**.

Exercise 2.9   Rounding the Tight Corners

Whoa! Did you think I'd let you get by without doing the most important thing—you guessed it—rounding those tight corners out? Don't worry. It's a snap.

1. Zoom in on the letter N in the word *HIDDEN*, as shown in Figure 2.27.

    Yep, those tight corners are a disaster waiting to happen. Let's fix them so we get nice rounded corners. We don't want anyone calling us rookies, do we?

2. With the Vertex level of the Sub-Object selected, click the Refine button and add a vertex on each side of both tight Corner vertices. Right-click to exit the Refine mode (see Figure 2.28).

3. Select the new vertices that you added with Refine and change their types from Corner to Bézier. Select and delete the old tight Corner vertices (see Figure 2.29).

Figure 2.27   The tight corners of the letter N in the word *HIDDEN*.

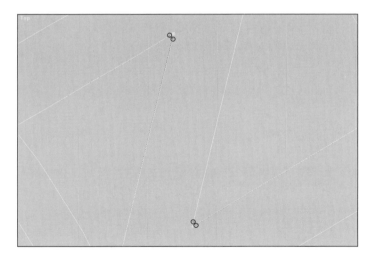

Figure 2.28   Tight corners with two new vertices added, one on each side of the original corner vertices, with Refine.

When the old tight Corner vertices are deleted, the tight corners should be rounded (see Figure 2.30).

4. Let's do the same thing to the other tight corner, in the letter Y in *EYES*. Repeat steps 1 through 3 on this corner.

5. Save your work as **ch02-04.max**.

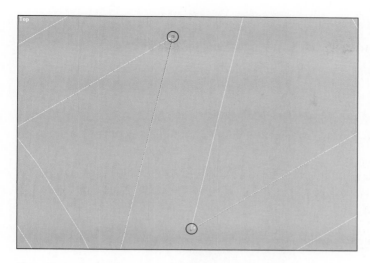

Figure 2.29   Select and delete the old tight Corner vertices

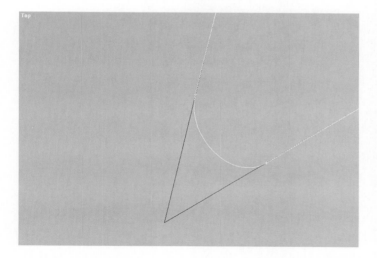

Figure 2.30   Extreme close-up of one of the newly rounded tight corners with the old tight Corner vertex deleted.

Using a Boolean Operation

You've done the better part of the spline editing on the logo shape. The only thing left to do is to join all the splines together using a Boolean operation.

A *Boolean operation* is a tool that is used when joining splines to other splines or objects to other objects. There are three types of spline Boolean operations:

- *Union.* Joins two splines and removes anything inside of the intersection.
- *Subtraction.* Subtracts the intersected area of spline B from spline A.
- *Intersection.* Creates a new spline using only the intersected area of splines A and B.

Exercise 2.10   Using the Subtraction Boolean Operation

We will use the Subtraction Boolean operation in this example to join the letters to the rings. Let's begin.

1. Load ch02-04.max and select the Logo-Font object. In the Modify panel, activate the Sub-Object/Spline level.

2. Select the second circle spline from the outside (see Figure 2.31).

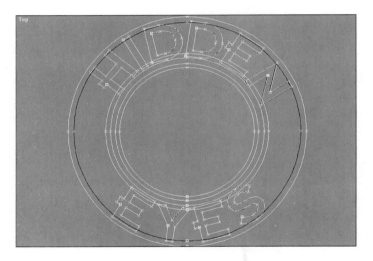

Figure 2.31   Select this circle spline.

3. Activate the Boolean button in the Geometry rollout, activate the Subtraction button, and then click the H in word *HIDDEN*. The Boolean operation subtracts the H from the circle.

4. To do the same for the rest of the letters, select the circle again, activate the Boolean button, and click the letter I in *HIDDEN*. The Boolean operation subtracts the letter I from the circle spline.

5. Subtract the rest of the letters of both words from the circle. Make sure the outer ring is selected and the Boolean button is on before you click each letter. Your Top viewport should look like the one in Figure 2.32.

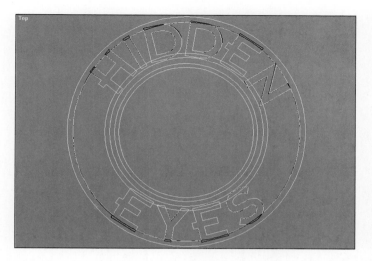

Figure 2.32 The circle spline after the letters have been subtracted with Boolean operations.

All that is left to do with this example is to subtract the circle that overlaps the bottom of the word *HIDDEN* and the top of the word *EYES*. That's easy to do.

6. Make sure the circle with the letters subtracted is selected, and then activate the Boolean button. Make sure Boolean is still set to Subtraction and click the circle that is overlapping the bottom of the word *HIDDEN*.

    The logo shape is finished, but before you jump for joy and high five yourself, you should double-check your work.

7. Make sure the shape of the letters matches the shapes of the frozen template. The Boolean operation has a tendency to throw in a surprise or two every now and then. Pay particular attention to the curves in the Ds. If the letters seem incorrect, enter the Sub-Object/Vertex level and fix the control tangent.

8. Make sure the Bézier vertices are, in fact, Bézier vertices, and make sure the Bézier Corner vertices are only where they belong.

Note

It is a good practice to go in and fix the new tight corners created with the Boolean operation (for example, where the curved letters meet the circles).

9. When your logo shape looks like the one in Figure 2.33, save your work as **ch02-05.max**.

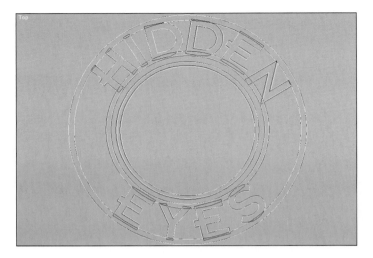

Figure 2.33   The finished logo shape.

Adding a Touch of Class: The Rounded Bevel

One of the most frustrating things for a person modeling logos or any other lofted shape is creating effective rounded bevels. MAX offers three ways to round a bevel; not knowing which one to use can be very frustrating. However, once you become familiar with all three, you'll find it quite easy to get the rounded bevels you want. Before moving on with the tutorial, let's look at three ways to create a rounded bevel with MAX.

From the accompanying CD, open the file \ch02\RoundedBevel.max. The file has three letter Ts in a large Perspective viewport and three smaller viewports with cross-section views of the bevel of each T (see Figure 2.34).

The three letter Ts are beveled three completely different ways. The quality of the three methods is shown in ascending order, the lowest being the poorest quality rounded bevel. Let's start from the bottom and work our way up:

- *Bevel_Modifier*. This object (the bottom one) has a Bevel modifier applied to a shape. From the Bevel modifier's Surface group, the Curved Sides feature is selected. As you can see, it's a poor rounded bevel at best. The extruded side should be straight!

- *Loft*. The middle T shows a sensible approach to making a rounded bevel. This bevel is totally acceptable, but it's a pain to configure, and it adds extra faces to the extruded side making an unnecessarily high polygon count. To create this bevel with a loft, you create a Line from the Create/Splines panel and assign the proper height of the complete extrusion (including bevels). You then assign the T shape to be a Loft from the Create/Loft Object panel. Using the Get Path command, select the extrusion Line as a Path. After the object is created, access the Loft Parameters from the Modify panel, open the Deformations rollout, open the Bevel Deformation dialog box, and draw a deformation spline to make the bevel.

- *Bevel_Profile_Modifier.* This is an example of the easiest and best way to create a beautiful, polygon-count-savvy, rounded-bevel object. With this method, you draw a spline, creating an accurate profile of the rounded bevel. First, select the letter T spline, and then apply a Bevel Profile modifier and select the profile spline as the profile. (You may need to adjust the Sub-Object gizmo of the Bevel Profile modifier to position the bevel properly on the object.)

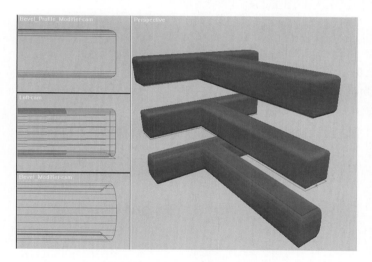

Figure 2.34   RoundedBevel.max illustrates the three most popular ways to make rounded bevels.

Warning

There is one major drawback to working with the Bevel Profile modifier. It can be very fussy about which viewport the shape is created in. It is good practice to build all the shapes to be beveled in the Top viewport. Draw the Bevel Profile spline in the Front viewport, starting where the extrusion is to begin, and work to the right and up for the bottom bevel, straight up for the extruded side, and up and to the left for the top bevel. This method ensures predictable results. While I am sure there is a combination for every viewport, this is mine.

Exercise 2.11   Making a Reference Bevel Object

With this information in mind, let's put a rounded bevel on the logo shape that we sweated to make perfect. Of course, we will be using the Bevel Profile modifier to do so. Why settle for anything less than perfection?

1. Open ch02-05.max, the slick logo shape that we created.

   We need a plan of attack for creating a rounded bevel on this object. We'll start by putting a Bevel modifier on the object and setting it up to make it look exactly how we want it to before applying the Bevel Profile modifier. This way we'll have something to trace when we create the profile spline.

Tip

I created a specific set of modifiers for working with logo elements. You can create your own set by clicking the Sets button in the Modify panel, entering the number of buttons, and assigning modifiers to each button. The set I created has six buttons: Edit Spline, Edit Mesh, Bevel, Bevel Profile, Xform, and UVW Map. These are the six tools I use most often.

2. Select the Logo-Font shape, and then, from the Modify panel, apply a Bevel modifier. Use the following settings to achieve the view shown in Figure 2.35:

   Start Outline: **0**

   Level 1: Height: **1.5**

   Level 1: Outline: **1.5**

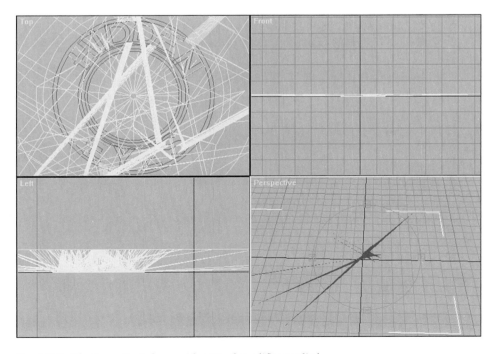

Figure 2.35   The Logo-Font shape with a Bevel modifier applied

What happened to our beautiful shape? That bevel is huge! We will have to enter very low numbers to make the desired bevel—or will we?

The shape looks miserable because the Adobe Illustrator file that we imported is very small; in fact, it's only around five units wide. It's my experience that Adobe Illustrator files import very small. We are going to have to make the logo shape much bigger before we apply the bevel. I, for one, don't want to have to mess with tiny numbers to get the bevel I want.

To make the Logo-Font shape larger, we have to apply an XForm modifier and scale the gizmo up. We can't just use the Select and Scale tool to scale up the shape because MAX applies the object level scale transform after the modifier stack has been evaluated and remembers that the object is five units wide. In this case, we need to scale the geometry of the object before it is acted on by the Bevel modifier. Placing an XForm modifier below the Bevel modifier allows us to scale the shape before it is passed into the Bevel modifier.

3. From the Modify panel, click the Remove Modifier From the Stack button to delete the Bevel modifier you added to the Logo-Font object.

4. Apply an XForm modifier to the Logo-Font shape. Make sure the Selection Level: Sub-Object gizmo is active. Then, with Use Selection Center active, use the Select and Uniform Scale tool to scale the gizmo up 3500%. Turn off Sub-Object.

Scaling the XForm gizmo up 3500% makes the logo shape roughly 200 units wide. This size is perfect for working with the Bevel modifier now.

 Note

Another reason for using the XForm modifier to scale up the shape is because it is very hard to animate tiny objects accurately. MAX displays distance down to only 1/1000 of a unit, and units that small are complicated to work with. In addition, when a camera is added to the scene, the camera has to be extremely close to the object in order for it to fill the Camera viewport. The default setting for clipping planes for a camera may clip out part of the logo, creating an unwanted result.

Since the XForm modifier has served its purpose, we can collapse the modifier stack.

5. Click the Edit Stack button to open the Edit Modifier Stack dialog box. Click the Collapse All button to collapse the stack back down to Editable Spline. Then click Yes at the warning prompt and click OK to exit the Edit Modifier Stack dialog box.

6. Click Zoom Extents and apply a Bevel modifier to the Logo-Font shape again.

The Bevel modifier should still remember the Level 1 settings we entered earlier: Height: **1.5** and Outline: **1.5** (see Figure 2.36).

7. Check Level 2 and enter Height: **10**, to make the extruded side 10 units high. Leave Outline: **0**.

8. Check Level 3 and enter Height: **1.5** and Outline: **–1.5**.

9. In the Surface group of the Parameters rollout, activate Linear Sides and change Segments to **1**.

Figure 2.36   The scaled Logo-Font shape after the Bevel modifier is reapplied.

Note

The way the Bevel modifier works is simple. The Start Outline value allows the user to trim or add to the original outline of the shape. The Level 1 Height setting tells the Bevel modifier to extrude the shape *x* amount of units, and the Outline value tells the Bevel modifier how many units to trim or add to the new level of the extrusion (in essence, the width). Levels 2 and 3 work the same way.

This completes the bevel process. The finished object should look like the one in Figure 2.37.

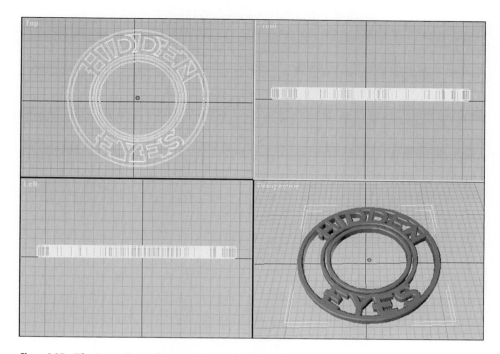

Figure 2.37   The Logo-Font object with completed Bevel modifier settings.

Exercise 2.12   Rounding the Bevel with Bevel Profile

Now we have a very nice looking logo object in front of us. But we want a rounded bevel. Well, let's use this bevel as our template.

1. In the Front viewport, use the Region Zoom tool to zoom in on the right side of the beveled object (see Figure 2.38). You may want to maximize the Front viewport with the Min/Max Toggle.

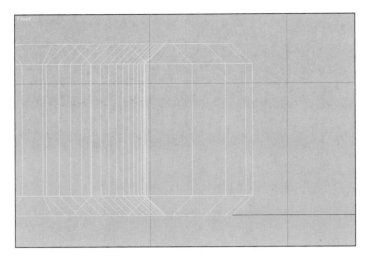

Figure 2.38   The Front viewport with the proper side zoomed in.

2. From the Create/Shapes panel, click Line. Then, in the Front viewport, click on the bottom corner of the bevel and drag to the right (about halfway to the exterior edge) to create a Bézier vertex.

3. Click on the corner of the first level and drag upward (about half the height of the first level) to create the second point.

4. Click on the corner of the second level and drag upward (about half way to the top level) to create a third vertex.

5. Click on the corner of the third level and drag to the left (about half the height of the top level) to create the forth and final vertex.

6. Right-click to exit the Create mode. Name the line **Logo-BevPro**.

7. Activate the Modify panel, enter the Sub-Object/Vertex level of the Line, and select the four vertices. Your viewport should look like Figure 2.39.

    Now we are ready to apply this profile spline to the logo shape and see the breathtaking rounded bevel in action.

8. Select the Logo-Font object and choose Edit, Clone to copy the object. Select Copy from the Clone Options dialog box and name the object **Logo-Font-Rounded**. Then click OK to exit the Clone Options dialog box.

    The new Logo-Font-Rounded object should now be selected.

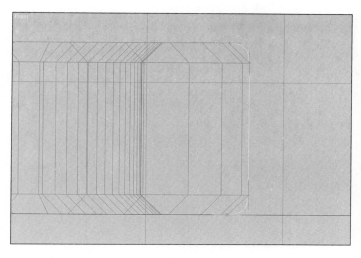

Figure 2.39   The proper profile spline.

9. Go to the Modify panel and remove the Bevel modifier from the stack to return to Editable Spline.

10. Add a Bevel Profile modifier to the Logo-Font-Rounded shape. Click the Pick Profile button and click the Logo-BevPro profile shape that you created (see Figure 2.40).

Note

The Bevel Profile Sub-Object gizmo is similar to the Start Outline of the Bevel modifier. Activating the Sub-Object gizmo of the Bevel Profile and moving the gizmo from left to right in the Front viewport adjusts the Start Outline of the beveled logo. We do not need to adjust the gizmo for our logo.

If you use a Start Outline value in your Bevel Modifier object, you will need to adjust your Bevel Profile gizmo the same value in units to achieve the same effect.

Good work, we have a beautiful logo with a rounded bevel! Let's clean up our workspace before we clean up the logo some more.

11. Click the Display tab and, from the Freeze rollout, click the Unfreeze All button. This will unfreeze the reference spline we traced earlier.

12. Open the Select by Name dialog box, either by clicking its button or by pressing H on the keyboard. Select Logo-Font and Logo-Template, and then click Select to exit the Select Objects dialog box.

Tip

You can use Ctrl+click to select multiple names.

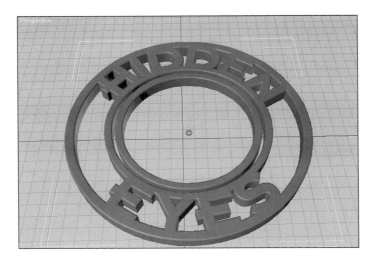

Figure 2.40   The rounded bevel logo object.

13. Press the Delete key on the keyboard to delete the template shape and the logo with the Bevel modifier.

Exercise 2.13   Optimize the Rounded Beveled Object

We can't delete the Logo-BevPro shape yet because the Bevel Profile modifier is still using it as a reference. The Bevel profile shape provides versatility to the logo object. Let's take advantage of it.

1. Select the Logo-BevPro shape and open the Modify panel. In the Front viewport, zoom in close to the right edge of the logo, where the Logo-BevPro spline is located.

2. From the Modify panel, uncheck the Optimize button in the General rollout (see Figure 2.41).

    The Optimize button optimizes the step interpolation of the spline. A straight edge is a straight edge whether it has 1 or 100 faces on it. The only reason we would need this unchecked is if we were going to modify the straight edge with conventional modeling methods later. We are going to leave it just the way it is, so let's turn Optimize back on.

3. Check Optimize to activate the Optimize feature and remove the unwanted faces along the straight extruded edge (see Figure 2.42). Notice in the Interpolation group that the Steps value is set to 6. This value tells MAX how many faces to add between two vertices on a curved spline. Let's see what happens if we set Steps to 0.

4. In the Modify panel, enter Steps: **0** in the General rollout as shown in Figure 2.43.

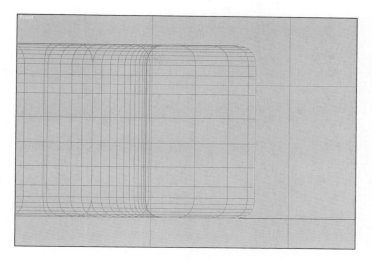

Figure 2.41   The logo with added faces along a straight extruded edge with Optimize unchecked.

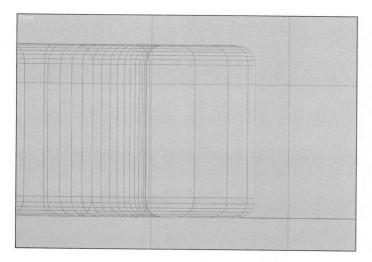

Figure 2.42   Logo-BevPro with Optimize active again.

Oh no, the dreaded straight bevel. The reason the profile turned into a straight Bevel Profile is because when the Steps value is zero, no interpolation occurs, making the shape linear from vertex to vertex. We certainly don't want that! But don't you think that six steps is too many? I am sure we can get away with three. Think of all the polygons we are saving.

5. Change the Steps value to Steps: **3** (see Figure 2.44).

6. Save your work as **ch02-06.max**.

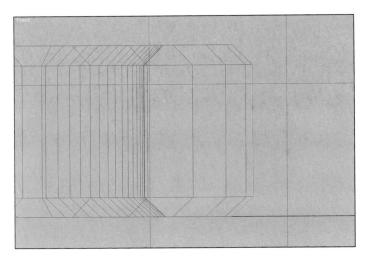

Figure 2.43   You can create a straight bevel with a Steps value of 0.

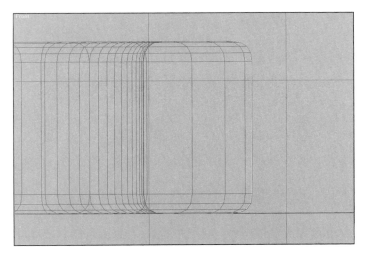

Figure 2.44   Rounded bevel with Interpolation set to Steps: 3.

The rounded bevel looks great with a Steps: 3 value. This completes the creation of the rounded bevel object. The logo object should have a rounded bevel and should have no missing faces, which are caused by overlapping faces. If your logo has missing faces, please go back and examine the logo spline for tight corners.

Completing the Logo

Now that we have created the major element of the logo, we can add the mysterious eye in the center of the logo. But before we do that, let's position the text element and stand it upright.

Now that our rounded bevel logo object has been created, we must stand it up in world space. It is good working practice to have the logo objects standing up in the scene: Standing the logo up allows us to understand its orientation in the viewports clearly. Also, when we apply a reflection bitmap to the object, which we will, we can see the "pinching" of the reflection bitmap caused by the spherical mapping coordinates (which occur at the top and bottom of world space).

Exercise 2.14   Positioning the Logo

Let's heave that logo into an upright position.

1. Open ch02-06.max.

2. Select the Logo-Font-Rounded object and click the Hierarchy tab. In the Adjust Pivot rollout, click the Affect Pivot Only button from the Move/Rotate/Scale group. With that button activated, click the Center to Object button in the Alignment group. Click the Affect Pivot Only button to turn it off.

   Now let's move the object to the center of the world coordinate system so we know exactly where it is, and the logo will be centered according to the world.

Tip

When I make any animation, I try to keep everything centered to the 0, 0, 0 world coordinates. Using these settings helps me keep track of everything and make things much easier to position in the long run.

3. Open the Move Transform Type-In dialog box and enter these Absolute:World coordinates to center the object on the world coordinates:

   XYZ: [**0,0,0**]

   Now let's stand the logo text upright in the world so we can see it in the Front viewport.

4. In the Rotate Transform Type-In dialog box, enter the Absolute:World coordinate X: **90** to rotate the object 90 degrees and stand it upright.

Exercise 2.15   Creating the Eyeball Objects

Let's create the eyeball that will be peering from the center of the logo, and then we will create the eyelids.

1. To create the eyeball, turn on the 3D Snap Toggle, click the Create tab, and click Sphere from Standard Primitives.

2. In the Front viewport, place the pointer over the intersection of the black lines (the X,Y coordinates of 0,0) and click and drag to create a sphere with a radius of **50**.

Note

To make sure the sphere is located at the XYZ coordinates [0,0,0], open the Move Transform Type-In dialog box and make sure the Absolute:World coordinates are all zero.

3. Name this object **Eyeball** (see Figure 2.45).

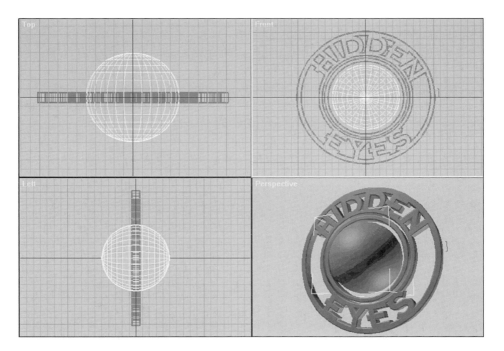

Figure 2.45   The Eyeball sphere.

4. Creating the eyelids is no problem. We make them by modifying the Eyeball.

   With the eyeball selected, Edit, Clone the eyeball, copy it, and name the new object **Eyelid-Top**.

   Well it doesn't look too much like an eyelid quite yet. We need to chop the sphere a tad bit less than half and rotate it into its closed position.

5. With the Eyelid-Top object selected, open the Rotate Transform Type-In dialog box and return the X coordinate to **0**.

6. Click the Modify tab and in the Sphere Parameters rollout, enter Hemisphere value of **0.52**. Make sure the Hemisphere method is set to Chop.

Note

The difference between Chop and Squash is simple. *Chop* simply slices the object at the Hemisphere value as if the object was chopped in half. *Squash* creates a hemisphere from the Sphere object and keeps the object segment value the same. We don't need to use Squash because it would add unnecessary faces.

Well, that made a reasonably cool top eyelid, but it is the same size as the eyeball. Let's make it a bit bigger.

7. From the Modify panel, enter Radius: **53**, making the eyelid slightly bigger than the eyeball (see Figure 2.46).

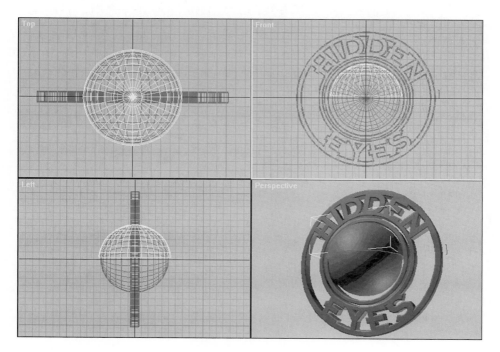

Figure 2.46 The Eyelid-Top object.

To create the bottom eyelid, let's just instance the top eyelid and turn it upside down.

8. With the Eyelid-Top object selected, use Edit, Clone to instance the top eyelid and call the new object **Eyelid-Bottom**.

Now we need to rotate the bottom eyelid so it is, in fact, on the bottom.

9. Open the Rotate Transform Type-In dialog box and enter the coordinate X: **180**. This rotates the object 180 degrees. Your model should look like the one in Figure 2.47 at this point.

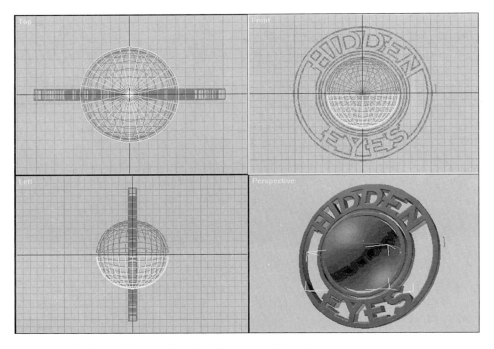

Figure 2.47   The logo objects as they should appear at this point.

Although these eyelids are acceptable, let's add a little lip to the edges to give the eyelids a slicker look.

10. Click on the Create tab and click Torus. Then using 3D Snap, click on the X,Y gridline intersection [0,0] in the Top viewport and drag to create the first radius. Move the mouse a little further in the same direction and click to create the second radius. Enter these values:

    Radius 1: **53**

    Radius 2: **3.0**

    Segments: **30**

    Sides: **8**

11. Name this object **Eyelid-Top-Lip** (see Figure 2.48).

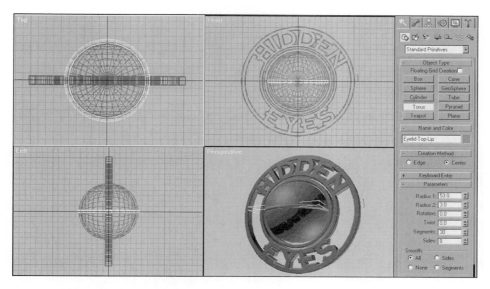

Figure 2.48   The Eyelid-Top-Lip object.

Let's move the torus up so it matches the top eyelid.

12. In the Move Transform Type-In dialog box, enter these Absolute:World coordinates to center the lip object over the edge of the eyelid:

     XYZ: [**0,0,3**]

It's time to create the lower eyelid lip. Any suggestions? Instance the top one, you say? Sounds good to me.

13. With the Eyelid-Top-Lip object selected, use Edit, Clone to instance the eyelid and call it **Eyelid-Bottom-Lip**.

14. In the Move Transform Type-In dialog box, enter these Absolute:World coordinates to center the lip over the edge of the bottom eyelid, as shown in Figure 2.49:

     XYZ: [**0,0,–3**]

This looks pretty good, except that the lip travels all the way around the eye. Let's fix it so the lip covers only the facing edge of the eyelid.

15. With either eyelid lip object selected, click the Modify tab. In the Torus Creation Parameters rollout, select Slice On to turn on Object Slicing. Enter Slice From: **–90** and Slice To: **90** to remove the eyelid lip from the back of the eyeball (see Figure 2.50).

16. Save your work as **ch02-07.max**.

This completes the modeling phase of the objects. All we need to do now is set up a few hierarchies and texture these objects. Then they are ready to be animated. Let's not waste any time but begin immediately to set up the hierarchy of the objects.

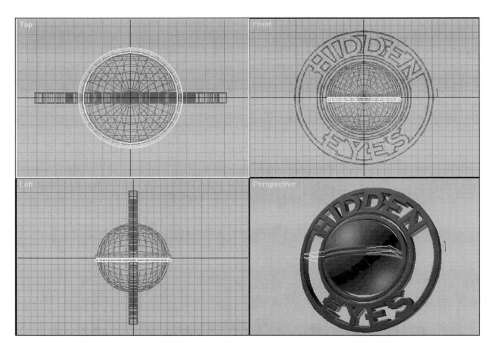

Figure 2.49   The Eyelid-Bottom-Lip object.

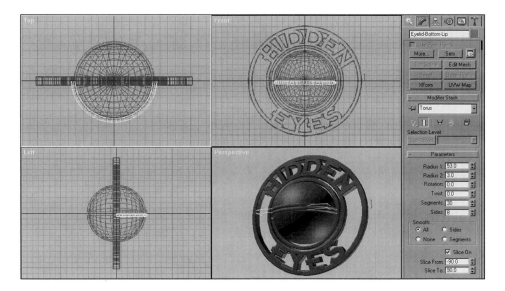

Figure 2.50   The finished logo object.

Creating the Link Hierarchy for the Logo Objects

To animate the logo in the scene, we need to create a hierarchy to hold it all together. We'll make the Logo-Font-Rounded object the parent of the hierarchy because it's the main element of the logo objects. We'll then link the Eyeball, Eyelid-Top, and Eyelid-Bottom objects to the Logo-Font Rounded object so that no matter where the Logo-Font-Rounded object goes, those objects will follow. The eyelid lip objects need to be linked as children to their corresponding eyelid objects because we want them to rotate and move with the eyelid objects.

Here is the hierarchy tree we want to establish for these objects:

Logo-Font-Rounded

    Eyeball

    Eyelid-Top

        Eyelid-Top-Lip

    Eyelid-Bottom

        Eyelid-Bottom-Lip

Exercise 2.16   Creating the Hierarchy

To create the hierarchy, we need to select the child or sibling first and then select the intended parent object. Let's start building the hierarchy.

1. Press the H key to open the Select Objects dialog box, and then select the Eyeball and eyelid (Eyelid-Bottom and Eyelid-Top) objects because they are the first children in the hierarchy tree. Click Select to exit the dialog box. Then click the Select and Link button and press the H key to open the Select Parent dialog box. Select Logo-Font-Rounded and click the Link button to create the link.

   Now we will link the eyelid lips to the eyelids. We need to link them separately.

2. Click the Select Objects button and press the H key to open the Select Objects dialog box. Select Eyelid-Top-Lip and click Select to exit the dialog box. Then click the Select and Link button and press the H key to open the Select Parent dialog box. Select Eyelid-Top and click Link to create the link and exit the dialog box.

3. To link the bottom eyelid lip to the bottom eyelid, click the Select Objects button and press the H key to open the Select Objects dialog box. Select Eyelid-Bottom-Lip and click Select to exit the dialog box. Then click the Select and Link button and press the H key to open the Select Parent dialog box. Select Eyelid-Bottom and click Link to exit the dialog box.

   We've finished creating the object hierarchy of the logo. However, we'll all feel better if we check to make sure the hierarchy is correct.

4. Click the Select Objects tool and press the H key to open the Select Objects dialog box. Check the Display Subtree box, and the hierarchy of the objects will be displayed (see Figure 2.51).

Figure 2.51   The correct object hierarchy of the logo objects.

5. Save your work as **ch02-08.max**.

Texturing the Logo Objects

It is time to texture the logo objects we created. Because the logo and eyelids will have metal textures, there is no need for explicit mapping coordinates. The eyeball, however, will have a texture map of an eye mapped onto it. No mapping coordinates have been applied to the eyeball object, however. So before we add the texture, we need to apply UVW mapping coordinates.

The object that will certainly grab the viewer's attention is going to be the eyeball object. The eyeball is going to be mapped with an eerie, hyper-realistic texture. Because the eyeball texture is centered on the middle of the eye, it is most practical to apply a Planar UVW Map to the eyeball object. Any stretching or distortion around the sides of the object will not be apparent because the texture in those areas has a relatively uniform color.

Exercise 2.17   Adding Texture to the Eyeball

The eyelids and eyelid-lips are blocking our view of the eyeball, so first let's hide the eyelid objects. Then we'll add texture coordinates to the eyeball object and apply the eyeball texture.

1. With ch02-08.max open, click the Display tab. Then from the Hide rollout, click Hide By Name to open the Hide Objects dialog box. Select the eyelid and eyelid-lip objects and click Hide to exit the dialog box and hide the objects.

Now that we have a nice view of the eyeball, we can add the texture coordinates and apply the texture.

2. Highlight the Front viewport, select the Eyeball object and, from the Modify panel, add a UVW Map modifier.

    The default mapping gizmo is the Planar gizmo, which is exactly what we need. Because the Front viewport was selected, the mapping gizmo was automatically aligned to face forward. The UVW Map modifier has automatically scaled the gizmo to precisely fit the Eyeball object as we need it to. Now let's create the material.

3. Open the Material Editor and click the second material slot (we are reserving the first slot for the logo material). In the Shader rollout, enter these values to create a nice, artificial plastic-looking material:

    Shader: **Phong**

    Glossiness: **50**

    Specular Level: **100**

4. Name this material **Eyeball**.

    Now we need to apply the eyeball texture to the Diffuse channel.

5. Open the Maps rollout and click the None button for the Diffuse Color. From the Material/Map Browser, set Browse From: **New**, choose Bitmap, and click OK to exit the browser. In the Select Bitmap Image File dialog box, choose ch02\maps\eyeball.jpg on the accompanying CD. Name this map **Eyeball-dif**. Make sure the Eyeball object is still selected and click the Assign Material To Selection button.

 Note

In eyeball.jpg, notice that the whites of the eyes are a grayish purple. A common mistake new animators and artists make is to assign a texture the color they "think" it is rather than assigning a color that will add a more dramatic effect. I always try to avoid using the obvious color.

6. To make the sphere look more like an eyeball in the shaded viewport, click the Show Map In Viewport button. Figure 2.52 shows how the eyeball texture should appear in the shaded viewport. Click the Go to Parent button to return to the root of the material.

Figure 2.52   The Eyeball texture is displayed on the Eyeball object in the shaded Perspective view.

Assigning Proper Material IDs to the Logo Object

To create the material for the Logo-Font-Rounded object, we will be assigning three separate material IDs to the logo object so that we can isolate the three main sections of the object. We will be isolating the following sections:

- *Face.* The readable face of the object; the part of the logo that is read and is most visible to the viewer.
- *Bevel.* The rounded bevel edge of the object.
- *Side.* The extruded side of the logo object.

We isolate these three sections so that three separate materials can be added to the model. If one material is applied to the model, it's very hard to tweak a highlight or control the highlights on the sides without changing the highlights on the face. Using three separate materials gives us maximum control over the highlights.

Exercise 2.18   Assigning Proper Material IDs

First, let's hide the Eyeball object so it doesn't get in the way. Then, in order to isolate the three sections of the model, we must apply an Edit Mesh modifier and change the Face settings.

1. Click the Display tab and choose Hide by Name to hide the Eyeball object. While you're at it, hide the Logo-BevPro shape (our bevel profile spline) because you don't need it visible anymore. Click Hide to exit.

2. Select the Logo-Font-Rounded object and, from the Modify panel, add an Edit Mesh modifier.

3. Maximize the Left viewport and activate Sub-Object/Polygon level. Use Edit, Select Invert to select all the faces of the object. Then move down to the Edit Surface roll-out in the Modify panel and enter the extruded edge (or side's) Material:ID: **3**.

4. To select the front and back bevels of the logo (see Figure 2.53), use the Rectangular Selection Region (Window Selection) to select the back faces, and then hold down the Ctrl key (to add to the selection) and use the Rectangular Selection Region to select the front faces. In the Edit Surface rollout, enter Material:ID: **2** as the beveled edge material assignment.

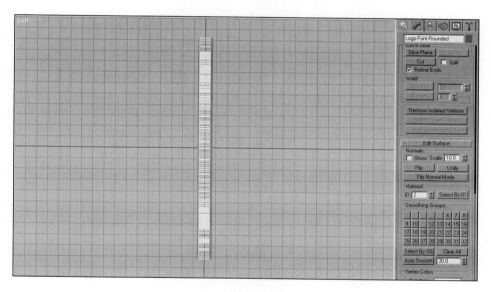

Figure 2.53   Assign Material:ID: 2 to these faces.

Now the extruded edge has a Material ID of 3, and the beveled edge and readable face of the object have a Material ID of 2. We need to select the readable face of the object and change its Material ID to 1. It would be quite hard to try to select the thin front and back faces of the object without accidentally selecting some of the bevels using the method we used to select the side and the bevel. Therefore, we need to implement another method of selecting the front and back faces.

5. Click the Min/Max Toggle to see all four viewports again. Highlight the Perspective viewport and Maximize it. Right-click on the Perspective viewport's name and select Edged Faces.

6. To select the front faces as shown in Figure 2.54, continue in Sub-Object/Polygon. Click on one of the front faces to select it and all coplanar faces. If the faces do not turn red, click in another spot until the front faces are selected. You will also need to select the inner ring's front faces in the same manner. Once the front faces are selected, assign Material:ID: **1**.

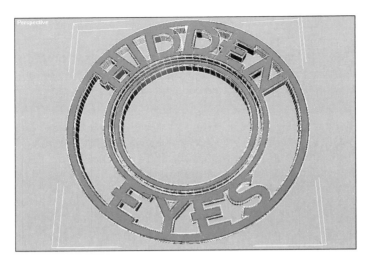

Figure 2.54   The logo object with front faces selected.

7. Choose Views, Save Active Perspective View to save the Perspective's viewpoint so you can return to it later.

8. To select the backside of the logo object (see Figure 2.55), use Arc Rotate Selected to see the back of the object in the Perspective viewport. Select the back faces of the object, assign Material:ID: **1** to the back faces, and turn off the Edit Mesh Sub-Object button.

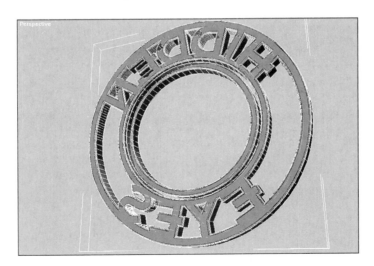

Figure 2.55   The logo object with back face selected.

9. Load the saved Perspective view from Views, Restore Active Perspective Viewport.

10. Save your work as **ch02-09.max.**

Exercise 2.19   Creating the Logo Material

Now that the logo object has the proper Material IDs, we are ready to create the material. This logo will have a gold material on the face and sides, and the bevel will have a bluish silver material.

1. With ch02-09.max loaded, open the Material Editor, click the first material slot, and name this material **Logo**. To change the material type from Standard to Multi/Sub-Object, click the Type: Standard button, set Browse From to New, and select Multi/Sub-Object. Click OK to exit the Material/Map Browser. From the Replace Material dialog box, choose Discard Old Material? and click OK to exit.

2. From the root of the Logo Material, click the Set Number button and enter Number of Materials: **3** (to account for the face, bevel and side). Click OK to exit the Set Number of Materials dialog box.

3. Click the first material slot to open Material 1's Basic Parameters, and name this material Logo-Face. To make a gold material, use these settings:

   Shader: **Metal**

   Ambient color swatch: RGB (**34,21,8**)

   Diffuse color swatch: RGB (**139,106,34**)

   Specular Level: **80**

   Glossiness: **80**

4. To make this material slightly reflective, open the Maps rollout, click the None next to the Reflection map, set Browse From to New, select Bitmap, and click OK to exit the Material/Map Browser. In the Select Bitmap Image File dialog box, choose the file ch02\maps\sunset90.jpg and click OK to exit. Name this texture map **Logo-Face-rfl** and click the blank next to Bitmap in the Bitmap Parameters rollout.

5. This makes a very nice refection, but it's too focused and intense. To make the reflection more subtle, enter Blur Offset: **0.012** in the Coordinates rollout.

 Note

Make sure the Mapping type is set to Environ Mapping: Spherical Environment for all the refection maps in this tutorial. The Spherical Environment simply wraps the bitmap around an imaginary sphere that surrounds the scene.

6. Click the Go to Parent button once to return to the top level of the Logo-Face material. To make the reflection less obvious, enter Reflection: **50** in the Maps rollout.

   This completes the face material. Let's work on the bluish silver material now.

7. Click Go to Parent to return to the root of the Logo Multi/Sub-Object material. Click the second material slot and name this material **Logo-Bevel**.

8. To make the bluish silver material, use these settings:

    Shader: **Metal**

    Ambient color swatch: RGB (**6,7,26**)

    Diffuse color swatch: RGB (**141,201,210**)

    Specular Level: **75**

    Glossiness: **70**

Note

You can create a much more realistic material if the hue of the Ambient and Diffuse colors are different.

9. To add a refection map, click the None next to the Reflection parameters in the Maps rollout, set Browse From to New, select Bitmap, and click OK to exit the browser. Choose ch02\maps\refmap.gif and name this refection **Map Logo-Bevel-rfl**. Enter Blur Offset: **0.05** to blur the map slightly. Then click the Go to Parent button to return to the top level of the Logo-Bevel and enter Reflection: **65** in the Maps rollout.

    This finishes the Bevel material; all that is left of finishing the textures for the Logo-Font-Rounded material is to create the side texture (#3).

10. In the Material Editor, click the Go to Parent button to go to the root of the Logo Multi/Sub-Object material. Click the third material slot to open the Basic Parameters.

    Because this material is going to be similar to the material on the face, let's just copy the face material and change its parameters to make it less shiny.

11. Click the Type: Standard button. Then, in the Material/Map Browser, set Browse From: Mtl Editor and uncheck the Root Only option. Select [1]: Logo-Face (Standard2) and click OK to exit the Material/Map Browser. At the Instance Or Copy? prompt, choose Copy and click OK.

12. Name this material **Logo-Side** and enter Specular Level: **70** and Glossiness: **65**.

13. To make the refection more obvious on this material, enter Reflection: **100** in the Maps rollout. Right-click the Perspective viewport name and uncheck Edged Faces.

    The Logo material is finished. Let's apply it to the model.

14. Click the Assign Material To Selection button to assign the material to the logo object.

Exercise 2.20   Texturing the Eyelid Objects

Before texturing the eyelids, we need to unhide them and position them correctly. Right now they're covering the eyeball object, and it would be nice to see all our objects as we work on the textures.

1. Click the Display tab and click Unhide By Name. From the Unhide Objects dialog box, select all the objects except the Logo-BevPro shape and click Unhide to unhide the objects and exit the dialog box.

   Let's open the eyelids up a bit so they aren't covering the eyeball.

2. Select the Eyelid-Top object and use the Rotate Transform Type-In dialog box to rotate it. Enter the coordinate X: **–30**. Select the Eyelid-Bottom object and enter the coordinate X: **–150**.

Note

The eyelid-lip objects rotate with the eyelids because of the hierarchy we set up earlier.

Now we can texture the eyelid and eyelid-lip objects. The eyelid objects will have a gold material on them, so we can use the gold material we created for the face of the logo.

3. Open the Material Editor and select the first material slot in the second row. Name this material **Eyelids** and click the Type: Standard button to open the Material/Map Browser. Set Browse From to Scene, uncheck Root Only, and select the [1]: Logo-Face (Standard2) material. Click OK to exit the browser. Then, from the Instance Or Copy? prompt, choose Method Copy and click OK to exit.

Note

This copies the material from the Multi-Sub-Object type as a Standard2 material type.

4. Click and drag the Eyelids material slot from the Material Editor and move the cursor over the Eyelid-Top object until its nametag is displayed. Release the mouse button to assign the material to Eyelid-Top. Do the same to assign the material to the Eyelid-Bottom object.

5. The eyelid-lip objects will have the bluish silver material applied to them. Select the second material slot in the second row and name the material **Eyelid-Lips**. Click the Type: Standard button to open the Material/Map Browser. Set Browser From to Scene, uncheck the Root Only option, select [2]: Logo-Bevel (Standard), and click OK to exit the browser. From the Instance Or Copy? prompt, choose Copy and click OK to exit.

6. To assign the material to the eyelid-lips objects, click and drag the material slot over the Eyelid-Top-Lip and Eyelid-Bottom-Lip objects and release the mouse to assign the material.

   This completes the texturing process of the logo. If you render a frame of the scene, it should look like Figure 2.56.

Figure 2.56 The rendered textured logo objects.

7. Save your work as **ch02-10.max**.

Lighting the Logo Objects

Now that the logo has beautiful materials on it, it's time to set up a camera and start placing lights in the scene. Remember your crash course in Three-Point Lighting? I hope so; you are going to need it.

Exercise 2.21   Placing Lights in the Scene

In this tutorial, we set up the Key light, the Fill light, the Back light and even a Special light for the logo. Let's put our knowledge of Three-Point Lighting to use.

1. With ch02-10.max open, create a Free Camera in the Front viewport and use the Move Transform Type-In dialog box to move the camera to these Absolute:World coordinates:

    XYZ: [**0,–400,0**]

2. Change the Perspective viewport to the Camera viewport.

    Now that we have a camera, let's add some lights to the scene.

3. Create an Omni light (the Key light) in the Top viewport and use the Move Transform Type-In dialog box to move the light to these coordinates:

    XYZ: [**–200,–620,150**]

    Name this light **Omni-Key** and use the Color Selector to enter these color values:

    RGB: (**135,116,61**)

Note

Usually when I am positioning lights, I set the Multiplier to 10 to make the highlights more obvious in the Camera viewport. Just remember to set the multiplier back to 1 before you move on.

3. For the Fill light, create an Omni light in the Top viewport (or just copy the Key Light), name it **Omni-Fill,** and use the Move Transform Type-In dialog box to move the light to these coordinates:

   XYZ: [**90,–620,–150**]

   Use the Color Selector to enter these color values:

   RGB: (**100,68,13**)

4. Create an Omni light in the Top viewport for our Back light. Name the Omni light **Omni-Back** and use the Move Transform Type-In dialog box to move the light to these coordinates:

   XYZ: [**–130,680,190**]

   Use the Color Selector to enter these color values:

   RGB: (**15,72,150**)

   The Back light will be a bluish color to mimic the blue hue of the filmstrip background.

5. Render the Camera viewport (see Figure 2.57).

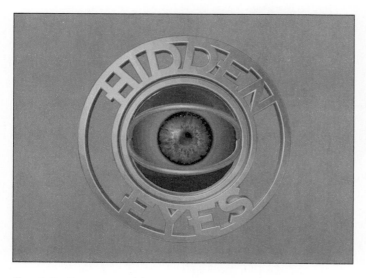

Figure 2.57 Frame zero of the Camera viewport rendered.

It looks pretty good, but it would look much better with a few extra highlights here and there. Let's add a bright white highlight to the eyeball object. It's time to add some Special lights.

6. Create an Omni light in the Top viewport, call it **Omni-Special-Eyeball**, and move the light to these coordinates:

   XYZ: [**−770,−440,−380**]

   Enter these color values:

   RGB: (**180,180,180**)

   Let's create an Include list for this light to ensure this light casts a highlight on the Eyeball object only.

7. Click the Exclude button from the Omni light's General Parameters rollout. In the Scene Objects, select Eyeball, click the arrow pointing to the right, and click the Include radio button to change it to an Include list. Click OK to exit the dialog box.

   Now this light will cast light on the Eyeball object only.

8. Render the Camera viewport to see the results (shown in Figure 2.58).

Figure 2.58   The Camera viewport rendered with highlight from the Special light on the Eyeball object.

To add more dramatic contrast, we will add one more Special Omni light to the scene to cast a nice highlight on the top eyelid.

9. In the Top viewport, create an Omni light, name it **Omni-Special-Eyelid-Top,** and move the light to these coordinates:

   XYZ: [**−250,580,330**]

   Enter these color values:

   RGB: (**137,114,20**)

10. To create an Include list for this light, click the Exclude button, select Eyelid-Top, click the arrow pointing to the right, and click the Include radio button. Click OK to exit the Exclude/Include dialog box.

11. Render the Camera viewport; it should look like Figure 2.59.

12. Save your work as **ch02-11.max**.

Figure 2.59   The finished rendered logo object.

In Summary

This completes this chapter and part of the tutorial. We are now ready to take this textured logo file and apply it over the filmstrip background we created in Chapter 1.

Chapter 3

Using Motion Capture

The MAX Motion Capture utility is not just for moving elements in your scene. It can also capture data for all the animatable parameters within your scene.

From moving something through your scene, to turning on lights, to adjusting the intensity of maps or the number of faces on an object, the uses for Motion Capture are practically limitless.

In this chapter, we experiment with using two common input devices, the mouse and the keyboard, to capture motion. We also take a close look at adjusting the parameters of the controllers to get the maximum realistic effects.

Let's examine the logo elements and plan their animation. The main logo element is straightforward, so we will be able to easily key its motion by hand. However, for the eyeball and eyelids, we may have some trouble creating a realistic and believable animation. The eyeball needs to be able to look around with a fluid multi-axis rotation. This rotation is complicated to key by hand, but with Motion Capture, we have a simple and quick solution for creating realistic animation.

3D Studio MAX has a very versatile Motion Capture interface that provides the user flexibility that can be applied to many aspects of animation. Motion Capture enables the MAX user to create keys in real time using a data input device such as the mouse or keyboard. In order for Motion Capture to work, the correct motion controllers and parameters must be assigned. Correctly configured, Motion Capture easily creates complicated motion quickly and effectively.

When you use Motion Capture, an external device attached to the computer (such as the mouse, keyboard, or joystick) acts as an input device, recording and inputting motion data into the computer. The Motion Capture utility then converts this motion input data into keys or motion sets that are applied to objects in the scene.

Viewing an Animation Created with Motion Capture

First, we'll view an animation that was created completely with Motion Capture inside 3D Studio MAX, load the file in which the animation was created, and quickly examine its controllers.

View desk.avi from ch03\images on the included CD.

 Note
Use the File, View command on the 3D Studio MAX toolbar to view the file.

When you play the animation, you should see a busy office desktop currently occupied by an invisible man. As you can see in the animation, the invisible man is writing with a pencil and taking a sip of Joe from his coffee mug. He is presumably writing a letter of complaint to the manufacturer of the faulty desktop lamp that is flashing on and off irregularly.

Believe it or not, not one key in this animation was animated by hand. Motion Capture input data controlled every animated object.

Exercise 3.1   Examining Motion Capture in Action

To understand how this animation was created, let's open the office desktop scene with the Motion Capture controllers already assigned to familiarize ourselves with how Motion Capture works.

1. From the ch03 directory of the accompanying CD, load desk.max. You should see the desktop, the coffee mug, the pencil, and the desktop lamp objects as they appeared in the rendered animation (see Figure 3.1).

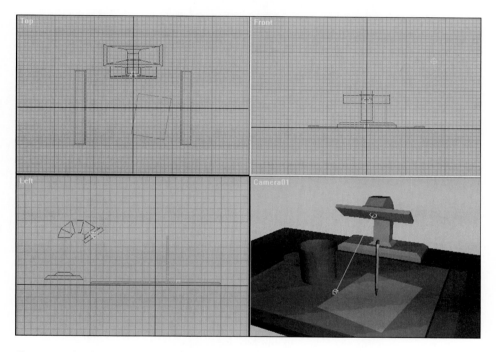

Figure 3.1   The desk.max file from the ch03 directory.

2. To view the Motion Capture controllers, click the Utilities tab, and select Motion Capture from the Utilities rollout.

Note

If you can't find Motion Capture in the list, click More and select it from the resulting options.

In the Motion Capture rollout shown in Figure 3.2, you will see the Record Controls and Tracks groups. The Record Controls group holds all the recording and testing controls for the Motion Capture interface. The Tracks group displays the motion controller tracks that have been added to the scene.

3. Double-click a track in the Tracks group to open the tracks Motion Capture controller dialog box. This scene has six Motion Capture tracks:

DeskLight\Self-Illumination is assigned to the Z key on the keyboard. The motion capture controller was assigned to the self-illumination of the desk light material. Pressing the Z key during Motion Capture changes the self-illumination of the material to 100 percent. Releasing the key returns the self-illumination back to 0 percent.

Pencil\Position is assigned to mouse input data. Moving the mouse up and down moves the pencil along the object's local Y-axis coordinates. Moving the mouse right to left moves the pencil along the object's local X-axis accordingly.

Pencil\Rotation is assigned to mouse input data. Moving the mouse up and down rotates the pencil on the object's local X-axis. Moving the mouse right to left rotates the pencil on the object's local Y-axis.

Spot01\Multiplier is assigned to the Z key on the keyboard. Pressing the Z key during Motion Capture testing or recording changes the multiplier value of Spot01 (simulating the light from the desktop lamp) from 0 to 1. Releasing the Z key returns Spot01's multiplier setting to 0.

CoffeeMug\Position is assigned to the X key on the keyboard. Pressing the X key during Motion Capture testing or recording moves the CoffeeMug object a predetermined distance (−20 units) along the object's local Y-axis and (50 units) along the object's local Z-axis. Releasing the key returns the mug to its place of origin.

CoffeeMug\Rotation is also assigned to the X key on the keyboard. During Motion Capture, pressing the X key rotates the CoffeeMug object on the object's local X-axis. The rotation has been slightly delayed because we want the mug to actually lift to a drinking position before rotating. Releasing the key will return the object to its original rotation.

Figure 3.2 The Motion Capture rollout for desk.max.

4. Make sure all the controllers in the Tracks group are selected. Then, in the Record Controls group, click the Test button.

Note

A track is selected when the box next to the track is filled with a red color. Deselecting a track removes it from the active tracks. Inactive tracks will not respond to the input data nor will they record keys during Motion Capture recording. This enables the user to record each track individually.

5. Move the mouse to control the pencil's position and rotation in the scene. Press the Z key on the keyboard to "turn" the light on, and then press the X key to make the invisible man take a drink. Releasing the Z key turns the light off, and releasing the X key returns the mug to its original position. Right-click to exit testing.

In order to fully understand how this Motion Capture works, let's look at the Motion Capture controllers.

Motion Capture Controllers

When setting up Motion Capture to create an animation, we have several things to consider. The Motion Capture solution is only as good as the input device and how the controller is configured for Motion Capture. When you're planning a Motion Capture animation, it's crucial that you ask "How do I want the device to affect the track parameters?" before you assign Motion Capture controllers to a track. Certain devices provide a mechanical "on/off" response in a track; others provide a free-form multi-value control. Knowing what device will work best to create the desired Motion Capture result is critical to the success of the animation.

MAX can assign controllers to four types of input devices:

- The *mouse input device* captures data from the motion of the mouse. The parameters in the Mouse Input Device dialog box enable you to adjust the effect the motion of the mouse has over any animatable parameter. This input device is very handy for creating fluid track data such as freeform multiaxis motion or rotation.

- The *joystick input device* captures data from the motion of the joystick, much like the mouse input device, but additional axis controls depend on the features of the individual joystick, button triggers, and the capability to increment based on the direction of an object. The joystick input device also enables the user to use accumulated or non-accumulated (as in Mouse Motion Capture) input values.

- The *MIDI (Musical Instrument Digital Interface) input device* captures data from an external MIDI device, such as a synthesizer. The controller can be configured to capture data from the note of the musical key pressed, the speed the key is pressed, the velocity at which the key is pressed, or the Pitch Bend data. The MIDI is a versatile capture device.

- The *keyboard input device* captures data from the computer keyboard by way of an Envelope Graph assigned to any key that represents a character. The keyboard input device is ideal when a mechanical animation is required. The Envelope Graph within the keyboard input device is interpreted by MAX, as illustrated in Figure 3.3.

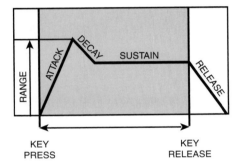

Figure 3.3   The Envelope Graph.

The Envelope Graph can be broken down into the following components:

> *Attack.* The Attack value is how quickly the controller reaches the specified value, which is assigned in the Range field of the Parameter Scaling group.

> *Sustain.* The Sustain value is the fraction of the total Range value that the controller value will return to while the key is held down.

> *Decay.* The Decay value is the time in which the Sustain value is achieved.

> *Release.* The greater the Release value, the longer it takes for the controller value to return to 0 when the key is released.

> *Range.* The Range value in the Parameter Scaling group is the numeric value of distance in units, angle of rotation, or numeric value of the controller, depending on the type of controller.

Time. The Time value specifies the scale of the Attack, Decay, and Release values. The value represents the number of seconds that 1 unit is. For example, if this value is 1.0, an Attack value of 1.0 equals 1 second.

The mouse and keyboard generally provide the versatility needed for most projects.

Experimenting with Motion Capture Controller Settings

Later in this chapter, you will learn how to correctly assign and configure the Motion Capture controllers to logo objects. But for now, let's take a look at settings of the Motion Capture controllers of the desk.max file. If you want, you can enter new values and test them to see how the new values react.

Exercise 3.2   Checking Out the Settings

1. With desk.max open, open the Utilities panel and select the Motion Capture rollout. The controller tracks are already assigned in the scene.

2. In the Tracks group in the Motion Capture rollout, double-click a track to open the controller's dialog box. The Motion Capture dialog box for the selected transform opens (see Figure 3.4).

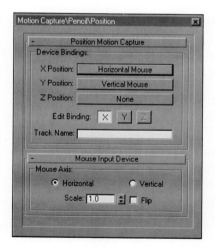

Figure 3.4   The Motion Capture dialog for the Pencil\Position transform track.

Tip

If you don't want a track to be affected by the Motion Capture testing or recording, you can deselect the red box next to the track.

3. With the Test button inactive, adjust the settings for the controller. For example, you can change the attack and decay of the DeskLight\Self Illumination and Spot01\Multiplier to make the light flicker on and off. Or you can adjust the height to which the coffee mug rises.

4. Click the Test button to see how the change you made affects the animation.

Note

The Test button allows you to test the Motion Capture bindings without actually recording keys.

5. When you finish testing, right-click to exit the Test mode.

When you are finished practicing and wish to record a track or tracks, click Start, and MAX will record a key for each frame of the animation for the tracks that are activated in the Tracks group.

Assigning Motion Capture to the Hidden Eyes Logo

Now that we have a better understanding of how Motion Capture works, it is time to load our logo and start assigning Motion Capture controllers to the elements that make up the eye.

Exercise 3.3   Binding the Eyeball to Motion Capture

Let's assign the Rotation Motion Capture with the mouse as the input device to the eyeball object.

1. Open ch02-11.max (the logo object we created earlier) and save it again as **ch03\ch03-01.max**.

2. We don't need to see the lights or the camera anymore, so click the Display tab, go to the Hide by Category rollout, and check Lights and Cameras. Then click Zoom Extents All to enlarge and center the logo in all the viewports (see Figure 3.5).

3. Select the Eyeball object and click the Motion tab. In the Assign Controller rollout, select the Rotation track (as shown in Figure 3.6) and click the Assign Controller button. In the Assign Rotation Controller dialog box, choose Rotation Motion Capture. Then click OK to exit.

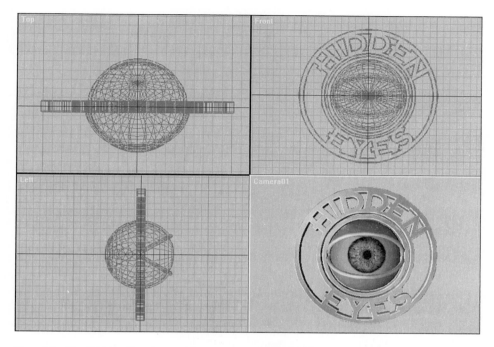

Figure 3.5 The Hidden Eyes logo, with cameras and light hidden and Zoom Extents All applied.

4. Select the Rotation: Rotation Motion Capture controller, right-click, and select Properties to open the Rotation Capture\Eyeball\Rotation dialog box.

   To match the vertical rotation of the eyeball to the vertical motion of the mouse, we need to bind the vertical mouse motion to the X Rotation of the eyeball.

5. In the Device Bindings group of the Rotation Motion Capture rollout, click None next to X Rotation to access the Choose Device dialog box. Choose Mouse Input Device and click OK to exit.

6. As a default, the Mouse Axis group is set to Horizontal. It needs to be set to Vertical for this scene. Therefore, in the Mouse Input Device rollout, select Vertical in the Mouse Axis group. Leave the Motion Capture\Eyeball\Rotation dialog box open.

7. Now it's time to test our Motion Capture binding. Click the Utilities tab. From the Utilities rollout, click Motion Capture, and in the Tracks group of the Motion Capture rollout, select the box next to Eyeball\Rotation to activate it (see Figure 3.7). Click Test and move the mouse up and down slowly to see how it works. Right-click when you finish testing it.

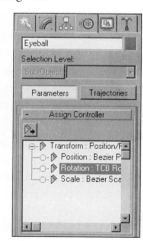

Figure 3.6 Select the Rotation track from the Assign Controller rollout.

Something seems to be wrong with our input data—the eye's rotation. The eyeball looks down when the mouse is pushed upward. Let's fix the rotation direction problem.

Figure 3.7   Select the box next to Eyeball\Rotation to activate it.

8. In the Motion Capture\Eyeball\Rotation dialog box, check Flip in the Mouse Axis group of the Mouse Input Device rollout. This reverses the rotation direction.

9. In the Motion Capture rollout of the Utilities panel, make sure Eyeball\Rotation is still activated and click Test again. Move the mouse up and down slowly. Right-click when you finish testing. Much better.

10. Let's make the horizontal bindings now. In the Motion Capture\Eyeball\Rotation dialog box, click None next to Y Rotation. From the Choose Device dialog box, select Mouse Input Device and click OK to exit. The Y Rotation binding should default to Horizontal Mouse (see Figure 3.9).

11. To test the bindings, click the Test button in the Record Controls group of the Motion Capture rollout in the Utilities panel. Move the mouse up and down and side to side. The Eyeball object's rotation should track the motion of the mouse. The eyeball now has the correct Motion Capture bindings.

12. Close the Motion Capture\Eyeball\Rotation dialog box and save your work as **ch03-02.max**.

Exercise 3.4   Binding Eyelid-Top to Motion Capture

Now that we have an understanding of how to bind objects to Motion Capture, the eyelids should be a breeze. Let's start with the Eyelid-Top object. Because the rotation is only on one axis and will be a very mechanical open or shut rotation, we can assign a key on the keyboard to be the controller.

1. Select the Eyelid-Top object, click the Motion tab, select the Rotation track in the Assign Controller rollout, and click the Assign Controller button. This opens the Assign Rotation Controller dialog box. Select Rotation Motion Capture in the Assign Rotation Controller dialog box and click OK to exit.

2. Select the Rotation: Rotation Motion Capture in the Assign Controller rollout, right-click it, and select Properties to open the Motion Capture\Eyelid-Top\Rotation dialog box.

3. In the Device Bindings group of the Motion Capture\Eyelid-Top\Rotation dialog box, click None next to X Rotation. In the Choose Device dialog box, choose Keyboard Input Device and click OK to exit.

4. To assign a key on the keyboard to be the controller, click the Assign button in the Key Assignment rollout. Then, when you are instructed to "Press to assign key," press the spacebar on the keyboard.

5. Set the rotation range by entering Range: **30** in the Parameter Scaling group (to rotate the eyelid 30 degrees to its closed position). Leave the Motion Capture\Eyelid-Top\Rotation dialog box open (see Figure 3.8).

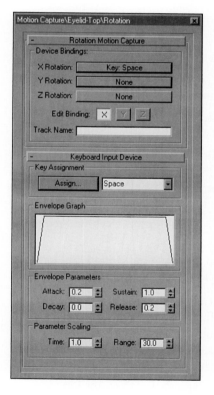

Figure 3.8   The correct settings in the Motion Capture\Eyelid-Top\Rotation dialog box (so far).

6. To test the bindings, click the Utilities tab to enter the Motion Capture controls. Click Eyelid-Top\Rotation to activate the track, and then click Test. Press the spacebar to see the eyelid close; release the spacebar to see the eyelid raise. Right-click when you finish testing.

The top eyelid is closing and opening, but the speed of the rotation seems to be a little bit off. Adjusting the Envelope Parameters of the rotation controller will help solve this problem.

7. With the Motion Capture\Eyelid-Top\Rotation dialog box still open, change the Attack: to **0.1** and the Release to **0.4** in the Envelope Parameters group. This will make the eyelid close more quickly and open more slowly.

8. Test the new settings by clicking the Test button in the Utilities panel. That is much better.

Note

You can turn off the Eyeball\Rotation during testing. To do so, click the red block next to its label to deactivate it before you click Test.

9. Save your work as **ch03-03.max**.

This completes the binding of the top eyelid object to Motion Capture.

Exercise 3.5   Binding Eyelid-Bottom to Motion Capture

To complete our Motion Capture bindings, we have to assign a Motion Capture controller to the Eyelid-Bottom object. Let's not waste any time.

1. With ch03-03.max and the Motion Capture\Eyelid-Top\Rotation dialog box still open, select the Eyelid-Bottom object. Click the Motion tab and assign a Rotation Motion Capture controller to the object in the Assign Controller panel.

2. Open the Motion Capture\Eyelid-Bottom\Rotation dialog box by selecting the object, right-clicking the Rotation: Rotation Motion Capture track, and selecting Properties.

3. In the Device Bindings group of the Motion Capture\Eyelid-Bottom\Rotation dialog box, click None next to X Rotation. Select Keyboard Input Device and click OK to exit.

4. In the Key Assignment group, click Assign and press the spacebar to assign it.

5. Make the same Envelope Graph changes you made to the last object by comparing the two Motion Capture dialog boxes (see Figure 3.9). However, for the Range, change it to **–30** so that the eyelid rotates up, not down.

6. From the Motion Capture settings in the Utilities panel, activate the Eyelid-Bottom\Rotation track and click Test to test the bindings.

7. Save your work as **ch03-04.max**.

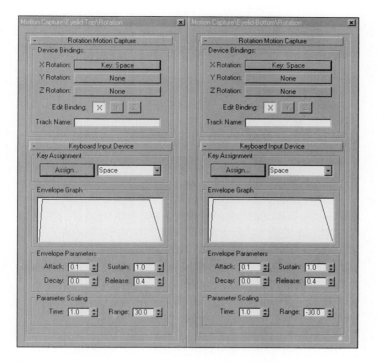

Figure 3.9   The correct Motion Capture settings for the two eyelid objects.

In Summary

This completes Chapter 3. For the eyeball object, a rotation Motion Capture controller is assigned to the mouse input device. For the eyelid objects, rotation Motion Capture controllers are assigned to the keyboard input device (the spacebar). The logo is now properly prepared for the animation needed in the next chapter.

Chapter 4

Animating the Logo

Animating a logo or corporate icon creates an eye-catching introduction that has many uses, such as the closing of a commercial, a splash screen, or a sponsor identifier. If the logo is animated, you capture the viewer's attention, making him want to know what is going to come next.

When it is done well, a moving 3D object is generally more interesting than a flat, static graphic.

The elements you use to surround the logo during the animation help create the mood. The use of certain colors and lighting techniques also aids in creating the subtleties that enhance the message you are sending. By adding animated backgrounds to your main logo animation, you can create depth and interest while also including elements that complete the message. Selecting the best camera angles and moves to highlight the logo as it moves is very important to the success of your animated logo.

In this chapter, we will be finishing up our Hidden Eyes logo animation. All we need to do is animate the camera, insert the filmstrip background environment, render the frames, and kick back and enjoy the fruits of our hard work.

Different Approaches to Camera Animation

In logo animation, an appropriate camera motion is critical to its success. It is very easy to fall into the trap of always using the same type of motion to create all your animations. This may not always be the best way to get the job done, however. Always keep an open mind and be willing to experiment with new ideas. Different animation controllers, hierarchies with dummy helpers, and whatever else you can come up with can make the camera animation in your scene that much better. It is generally much easier to control the outcome and to experiment with various motions when you're animating the camera than when you're animating the logo object.

Before you start the production process, thoroughly examine the project, the elements, and the message the animation must convey. While you are creating the animation, keep this important criterion in mind: "Is it appropriate?" Even though an animation may have beautiful, complex textures and breathtaking effects, it may not be effective.

Make sure the color and texture emphasize the mood being created by the animation. A cold metallic logo element that would work great in a sports environment probably wouldn't work well for the opening of a soap opera.

The motion of the elements is also vital to creating a successful animation. An aggressive sports program would probably have a logo build with elements crashing down into place. A soap opera would probably have a more seductive, soft motion.

The examples in this chapter are from my personal arsenal of motion strategies for logo animation. Each has a specific purpose and use. Before animating a logo, I visualize the desired motion path I want the logo to take, and then I decide which of the following techniques will create the desired effect.

Before we animate our logo, let's examine some possibilities.

Launching a Free Camera

From the ch04 directory of the accompanying CD, load the file L-fc.max (see Figure 4. 1).
This scene has two objects: the Logo object and Camera01. Click the Play button and
watch the animation. The camera flies through the center of the first *o* in the word *Logo*
and gently stops at its end position.

Figure 4.1   Frame 20 of L-fc.max.

Did you notice that the Logo object is rotating slowly to an upward position and the
camera is always pointing forward? It would have been just as easy to leave the Logo
object upright and just rotate the camera to give the sense of perspective. However, if we
keep the camera pointing forward and rotate the Logo object, we can easily see in the
Front viewport if the camera collides with any of the logo's faces.

This type of logo animation works best when a dramatic result is needed. The logo flies
uncomfortably close to the camera, grabbing the viewer's attention immediately. This is
one of the quickest ways to fly in a logo dramatically because of the simple linear path
the object takes. It also instills confidence because of the straightforward approach and
lack of curving motion.

Using a Path Follow Controller

From the ch04 directory of the accompanying CD, load the file L-tc-tPath.max (see Figure 4.2). The contents of the scene are the Logo object, a Target camera, and a helix spline. Play the animation and study the motion.

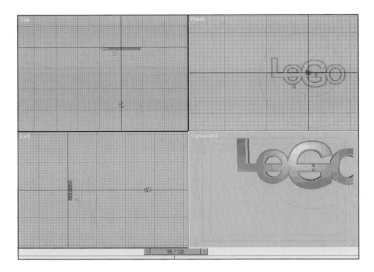

Figure 4.2   Frame 55 from L-tc-tPath.max.

Seems a bit over the edge, doesn't it? The logo and camera remain stationary, but the camera's target spins around the scene following a helix path. To assign the camera's target to the helix path, follow these steps:

1. Select the Camera01.Target object.

2. Click the Motion tab and select the Position track in the Assign Controller rollout.

3. Click the Assign Controller button and choose Path from the Assign Position Controller dialog box.

4. In the Path Parameters rollout, click the Pick Path button. Then, from any viewport, select the Helix path.

After you pick the path, the target is automatically animated to follow the helix spline from its first vertex to its last over the current animation length.

For this example, the target of the camera was assigned to the helix when the animation length was set to 100 frames. Extra frames were added to this example in the Time Configuration dialog box to allow the logo to rest before looping. Sometimes this controller gets confused, and the first and last frames do not calculate properly. To fix this problem, I opened Track View, opened the parameters for the Path's first key, and entered 0.01 in the Value field. I then changed the Value of the last Path key to 99.99. With these changes, the animation will play back properly.

Although this animation seems a little over the edge, I wanted to point out the power of the Path Follow controller and the many ways it can be used to make animating a camera much simpler.

Assigning the camera target to a path is a very powerful technique that has endless uses. It is smart to use this Path Follow on the target when you have a complex target motion. Sometimes when you key multiple keys to a camera or target, the overshoot of the key interpolation creates an undesired motion path. Instead of spending hours changing the key values to smooth out the path, it's very easy to create a path spline and assign a Path Follow controller.

Linking the Target Camera to a Dummy Helper

From the ch04 directory of the accompanying CD, load the file L-tc-dumy.max (see Figure 4.3). This scene contains the Logo object and a target camera, and both the camera and the target are linked to a dummy helper. Play the animation and study it.

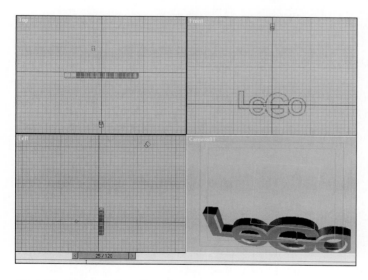

Figure 4.3 Frame 25 from L-tc-dumy.max.

As you can see, the camera is rotated from the top of the logo to the final position. The dummy helper is actually performing the rotation. The reason for this is that the rotating dummy keeps the camera a constant distance from the logo object. Animating the camera with only two keys from point A to point B would create animation with linear motion. That would not keep the camera equidistant from the target. The result would be an animation in which the camera moved closer to the logo before moving away.

The wobbling that occurs during the animation is caused by the target movement, which is animated from right to left and then back in the Top view. Although the effect of the target movement is nauseating, it was added as a good example of the flexibility and independence of the target from the camera. If you notice, the dummy's position is also animated, which also moves the camera target. If the dummy/target relationship was not created, it would be more complicated to animate the target to mimic this motion and maintain the smoothness of the animation.

This is a very popular technique for flying in logos. The motion is simple and dramatic, a neutral effect for flying in logos. It makes the logo appear big, but not "in your face."

Using a Free Camera with a Look At Object

From the ch04 directory of the accompanying CD, load the file L-fc-Dlook.max (see Figure 4.4). This scene contains a free camera, a dummy helper, and the Logo object. Play the animation and study the motion.

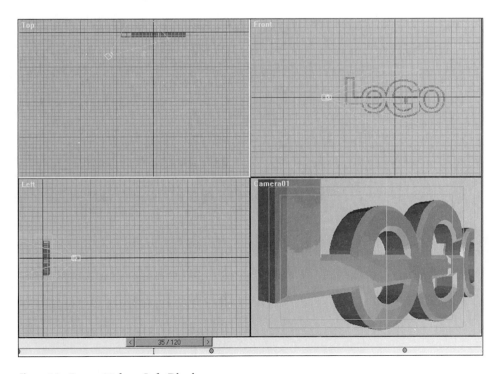

Figure 4.4   Frame 35 from L-fc-Dlook.max.

The camera motion pans across the logo object and then pulls back to its final position. This motion is generally a tricky one to get right because keying it by hand may use too many keys, and the interpolation between the keys can cause overshoot in the motion between closely positioned keys. One of the best ways to create this effect is with this camera/dummy relationship. In this example, the camera is looking at the dummy helper, much like a target camera looks at its target. The difference here is that the dummy helper is much larger than the target of a target camera, making it much easier to select and animate than the target.

To make the dummy the free camera's Look At object, I took the following steps:

1. I selected the Free Camera and entered the Motion panel.

2. In the Assign Controller rollout, I selected the Transform track. Then I clicked the Assign Controller button and chose Look At from the Assign Transform Controller dialog box.

3. In the Look At Target group of the Look At Parameters rollout, I clicked the Pick Target button and then clicked the dummy in any viewport (see Figure 4.5).

Figure 4.5   The Motion panel displaying the Look At settings.

Now, no matter where the free camera is moved, it will always be looking at the dummy helper.

This technique for animating a logo object works best for logos that are longer than they are high. The camera gets in close for a big dramatic shot that reads across the logo and then moves back to resolve the logo in full view. The move is smooth and comfortable to watch, and it adds mystery to the logo because the viewer is not able to read it because only a few letters are in view at any given moment. This grabs the viewer's attention by making him wait until the very end to receive the message.

Linking a Free Camera to a Dummy Helper

From the ch04 directory of the accompanying CD, load the file L-fc-dumy.max (see Figure 4.6). This scene contains the Logo object and a free camera that is linked to a dummy helper. This is the camera/helper relationship I use most often. Play the animation and study its motion.

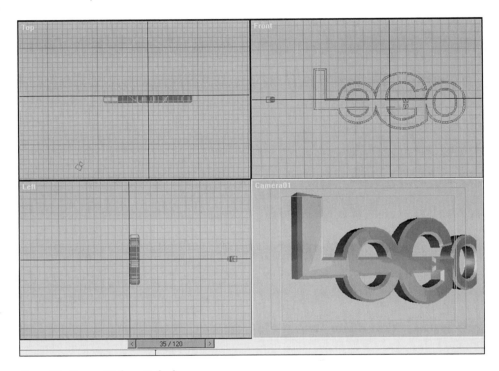

Figure 4.6   Frame 35 from L-fc-dumy.max.

The logo flies in from the right of the screen at an angle and gently rests in its final position. The logo in this scene is completely stationary. The animation is the result of a rotating dummy helper with a camera linked to it. The camera is also animated on its local Z-axis to zoom out as the dummy rotates. The result is a very graceful move with lots of drama.

This technique is almost identical to the earlier example that had the target camera linked to the dummy helper. The only difference between the two is that here we've lost the versatility gained by having the camera target. In most cases, the camera target is not needed because the desired move is simple and clean. This is another favorite I use when flying in logo elements in animation.

These are only a few of the many combinations and techniques available for animating a camera. Always be open to new ways of animating the camera, and experiment with combinations of linking the camera and target to objects, using path controllers, and using Look At controllers. Remember: The animation is only as good as its camera motion. After all the work you put into building your scene, it's always worth the extra time to make the camera motion perfect.

Animating the Hidden Eyes Logo

Now that we have examined a few possibilities for animating our logo, it's time to decide what our motion path should be. We want the logo to have a big presence with a heavy feel to make potential customers feel as though this company is solid and tough. From the previous motion examples, we decide that the best possible way to animate our logo is to use the technique in the last example—the free camera with the dummy parent object.

Exercise 4.1   Building the Relationship Between the Camera and the Dummy

Now that we have decided which way we are going to animate our scene, it's time to load the scene and build our camera/dummy relationship.

1. Load ch03-04.max from the previous chapter and save it as **ch04\ch04-01.max** (see Figure 4.7).

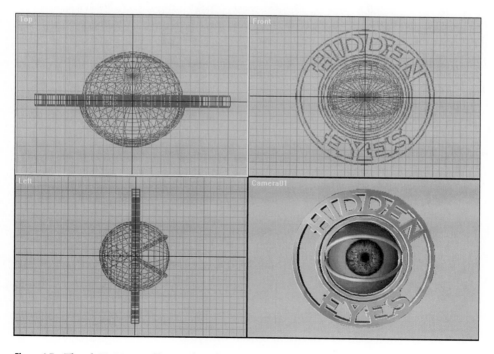

Figure 4.7   The ch03-04.max file saved as ch04-01.max.

2. Click the Create tab and click the Helpers button to open the Create/Helpers panel. Click Dummy and create a dummy in the Top viewport with XYZ at **[0, 0, 0]**. Make sure the Dummy object is larger than the Eyeball object (see Figure 4.8).

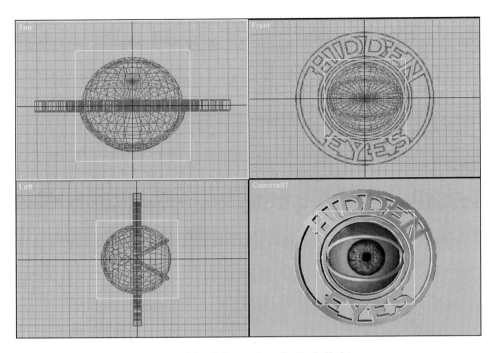

Figure 4.8   Make sure the Dummy object is larger than the Eyeball object.

3. To unhide the camera, click the Display tab and uncheck Cameras in the Hide by Category rollout. Click Zoom Extents All.

4. To link the camera to the Dummy object, activate the Select and Link tool, click on Camera01, and drag the mouse to the Dummy01 object. When the mouse is over the Dummy object (the cursor changes), release the mouse button.

Note

You can also link the camera to the dummy by activating the Select and Link tool, selecting the Camera, pressing the H key to open the Select Parent window, and selecting the dummy helper.

5. Save your work as **ch04-02.max**.

This completes the creation of the camera/helper relationship. When the dummy is rotated or moved, the camera moves in unison with it.

Animating the Camera with the Dummy

We are now ready to start making the keys to make the logo fly in. We will create a simple, yet dramatic motion that will make the logo seem very large and solid.

Remember that the background filmstrip animation we created was 210 frames (7 seconds at 30 frames per second). We don't want to make the logo fly in any longer than three seconds because we have only four seconds for the logo to be established before the animation ends. Three seconds of fly-in time should be more than enough to create the large effect we want to convey.

Exercise 4.2   Setting the Keys

Our Camera viewport already looks the way we want it to when the logo lands, so let's set keys to lock it there 90 frames (3 seconds) into the animation.

1. With ch04-02.max open, open the Time Configuration dialog box and set the End Time to 210.

2. Open the Track View and expand the tracks for the Dummy01 object (but not the hierarchy that includes the camera). Select the Transform title for the Dummy object. This highlights the entire track in the window and helps separate it from the other tracks.

3. Click the Add Keys button and click in the Transform track at frame 90 to create a key. Notice that it created keys for Position, Rotation, and Scale (see Figure 4.9).

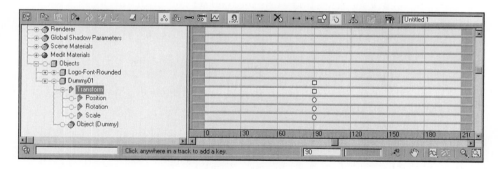

Figure 4.9   The Track View with the Dummy01 track expanded and a set of keys created at frame 90.

4. Close the Track View, make sure the time slider is at frame 0, and turn on the Animate button.

5. In the Top viewport, select Dummy01 and rotate it −40 degrees using the View Z coordinates (see Figure 4.10).

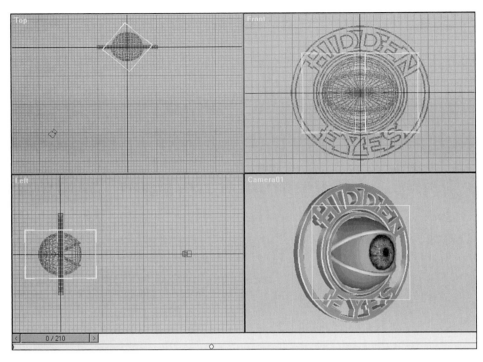

Figure 4.10   Dummy rotated –40 degrees in the Top viewport.

6. At frame 0, click the Select and Move tool and set the constraints to the View Y axis. In the Top viewport, move Dummy01 up approximately 230 units until the Logo object is no longer visible in the Camera viewport (see Figure 4.11). Turn off the Animate button.

7. Save your work as **ch04-03.max**.

8. Play the animation. The logo object should fly in at an angle from the right side of the Camera01 viewport and land at frame 90.

This animation isn't bad at all. However, it is a little slow, and we have given absolutely no time for the background element to be established. A good background, aside from added appeal, defines mood, perspective, and environment, all of which enhances the force of the logo.

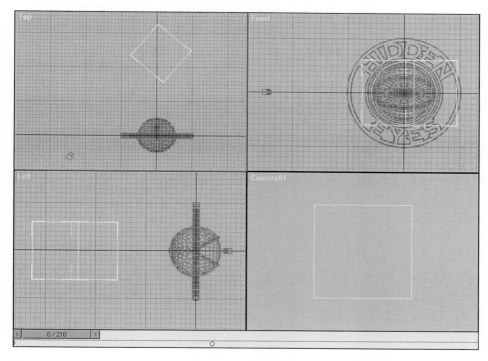

Figure 4.11   Dummy01 moved approximately 230 units from the Top viewport. Notice that the logo is no longer visible in the Camera viewport.

Exercise 4.3   Grooming the Keys

We need to add some time to the beginning of the animation where we don't see the logo at all. This space at the head of the animation is called "pre-roll." It is good practice to always add at least one second of pre-roll to every animation. One reason for adding pre-roll is to give a director time to dissolve or transition to the animation before the logo element appears. Another reason is to give the audience a moment to take in the background before the logo covers it.

1. With ch04-03.max still loaded, open the Track View and expand the Transform tracks for Dummy01. Select the Position and Rotation keys at frame 0 and move them to frame 30 (see Figure 4.12).

2. Play the animation again. Looks pretty good.

   The pre-roll added to this animation is just enough. However, the landing of the logo could be softer. Let's clean up the keys a bit and adjust the logo's "landing."

3. With the Track View still open, select the key in the Scale track and press Delete to remove the key.

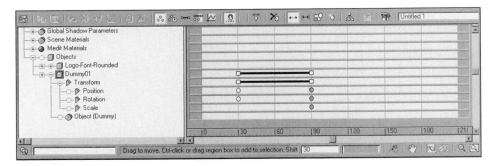

Figure 4.12   The Position and Rotation keys have been moved from frame 0 to 30.

4. To make the landing softer, right-click the Position key at frame 90 to open the Dummy01\Position dialog box (this assumes you are using the default Bezier Position Controller). Change the In: Tangent type to Slow (as shown in Figure 4.13) and close the dialog box. This will decelerate the motion as it approaches the key.

Figure 4.13   The Dummy01\Position dialog box with an In:Slow tangent type.

5. To make the end of the rotation softer, right-click the Rotation key at frame 90 to open the Dummy01\Rotation dialog box (this assumes you are using the default TCB Rotation controller). Enter an Ease To value of **25.0** (as shown in Figure 4.14) and close the dialog box. Then close the Track View.

 Tip

When editing the Ease To values of the TCB Controllers, I have found that the value 25 usually yields the best results. Entering a value of 25 provides a medium Ease amount. If it does not provide the desired ease, adjust the value plus or minus to add or remove ease (respectively).

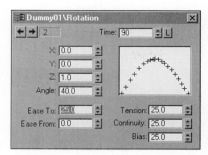

Figure 4.14   The Dummy01\Rotation dialog box with the correct Ease To setting.

6. Play the animation again. The logo lands much more smoothly now; it doesn't have such an abrupt stop as it did before.

   Now it's time to add pad to our animation. *Pad* is the term used to describe the length of time the animation sits in position. Because our logo lands by frame 90, we don't want it to sit motionless. Let's just rotate it slightly over time.

7. Move the frame slider to 210 and turn on the Animate button.

8. Select Dummy01 and activate the Select and Rotate tool. Set the coordinate system to Local and rotate the dummy object 5 degrees on the X axis to make the logo face upwards.

9. Rotate Dummy01 on its local Z axis 5 degrees to make the logo face the left side of the viewport (see Figure 4.15). Turn off the Animate button.

10. Play the animation. It looks pretty good except that the motion out of frame 90 is quick and jerky. Let's adjust the key so that the motion eases out of frame 90.

11. Open the Track View and expand the Transform tracks of Dummy01. Right-click the Rotation key at frame 90 to open the Dummy01\Rotation dialog box. Set the Ease From value to **25.0** (see Figure 4.16).

12. Play the animation once more. Notice that after frame 90, the logo wobbles instead of rotating slowly from the key at frame 90 to the key at 210. This is an easy thing to fix. In the Dummy\Rotation dialog box at frame 90, change the Continuity value to **0** and close the dialog box. Then close the Track View.

13. Play the animation once more. The rotation is perfect. Save your work as **ch04-04.max**.

The logo is now properly animated to fly into the scene. In summary, we have added pre-roll and animated pad to our animated logo. Now we are ready to use Motion Capture to animate the eyeball and eyelid objects.

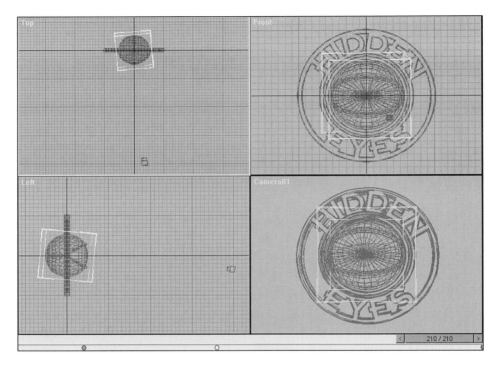

Figure 4.15   The correct rotation of Dummy01 at frame 210.

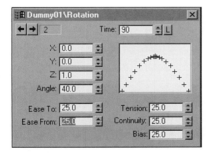

Figure 4.16   The Dummy01\Rotation dialog box with the correct Ease To and Ease From settings.

Recording Motion Capture

With our animation is almost complete, it is time to add the eyeball and eyelid animation to the scene. We have already set up the Motion Capture parameters, so all we have
to do is open the Motion Capture utility and record the Motion Capture input data.

Exercise 4.4   Getting Ready for the Motion Capture

Before you begin recording data, you must set up the animation range.

1. With ch04-04.max loaded, click the Utilities tab and open the Motion Capture panel.

2. To set the correct animation range, in the Record Range group of the Motion Capture panel, change the Out value to 210.

Now we are ready to record our Motion Capture data. There are two ways we can approach this. We can record all the data (mouse and keyboard) at once, or we can record each piece of data individually. For this example, we will record the eyelids with one pass using the keyboard and then go back and record the eyeball motion in a second pass with the mouse.

Recording the Eyelid Objects' Motion

How the eyelids are animated is entirely up to you. The tutorial is going to have the eye closed as the logo flies in, and then right before the logo lands, the eyelids will open. You can even throw in a blink at the end if you are moved to do so.

The problem with the eyelids is that they are already open. Because we set 30 frames of pad, we can hit the spacebar and close the eyelids before they appear in the Camera viewport. Later we will remove the unwanted keys from the Animation track.

Exercise 4.5   Fluttering The Eyelids

It's time to record the eyelid Motion Capture data. If you remember, we assigned the spacebar to the eyelids. All we need to do now is start recording and press the spacebar at the appropriate times.

1. From the Record Controls group, check Play During Test. This means the animation will actually play as if it was recording so you can get your timing down.

2. Click the red box next to the Eyeball\Rotation track to deselect it.

3. In the Record Controls group of the Motion Capture panel, click the Start button and immediately press the spacebar to close the eye. Wait until the logo has almost landed, and then release the spacebar. If you wish to add a blink to the eye, press the spacebar again.

4. Play the animation. If you are unhappy with the Motion Capture data, click the Start button and record it again. When you re-record input data, it automatically overwrites the previous keys and creates new ones.

5. When you are happy with your work, save it as **ch04-05.max**.

Exercise 4.6   Removing the Unwanted Keys

Although Motion Capture is convenient and fast, there is a downside. Motion Capture just recorded a key for every single frame of the animation. Not only does having a key for every frame make the MAX file unnecessarily large, but it also makes it nearly impossible to make changes to the animation by adjusting the keys manually. We have to optimize the keys to remove the unnecessary ones.

1. Open the Track View and open the Rotation\Data tracks for the Eyelid-Bottom and Eyelid-Top objects (see Figure 4.17).

   Notice that there is a key for each frame in both Data tracks. To remove the unwanted keys, we must enter the Edit Time settings and use the Reduce Keys tool.

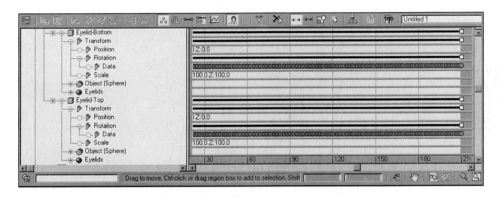

Figure 4.17   The Track View should currently look like this.

2. Click the Edit Time button on the toolbar of the Track View. If the entire length of animation is not in the Track View window, click the Zoom Horizontal Extents button in the lower-right of the Track View.

3. Select the Data track title of the Eyelid-Bottom object, and then Ctrl-click the Data track title of the Eyelid-Top object to add it to the selection. Both Data track titles should be selected. Click in the timeline window to the left of frame 0 and drag to the right of frame 210, highlighting all the keys, and then release the mouse button (see Figure 4.18).

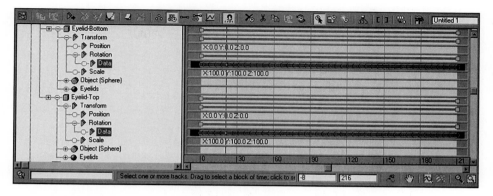

Figure 4.18   Now the Track View should look like this.

4. Click the Reduce Keys button on the toolbar of the Track View. In the Reduce Keys dialog box, set the Threshold to **5.0** and click OK to reduce the keys.

The value you enter in the Threshold field constrains how much 3D Studio MAX changes the selected tracks. The difference between the new animation and the original animation, at any frame, will be less than the Threshold value.

The animation tracks should look something those shown in Figure 4.19.

That's a bit more reasonable. You really need keys for only the open and closed positions of the eyelid objects.

Remember that we had to close the eyelids before the logo entered the screen? Well, let's remove those keys altogether to make a nice clean animation.

5. In the Track View toolbar, click the Edit Keys button and select the first group of keys in both data tracks (see Figure 4.20). Press the Delete key to remove these unwanted keys.

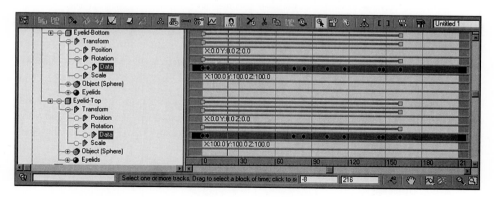

Figure 4.19   The Rotation Data tracks with Reduce Keys applied.

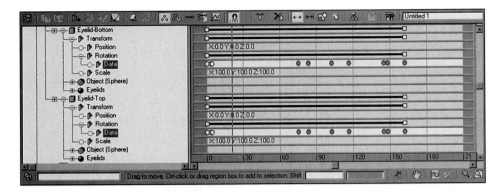

Figure 4.20   Select and delete these keys.

6. Close the Track View, save your work as **ch04-06.max**, and play the animation.

Looks great! If you made the eyelids blink, you may find that the eyes have closed over each other and overlapped. I won't tell if you don't tell! If the eyes are blinking quickly, no one is going to notice anyway. However, if you are a perfectionist, you can open the Track View and fix the keys. To clean up the keys a bit, you can move the position of each key to time the rotation precisely.

If the eyelids are rotating abruptly and aren't supposed to, the Continuity value of the key is probably set to 25. Right-click the key to open its dialog box and change the continuity to 0. Changing the continuity makes the rotation of the eyelids linear.

If you are changing the keys in anyway, make sure you change the keys for both the top and bottom eyelids. Otherwise their rotations will not be synchronized.

Exercise 4.7   Recording the Moving Eyeball

Only one major step remains before we can call this animation "finished." We have to record the Motion Capture data for the eyeball. This should be a breeze now that we are experts with Motion Capture.

For this example, I am going to have the eyeball start in a looking-down position. As the eyelids open for the first time, the eyeball will slowly look up and peer around the viewport. You can animate the eyeball to do anything you want it to do. I chose this because it's eerie and looks mischievous.

1. With ch04-06.max loaded, open the Motion Capture panel and deselect the Eyelid objects.

2. Activate the red box next to the Eyeball\Rotation title to activate the object.

Warning

Make sure the Eyeball object is the only one activated, or you may risk recording over your carefully animated eyelid tracks.

3. To practice your motion, check the Play During Test option and click Test.

   Before we start recording, let's use Reduce Keys in the Samples group so we can remove our unwanted keys when we finish recording.

4. Check the Reduce Keys option in the Samples group to enable the Threshold value. Set Threshold to **5.0** (the same value by which we reduced keys in the Track View for the eyelids). This will clean up the new keys considerably.

5. When you are ready to record your animation, click Start and use the mouse to control the direction you want the eye to look.

6. Play the animation. If you are unhappy with the results, try again. When you are happy with the results, open the Track View and expand the Eyeball\Rotation\Data track to see the keys (see Figure 4.21).

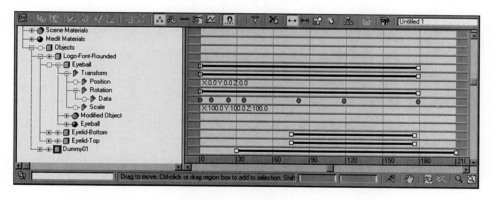

Figure 4.21 The Track View with Eyeball\Rotation\Data track keys displayed.

7. In the Track View, remove, add, or reposition any of the keys that were created with Motion Capture if you feel the need to do so. When you are happy with your animation, save your work as **ch04-07.max**.

Exercise 4.8   Adding the Background and Rendering the Animation

All our keys have been created, and we are thrilled with the results. It's time to add the background to the scene and render the animation.

1. From the Rendering drop-down, select Environment to open the Environment dialog box. In the Common Parameters rollout of the Environment dialog box, click the Environment Map slot. From the Material/Map Browser, choose Bitmap, and then click OK. In the Select Bitmap Image File dialog box, shown in Figure 4.22, open the Ch01\images directory (the directory that you rendered the background frames to) and select back0000.jpg in the File Name field. Check Sequence and click Open. Checking Sequence creates an .ifl file to animate the background images in our scene. Click OK to exit the Image File List Control dialog box.

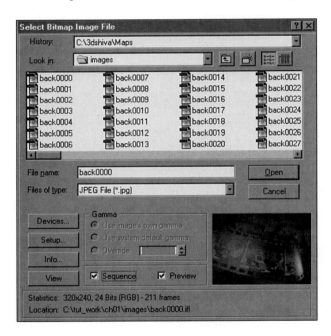

Figure 4.22   The Select Bitmap Image File dialog box.

2. Close the Material Editor and save your work as **ch04-08.max**.

3. Now we need to render the animation. From the toolbar, click the Render Scene button to open the Render Scene window. Because the background was rendered at 320 × 240, we should render this animation at the same resolution. In the Output Size group, change Width to **320** and Height to **240**.

4. In the Render Output group, click Files and choose the name and format for the final rendered file. For this example, we will be creating **hddneyes.avi**. If you prefer a different name or file format, feel free to change them.

5. In the Time Output group, select Active Time Segment.

6. When you are satisfied with the Render Scene settings, click the Render button to render your animation (see Figure 4.23).

Figure 4.23   The final rendered Hidden Eyes logo.

In Summary

This chapter has explained important concepts of animation that can be used when animating any type of scene. Such concepts included multiple ways to approach animating a camera and their uses. This chapter also explained the process of using Motion Capture to animate your scenes and showed you how to apply that knowledge.

The result of the last four chapters and your hard work is an animation that looks pretty darn good. The logo object flies in from the right side of the screen over the beautiful filmstrip environment we created. As the logo is landing, the center of the logo opens up revealing a looming and mysterious eyeball that will instill fear in the hearts of all. Seriously, it's a very nice animation. The lighting is effective, the background is appropriate, and the keys create a pleasing animation that doesn't distract the viewer.

Planetary symbols are
visible on side of G.
Camera slowly orbits
from left to right.

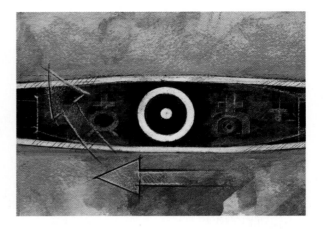

Camera continues left
to right orbit. G object
rotates upward.

Moon enters lower left
as camera continues orbit.
G continues upward
rotation.

Project II
Gravity Zone

Camera orbits slowly stops as G reaches its upright position. "Gravity Zone" title dissolves over animation.

designed by John Chismar and Amy Beth Jackson

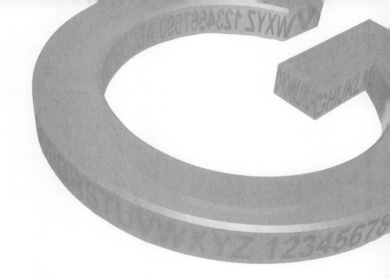

Chapter 5

Working with Complex Texture Mapping

Placing complex textures on objects can mean heartache if the correct approach is not implemented. For some projects, "close enough" is good enough. What can we do when the result must be precise?

A misunderstanding of UVW Maps can mean countless hours spent aimlessly exploring UVW Map modifiers and the effects they have on a texture. It's then that a deep understanding of UVW Map modifiers and the Material Editor's power come in quite handy.

This chapter presents a complex mapping project where the end result must be precise. The success of the animation depends on accurate texture mapping and carefully prepared materials. Attention to detail and a well thought out production process will be rewarded in the final animation.

We just heard word that we landed the Gravity Zone account. As a new company, Gravity Zone wants to ensure its position in the industry as a cutting edge, yet reputable, company. The company representative is a stickler for details and has approached us to produce an animation that will represent his company for commercials, corporate videos and trade show kiosks.

Gravity Zone, a satellite communications company, has requested that its logo reflect its association with the universe. The capitol G, the company's corporate logo, needs to have planetary symbols incorporated on it in order to demonstrate this connection. A blue sky turning into a starry night sky establishes the idea that Gravity Zone is working for us 24 hours a day. Having the moon rising in the background places the viewer in the perspective of being on earth where gravity rules and where satellite communications are an integral part of everyday life.

For a sneak preview of what your finished animated Gravity Zone logo will look like, view the file Gravity.avi from the ch05\images directory of the accompanying CD.

In this chapter, we will be texturing planetary symbols on the extruded side of the G logo object. The purpose of this tutorial is to map a single texture map around the G. By applying several UVW Map modifiers along the extruded side, we will wrap the texture seamlessly without stretching or distorting the bitmap texture. We will be using tape helpers and the Measure utility for measuring the exact length of each section. Using multiple UVW Map modifiers in the sub-object level, the object will be texture mapped seamlessly. And in the Material Editor, we will crop an image to make it fit perfectly in each face.

In the next chapter, we will finalize the logo's textures, create the moon, add the sky environment, and animate the scene.

Exploring Simple and Complex Texture Mapping

Quite often, applying a single standard UVW mapping coordinate type to an entire object does not provide the flexibility to create the desired texture coverage; many projects require more complex texture mapping. Fortunately, MAX offers several ways to apply complex texture maps to an object. The key to understanding the UVW mapping types is to learn about them through experimentation.

The tutorial in this chapter, texturing the letter G, gives us the perfect opportunity to conduct our experiment. We will start with a multi-colored rainbow texture with the letters of the alphabet and sequential numbers. This texture must wrap around the extruded side of the object like a piece of wallpaper. The rainbow colors and the sequence of numbers and letters will allow us to ensure that all of the maps are aligned correctly. In the next chapter, we will replace the rainbow map with the final production texture.

What is the best approach to applying the texture to the G? MAX offers two basic ways to apply texture coordinates to an object. We can do either of the following:

- Apply a single UVW mapping type to the entire object.
- Assign specific UVW Map modifiers to different areas of the object.

Applying a Single UVW Mapping Type

As stated earlier, applying a single UVW mapping coordinate type to an entire object often does not provide the flexibility to create the desired texture coverage. In order to understand the reasons why we need to apply several UVW Map modifiers to the object, let's look at the results we get when we experiment with four of the possible approaches for applying standard UVW mapping types to an entire object one at a time:

- Planar
- Cylindrical
- Shrink wrap
- Face map

If we were to just apply a planar UVW Map modifier to the extruded side of the G object the results would not yield the desired effect (see Figure 5.1). The texture would be applied unevenly and streak back along faces perpendicular to the mapping gizmo. You can examine the file that created this image by loading G-planar.max from the ch05 directory of the accompanying CD.

Figure 5.1   Using planar texture mapping on the G object causes streaking on faces perpendicular to the mapping gizmo.

Using a cylindrical UVW Map modifier is not a good idea, either. Figure 5.2 illustrates the stretching and distortion caused by applying cylindrical mapping. If you wish to view the file that created this example, load G-cylindrical.max from the ch05 directory of the accompanying CD.

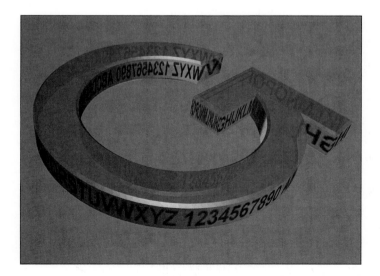

Figure 5.2   Using cylindrical texture mapping on the G object also causes streaking and distortion to the texture.

If you are thinking to yourself, "Shrink wrap texture mapping to the rescue!" I urge you to think again. Figure 5.3 illustrates the result of applying shrink wrap texture coordinates to the sides of the G object. If you would like to examine the file from which this image was created, load G-shrink.max from the ch05 directory of the accompanying CD.

Figure 5.3   The result from applying a UVW Map modifier with shrink wrap mapping to the extruded side.

Shrink wrap texture mapping applies texture coordinates to the external surface of the object. It attempts to stretch the texture over the surface of the object, usually with unpredictable results.

The final unsuccessful example that will be examined before moving forward with the chapter will be applying a face map gizmo to the faces of the extruded side of the G object. At first this seems like it could work, but Figure 5.4 shows the result, which quickly prove us wrong. If you would like to examine the file from which this figure was created load G-face.max from the ch05 directory of the accompanying CD.

Face map texture mapping applies the entire texture to each triangular face, whether the face has visible or hidden edges. It does, however, keep the texture rectangular and results with undesirable triangular cropping on the faces.

Figure 5.4   The result of applying a UVW Map modifier with face mapping to the extruded sides of the G object.

Measuring the G

Now that we understand the reason we need to apply several UVW maps to the G object in order to map it properly, it's time to begin the process. The first step in correctly mapping the extruded side of the G object is to accurately measure each face, or group of faces, to which we will be applying a UVW Map modifier.

Figure 5.5 shows the letter G that we will be texturing. To take a closer look, open the file Gsolve01.max from the \tutwork\ch05 directory on the accompanying CD. If you do open it, be sure to close it *without* saving it before we begin the tutorial: Gsolve01.max is the file we use to begin the tutorial. You need to make certain that you don't save any changes to it.

In the viewports, you should see a beveled letter G, splines in the shape of a G and tape helpers. There are also two hidden cameras in the scene.

The letter G was created by applying a Bevel modifier to a spline in the shape of the letter G. The splines that are floating above the beveled letter G were detached from the original spline and represent each Face Group to which we will be applying UVW Map modifiers. The tape helpers were added to measure each straight face we will be texturing, these were created by using Vertex Snap to the spline.

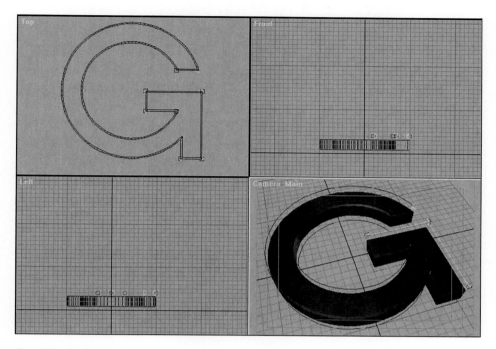

Figure 5.5   Gsolve01.max.

Examining the Measurements

Figure 5.6 illustrates the measurements for each Face Group.

Before explaining how these measurements were acquired, let's first examine how I chose their labels. Face Group #3 is the first group of faces labeled and the last is Face Group #11. The Face Groups were labeled starting with #3 because the top and bottom faces will be Face Group #1 and the bevel will be Face Group #2. Later in production, you may need to change the face and bevel material because they are likely to be the most important faces after the object reaches its final position in the animation. You used this technique when you applied Material IDs to the Hidden Eyes logo text in the previous tutorial:

- Readable Face = Material ID #1
- Bevel = Material ID #2
- Extruded Side = Material ID #3

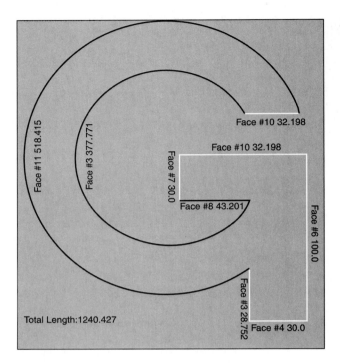

Figure 5.6   The measurements for each Face Group to which UVW Map modifiers will be applied.

Measuring Straight Faces

The measurements of the straight faces were acquired by creating a tape helper and using Vertex Snap to snap the base and end of the tape to the ends of the G spline straight faces. A brief explanation of tape helpers and Vertex Snap is in order:

- The tape helper is accessed from the Create/Helpers panel. A tape helper's major purpose is to measure the distance of a straight line. It creates two objects (much like a targeted camera) the first object created is the arrow and the second is the box, both connected with a line. When the arrow of the tape helper is selected, the Modify panel displays the measurement of the line.

- Vertex Snap is activated in 3D Snap by right-clicking the 3D Snap button and checking Vertex only. When Vertex Snap is on (and the snap button is active), the cursor will snap to all vertices in the scene. To measure the straight lines of the G, enable Vertex Snap and create tape helpers, snapping to the vertices of the G spline.

Measuring Curved Splines

To measure the curved splines, a different method must be implemented because a tape helper does not curve. The G spline was cloned twicebecause there are two curved surfaces. Using the EditSpline modifier, all but the curve to be measured was deleted in each. In this example the two cloned and modified splines are named curve_inside and curve_outside. When one of these splines is selected, you can go to Utilities/Measure and the length of the curved splines will be displayed. The total Length was determined by simply selecting the original spline G_spline and going to Utilities/Measure and looking at the displayed length.

Applying the UVW Map Modifiers

In this example, we are going to apply several UVW Map modifiers to the sides of the G so we can "wallpaper" the sides with a constant texture. For this part of the tutorial, we will be applying a rainbow of color with the alphabet and numbers on it. I chose this pattern so that we can accurately view our results to ensure that they are correct. (In the next chapter, we will be loading the production texture over this temporary texture map.) Every flat face will have a planar mapping gizmo and every curved surface will have a cylindrical mapping gizmo. The accurate measurements of all the sides are necessary during this process. The measurements will also be needed later in the Material Editor when we are applying the texture.

Exercise 5.1   Applying the Texture Mapping to Face Group #3

1. Open a fresh copy of Gsolve01.max from the \tutwork\ch05 directory on the accompanying CD. This removes any changes you may have made earlier in the tutorial.

   Let's start by adding a UVW Map Modifier to Face Group #3 of the G Object.

2. Activate the Camera_Main viewport and change it to the Perspective viewport. Select G_Object and use Arc Rotate Selected, Pan, and Zoom to get a good look at Face Group #3 (see Figure 5.7). Right-click the Perspective viewport's label and select Edged Faces to turn on Edged Faces. Now we can view the wireframe of the object in the shaded viewport.

3. To prepare this Face Group for UVW Map modifier, apply an Edit Mesh modifier, change the Sub-Object level to Polygon and select only Face Group #3 (see Figure 5.8). Change its Material ID to 3 if it is not already assigned. Click the Edit Stack button and highlight the Edit Mesh modifier name in the Edit Modifier Stack dialog box. Change the modifier name to **Edit Mesh Face 3** and click OK to exit. Leave the Sub-Object button activated.

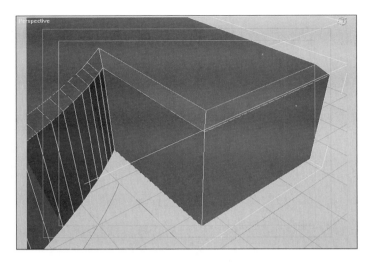

Figure 5.7   Face Group #3 of G_Object in the Perspective viewport.

 Note

It is not necessary to change the name of the modifier for this tutorial to work. However, doing so makes it easier to find the modifier for that particular face if you need to change it.

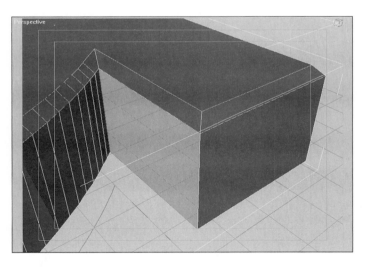

Figure 5.8   Face Group #3 selected in the Perspective viewport.

4. Apply a UVW Map modifier and, from the Mapping group of the Parameters rollout, choose Planar (see Figure 5.9). In the Alignment group, choose Y. Use these measurements:

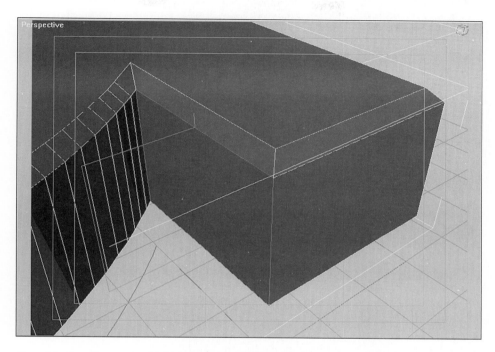

Figure 5.9   Face Group #3 with UVW Map modifier applied.

Length: **20.0** (the sides are 20 units high)

Width: **28.752** (the length we measured)

Height: **1.0** (the thickness of the gizmo—any positive number is correct for the height value)

5. Change the UVW Map modifier name to **UVW Face 3**.

When you change the UVW Map Alignment to Y, the mapping gizmo rotates so that it is upright and aligned to be correctly viewed in the Front viewport. This automatic alignment, which occurs because the spline was created in the Top viewport, has actually messed up the alignment we need in order to texture the G properly. We now need to rotate the UVW Map gizmo clockwise in the Top viewport to align the gizmo properly.

6. Activate the Sub-Object button gizmo is the only sub-object option) and in the Top viewport rotate the gizmo 90 degrees clockwise using the view's Z-axis (using angle snap may make it easier to be precise). Turn off the Sub-Object button.

7. Save your work as **ch05-01.max**.

This UVW Map modifier applied all of the necessary UVW mapping information that we need to correctly apply the texture to Face Group #3. The Edit Mesh modifier isolates Face Group #3 because the Sub-Object button was activated. Any modifier added to G_Object at this point would only affect the selected face. Adding the UVW Map modifier to the isolated Face Group #3 applied the correct UVW mapping to only that face.

Exercise 5.2   Applying the Texture Mapping to Face Group #4

Now that we have finished applying the UVW mapping information to Face Group #3, let's move on to Face Group #4. It is important to understand that in order to isolate each face, or group of faces, it is imperative to add a new Edit Mesh modifier. Leaving the Sub-Object level activated, with the appropriate face(s) selected, is what instructs MAX to apply the UVW Map modifier to only the isolated elements.

MAX lets you assign different Material IDs to individual faces of an object in just one Edit Mesh modifier. However, MAX does not let you assign varying UVW mapping coordinates to different faces in one Edit Mesh modifier. Because of this limitation, we will be assigning the Material IDs to the faces as we progress.

1. With ch05-01.max open, apply an Edit Mesh modifier to the G_Object and change its name to **Edit Mesh Face 4** (see Figure 5.10). Set Sub-Object selection level to Polygon and select only Face Group #4 (see Figure 5.11). You may need to adjust your viewport. Change its Material ID to **4**. Leave the Sub-Object button on.

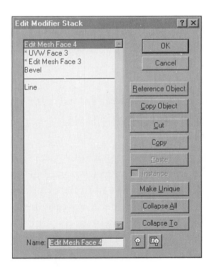

Figure 5.10   Change the Edit Mesh modifier's name to Edit Mesh Face 4 in the Edit Modifier Stack window.

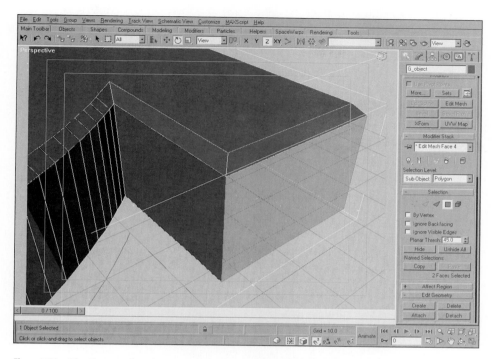

Figure 5.11 The Perspective viewport with Face Group #4 selected.

2. Leave Sub-Object/Polygon activated, apply a UVW Map modifier, and use these settings:

> Mapping: **Planar**
>
> Alignment: **Y**
>
> Length: **20.0**
>
> Width: **30**
>
> Height: **1.0**

3. Change the UVW Map's name to **UVW Face 4**.

Face Group #4's alignment is viewed correctly in the Front viewport; therefore, the UVW Map modifier gizmo does not need to be rotated.

4. Save your work as **ch05-02.max**.

Exercise 5.3   Applying the Texture Mapping to Face Group #5

The next Face Group we will be applying UVW mapping coordinates to is Face Group #5. Because we are familiar with this process we already know that we must apply an Edit Mesh modifier to the top of the stack, select Face Group #5, change its Material ID, and leave the Sub-Object button activated.

1. With ch05-02.max open, apply an Edit Mesh Modifier and name it **Edit Mesh Face 5**. Adjust the Perspective viewport to view Face Group #5 correctly. Set the Sub-Object selection to Polygon and select Face Group #5 (see Figure 5.12). Change the Material ID to **5**. Leave Sub-Object activated.

   We now know that, in this example, when we apply a UVW Map modifier to the G_object and set the Alignment to Y, the map gizmo is aligned to the Front viewport. When we apply the UVW Map modifier for Face Group #5, we will need to rotate it counter clockwise in the Top viewport for it to be applied properly.

2. Apply a UVW Map modifier and use these settings:

   Mapping: **Planar**

   Alignment: **Y**

   Length: **20**

   Width: **100**

   Height: **1**

3. Turn on Sub-Object and, in the Top viewport, rotate the gizmo 90 degrees counterclockwise using the view's Z-axis. Name the modifier **UVW Face 5**.

4. Save your work as **ch05-03.max**.

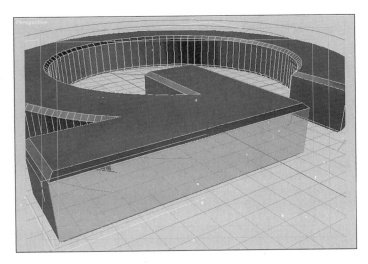

Figure 5.12   Adjust the Perspective viewport to view Face Group #5 to select it.

Exercise 5.4   Applying the Texture Mapping to Face Group #6

Let's select Face Group #6, preparing it for the UVW Map modifier.

1. With ch05-03.max loaded, adjust the Perspective viewport so Face Group #6 is visible, apply an Edit Mesh modifier and name it **Edit Mesh Face 6.** With Sub-Object/Polygon activated, select Face Group #6, change the Material ID to **6,** and leave the Sub-Object button active (see Figure 5.13).

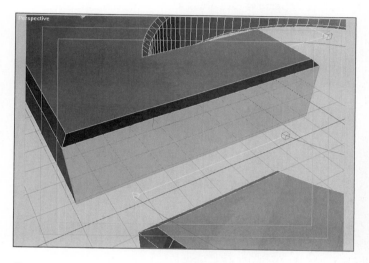

Figure 5.13   Adjust the Perspective viewport to view Face Group #6.

Assign the UVW Map modifier.

2. With Sub-Object/Polygon active and Face Group #6 selected in the Edit Mesh Face 6 modifier, add a UVW map modifier and name it **UVW Face 6.** Use these settings:

   Mapping: **Planar**

   Alignment: **Y**

   Length: **20**

   Width: **80**

   Height: **1.0**

   We now know that when we apply the UVW Map and set the alignment to Y, the gizmo is going to appear to be correct and aligned because this face is aligned to the Front viewport. However, the gizmo is backwards. On Face Group #4, we did not need to rotate the gizmo because it was aligned to the Front viewport. This face, although on the same plane as Face Group #4, is facing in the opposite direction. Instead of correcting the problem by rotating the gizmo 180 degrees, let's flip the U orientation.

3. In the Mapping group of the UVW Face 6 modifier, check Flip next to U Tile.

   This setting flips the right/left orientation instructions of the mapping gizmo, making it left/right, as though turning the gizmo 180 degrees on the V-axis. The top/bottom orientation does not change because V Tile is unchecked.

4. Save your work as **ch05-04.max**.

Exercise 5.5   Applying the Texture Mapping to Face Group #7

Now let's work with Face Group #7.

1. With ch05-04.max loaded, adjust your viewport so you can see Face Group #7. Apply an Edit Mesh modifier and name it **Edit Mesh Face 7;** select Face Group #7 and change its Material ID to **7** (see Figure 5.14). Leave Sub-Object/Polygon activated.

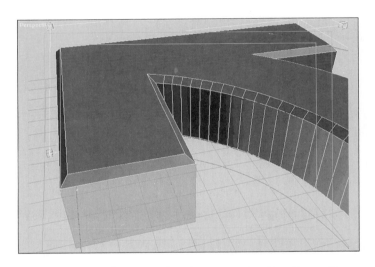

Figure 5.14   Adjust the Perspective viewport to view Face Group #7.

It's time to apply the UVW Map modifier.

2. Apply a UVW Map modifier and use these settings:

   Mapping: **Planar**

   Alignment: **Y**

   Length: **20**

   Width: **30**

   Height: **1**

3. Name the modifier **UVW Face 7**.

4. Activate Sub-Object and, in the Top viewport, rotate the gizmo with the view's Z-axis 90 degrees clockwise. Turn off Sub-Object.

5. Save your work as **ch05-05.max**.

Exercise 5.6   Using Clipping Planes

Sometimes there are cases when, during the modeling process, certain parts of an object are hard to view because other sections of that object are in the way. One of the ways to overcome this problem is to use a camera with clipping planes turned on. To illustrate this point, a camera has been added to the scene to facilitate the viewing of Face Group #8.

1. With ch05-05.max open, right-click the Perspective viewport's label and select Views, Camera_InsideClip as the current view. Now you should see the entire viewport filled with the bottom of the G. Not much help to us, but wait—it gets better!

2. To see the Camera_InsideClip's position in the scene, click the Display tab and in the Hide by Category rollout, uncheck Cameras so we can view them. Click Zoom Extents All to see the camera's position in the scene. You can see that the Camera_InsideClip camera is looking at the bottom of the G object at a slight angle (see Figure 5.15). You can hide the cameras again after examining their positions.

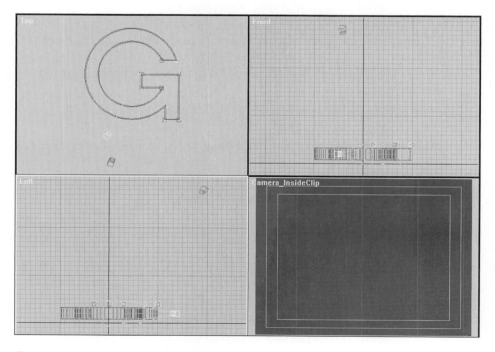

Figure 5.15   Camera_InsideClip selected in the scene.

3. Now for the cool part. Right-click the Camera_InsideClip label in its viewport. From the dropdown, activate Viewport Clipping. Two triangle pointers appear on the right side of the camera viewport. Slowly move the bottom pointer upward until the bottom of the G object clips from the view. Figure 5.16 shows the clipped Camera_InsideClip viewport.

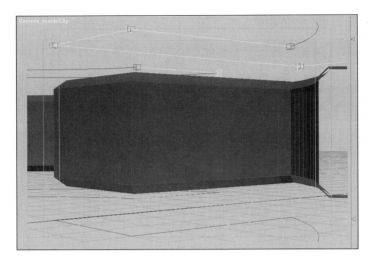

Figure 5.16   Camera_InsideClip viewport with Viewport Clipping activated and properly applied.

As you can see, Viewport Clipping comes in very handy when working with complex objects.

Now let's get back to adding those UVW Map modifiers!

4. Click the Display tab and hide the Cameras by Category. Select G_object, apply an Edit Mesh modifier and name it **Edit Mesh Face 8.** In the Camera_InsideClip viewport select Face Group #8, change its Material ID to **8**, and leave the Sub-Object button turned on (see Figure 5.17).

5. Apply a UVW Map modifier and use these settings:

   Mapping: **Planar**

   Alignment: **Y**

   Length: **20**

   Width: **43.291**

   Height: **1.0**

6. Name the modifier **UVW Face 8.**

   The mapping gizmo does not need to be rotated because Face Group #8 is aligned to the Front viewport correctly.

7. Save your work as **ch05-06.max.**

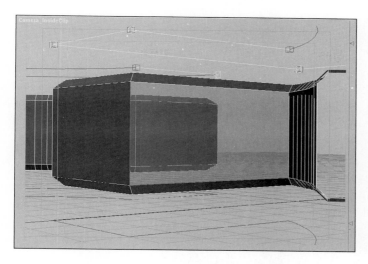

Figure 5.17 Face Group #8 selected in the Camera_InsideClip viewport.

Exercise 5.7   Working with the Texture Mapping of Face Group #9

Face Group #9 is where the game changes a bit. This group of faces is curved. These faces are going to require extra attention when we're adding the UVW map, positioning the UVW map, and especially in the Material Editor when cropping the texture map. For now, let's just add the mapping gizmo. We will return to adjust its position when we are actually texturing the object.

1. With ch05-06.max open, activate the Camera_InsideClip viewport, press P to change it back to Perspective, and click Zoom Extents All. Adjust your Perspective view so you can see the whole G, especially the inside curved edge (see Figure 5.18).

2. Select G_Object, apply an Edit Mesh modifier, and name it **Edit Mesh Face 9.** Set the Sub-Object level to Edge and select Edit, Select Invert to select every edge of G_object; every edge should turn red (see Figure 5.19).

3. In the Edit Surface rollout, click Auto Edge. Turn off Sub-Object.

Note

If we select all the edges and click Auto Edge, removing all of the stepping edges of the curve, the unnecessary edge lines of the curve are hidden from the viewports (see Figure 5.20).

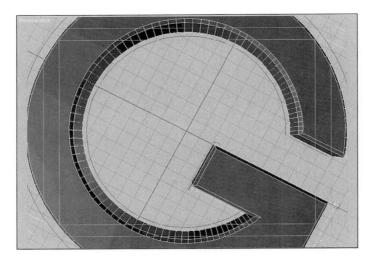

Figure 5.18   Adjust the Perspective viewport to view the inside curve of G_Object.

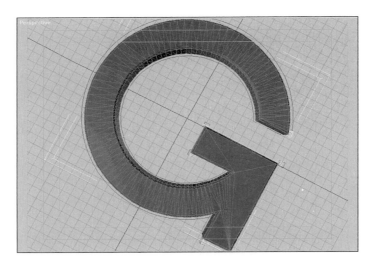

Figure 5.19   Every Edge of G_object should be selected.

The Auto Edge feature of the Sub-Object/Edge modifier reduces the visible edges within the Angle Threshold. This means that if the angle two faces create at their edges is less than 24 degrees (the current Angle Threshold value), the edges are hidden.

Now let's select the inside face. It should be much easier now because we won't have to select all the tiny individual faces.

4. Activate Sub-Object/Polygon and click anywhere in the inside curved surface. The entire curve should be selected now (see Figure 5.21).

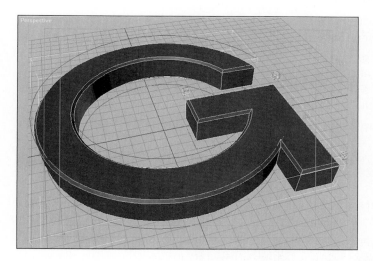

Figure 5.20   The G object with Auto Edge applied and Sub-Object disabled. Notice that the extruded side faces are invisible.

Figure 5.21   Perspective viewport with inside curve faces of G_Object selected.

Just one click, and all of those faces are selected. All of the interior faces are still there, but because we applied Auto Edge, the interior faces act as one polygon. Pretty cool.

5. Change the selected faces' Material ID to 9. In the Perspective viewport, Arc Rotate around to make sure that the entire curve is selected. Leave the Sub-Object button active.

Now it's time to apply the UVW Map modifier.

6. Assign a UVW Map modifier and name it **UVW Face 9.** Set Mapping to Cylindrical. Turn on Sub-Object.

7. Select Tools, Transform Type-In to open the Transform Type-In dialog box and highlight Select and Move. In the Transform Type-In dialog box, enter these Absolute World XYZ coordinates: (**0,0,20**) to place the gizmo in the direct center of the G. Close the Transform Type-In dialog box and turn off Sub-Object.

8. In the UVW Map Parameters rollout, enter these values:

    Length: **140**

    Width: **140**

    Height: **20**

    These values put the gizmo right up against the faces. Check the Flip box next to U Tile, and leave Alignment set to Z.

    U Flip needs to be checked because the mapping coordinates are facing outward from the gizmo (see Figure 5.22). It was necessary to check the U Tile Flip so the mapping coordinates would face inside (see Figure 5.23).

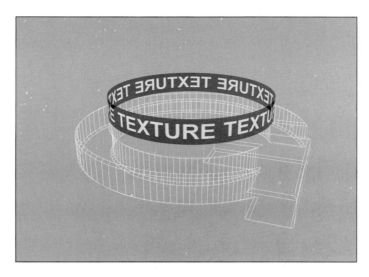

Figure 5.22   Example figure displaying the default cylindrical mapping gizmo applied to a cylinder floating above the G_object. The texture reads correctly on the outside.

9. Save your work as **ch05-07.max**.

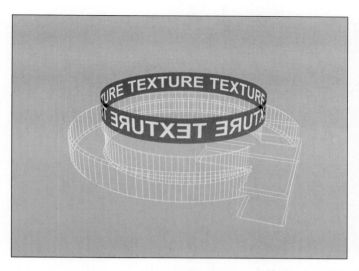

Figure 5.23   Example of figure displaying the effect of checking U Flip, the texture reads correctly on the inside.

Exercise 5.8   Applying the Texture Mapping to Face Group #10

Now it's time to work on Face Group #10.

1. With **ch05-07.max** loaded and G-Object selected, adjust your viewport so Face Group #10 is visible. Assign an Edit Mesh modifier and name it **Edit Mesh Face 10**. Activate Sub-Object/Polygon, select Face Group #10, and change its Material ID to **10**. Leave Sub-Object turned on (see Figure 5.24).

2. Apply a UVW Map modifier and use these settings:

   Mapping: **Planar**

   Alignment: **Y**

   Length: **20**

   Width: **32.198**

   Height: **1.0**

3. Name the modifier **UVW Face 10**.

   The gizmo does not need to be rotated because it is aligned properly to the Front viewport.

4. Save your work as **ch05-08.max**.

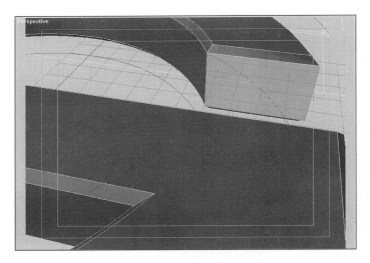

Figure 5.24   Perspective viewport with Face Group #10 selected.

Exercise 5.9   Applying the Texture Mapping to Face Group #11

The last face that we need to apply a UVW Map modifier to is the big outside curve of G_object. Because we applied Auto Edge to the entire object when we were working on Face Group #9, this should be a breeze.

1. With ch05-08.max open and G_object selected, apply an Edit Mesh modifier, name it **Edit Mesh Face 11**, and set the Sub-Object level to Polygon. Adjust your Perspective viewport so you can see the outer curved set of faces on the G, and then click to select it (see Figure 5.25).

   Nice! Just in case the entire outside curve didn't select, take a quick spin around it with the Arc Rotate Selected tool. It should be fine.

2. Change the Material ID of the selected faces to **11** and leave Sub-Object active.

   Now it is time to add the final UVW map of this tutorial. Because we have already dealt with a rounded face, these last few steps should be a piece of cake.

3. Apply a UVW Map modifier and use these settings:

   Mapping: **Cylindrical**

   Alignment: **Z**

   Length: **200**

   Width: **200**

   Height: **20**

4. Name the modifier **UVW Face 11**.

5. Activate Sub-Object gizmo, open the Transform Type-In dialog box again (Select and Move should still be selected), and enter the Absolute:World XYZ coordinates (**0,0,20**).

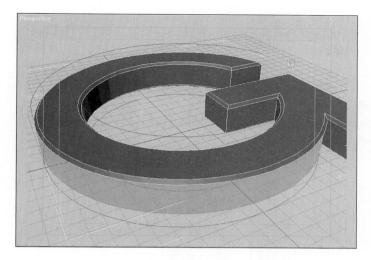

Figure 5.25   Face Group #11 selected in the Perspective viewport.

6. As you can see, the gizmo is resting nicely against the curved surface. You can close the Transform Type-In dialog box now and turn off Sub-Object.

7. Apply one last Edit Mesh modifier and turn off Sub-Object. This will remove the dotted edge lines from the viewport.

8. Save your work as **ch05-09.max**.

We have correctly assigned multiple mapping gizmos to one object in order to create a seamless texture around the entire edge of the G_object object. There is one last step to perform before beginning texture mapping and achieving the visual payoff.

Note

When doing this on your own, you may want to apply a texture with a visible bitmap in the shaded Perspective view so you can make sure the images aren't upside-down or inverted right to left.

If you choose not to, as we did, it is always very easy to move through the Modifier Stack to the incorrectly applied UVW Mapping gizmo and make the adjustments because we have given each UVW Map modifier a specific name.

Exercise 5.10   Cleaning Up the Viewports

Because we are getting closer to finishing our object and its textures, let's clean up the viewports a bit and finish off the Material IDs of the G_object by adding the face and bevel Material IDs.

1. With ch05-09.max open, click the Display tab. Then, from the Hide by Category rollout, check Shapes and Helpers to hide them.

We were so excited about applying the UVW Map modifiers to the G_Object that we almost forgot to apply the correct Material IDs to the readable face and bevel. Let's do that now.

2. Maximize the Left viewport and make sure G_object is selected. Click the Modify tab and activate the Sub-Object/Polygon level of the uppermost Edit Mesh modifier in the stack.

3. Using Window Selection with the Rectangular Selection Region, select the center section (the extruded side), the readable face (the top of the object) and back-faces of the readable face (the bottom of the object) (see Figure 5.26).

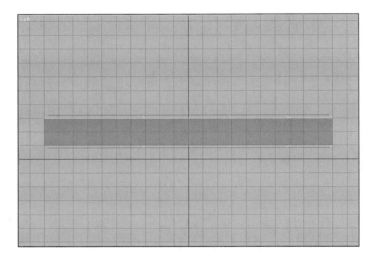

Figure 5.26   Select these faces using Window Selection and the Rectangular Selection Region.

4. From the Edit drop-down, choose Select Invert to select just the bevel faces. Change the Material ID on those faces to **2** (see Figure 5.27).

5. Using Window Selection with the Rectangular Selection Region select the readable faces of the object, both front and back (see Figure 5.28), and change their Material IDs to **1**.

6. Turn off Sub-Object and save your work as **ch05-10.max**.

Now the readable face and the bevel have the correct Material IDs and they are colored correctly.

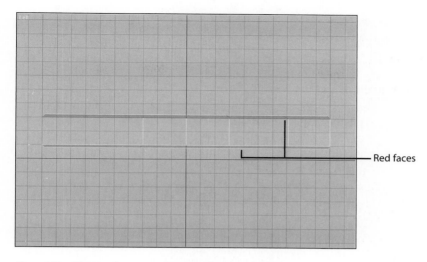

Figure 5.27   Change the Material on these faces to **2**.

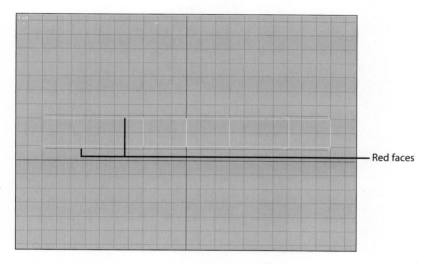

Figure 5.28   Select these faces and change the Material ID to **1**.

Texturing the G

To texture the G_object object, we must now pay close attention to the measurements that we acquired earlier in this tutorial. We will be applying one bitmap image that will cover the extruded side (the faces to which we added UVW Map modifiers) of the object. If we were to make a material now and just apply the texture to the object, the texture would appear in its entirety on each of the UVW Mapped faces. If the bitmap is to appear correctly, we must instruct the Material Editor to crop the bitmap exactly for each section. First, however, we must examine our measurements closely (see Table 5.1).

Table 5.1   Measurements of the G Faces

Face Group Number	Face Length	Percent of Path	Measured Start	Measured Finish
Face Group #3	28.752	.023	.000	.023
Face Group #4	30.000	.024	.023	.047
Face Group #5	100.000	.080	.047	.127
Face Group #6	80.000	.064	.127	.191
Face Group #7	30.000	.024	.191	.215
Face Group #8	43.291	.035	.215	.25
Face Group #9	377.771	.305	.25	.555
Face Group #10	32.198	.026	.555	.581
Face Group #11	518.415	.418	.581	1.0
Total Length	1240.427			

Note

You need to know that .001 was added to the Measured Finish of Face Group #11 because that is how much was left over from all of the rounding to the third decimal place. This will not make a noticeable difference because it was added to the longest face. No squashing will be apparent.

I guess an explanation is due (just don't close the book and run away): It's much easier than it looks. Remember that in the first part of this tutorial the total length of the spline is 1240.427. This number becomes our reference length for 100%. We need to know the length percent (Percent of Path) for each face so we can accurately crop the image in the material editor for accurate placement. The formula used to achieve the Percent of Path for each face group (or its fraction relative to the total length) is the length of the face divided by the total length of the entire spline. In other words, to get Face Group #3's Percent of Path, we take its length (28.752) and divide by the total length of the spline (1240.427). Here's the solution: 28.752 [db] 1240.427 = .023.

If we were in math class, we would get an F for this answer because it's not .023% it's 2.3%; we forgot to move the decimal. However, with MAX, we don't want to move the decimal because the crop function range is from 0.0 to 1.0; the Material Editor doesn't accept the values to 100%. There is no need to move the decimal at all. In fact it's quite nice that this formula works out this way.

When entering the U and W values for cropping into the Material Editor, we need to be concerned with the Measured Start and Percent of Path of each face. The U value is the point at which the crop begins and the W value is the length of that face as percentage of the entire length of all the faces combined. So in essence, we have to tell the Material Editor where to start the crop and how far to go along the length of the bitmap. Determining the Measured Finish is only necessary because that value becomes the Measured Start of the next face.

To further illustrate this point, imagine that you have been given a piece of wallpaper that is exactly the right size to paper a room. The room is rectangular with the short walls being 15 feet long and the long walls being 35 feet long. Do not figure in the doors and windows. The total length of the walls is 100 feet (see Figure 5.29).

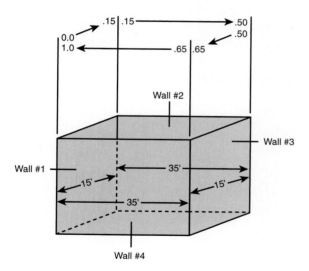

Figure 5.29 The room to be wallpapered.

Figure 5.30 depicts the piece of wallpaper as it would be cut and shows the measurements and percentages as they would be entered into the Material Editor in MAX.

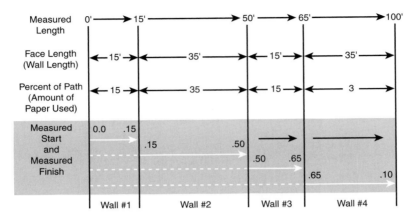

Figure 5.30   The wallpaper as it would be cut with all the values included.

Exercise 5.11   Using the Material Editor

Now that it is time to start applying our textures to the G_object object, let's open the Material Editor and get started.

1. With ch05-10.max loaded, open the Material Editor. Make sure the first material slot is selected, click the Type Standard button, and change it to a Mult/Sub-Object material. Discard old material, click the Set Number button, and set the number to **11** (remember, we have 11 face groups). Name the material **G**.

2. Click the first material slot and name this material **G_Face01**. Use these parameters:

   Shading: **Phong**

   2-Sided

   Specular Level: **75**

   Glossiness: **25**

   Self-Illumination: **50**

   Opacity: **80**

   Ambient color RGB values: (**27,12,4**)

   Diffuse color RGB values: (**201,86,29**)

   You created an orange color.

3. Click Go To Parent to return to the root of the material. Drag the material from slot #1 to #2 and select Copy from the Instance (Copy) Material window. Copy it once more to material slot #3. Go back and name the material in slot #2 **G_Face02**, and then go to slot #3 and rename it **G_Face03**.

Exercise 5.12   Applying Material to Face Group #3's Material

For the next section, you will need to copy the contents of the ch05/maps directory onto the working tutorial directory on your hard drive. Earlier in this chapter, we learned that we will be adding a temporary bitmap to Face Group #3 through #11 to insure the mapping was correct. This temporary bitmap (G1240x20.jpg) image is a sequence of letters and numbers on a rainbow colored background. We will be loading this bitmap included in an .ifl (image file list). G1240x20.jpg is the first frame (frame zero) in the IFL sequence. The following images are the actual production images we will be using. Remember to stay at frame zero on your timeline while working on this section of the tutorial; otherwise, the production images will appear on your geometry. When we are ready to render our final animation, we will simply delete the G1240x20.jpg from the .ifl, leaving only the final production image sequence.

Using an IFL will eliminate the need to enter the material editor, when we are ready to render, and change the diffuse bitmap for Face Groups #3 through #11. All we will need to do is modify the IFL and re-open the scene.

1. While the G_Face03 material is open, open the Maps rollout and click the Diffuse button. Choose Bitmap from the Material/Map Browser. Load plnt0000.ifl from your tutorial maps directory on your hard drive and name this map **G_Face03-dif.**

   If you were to look at G1240x20.jpg, you would see a 1240x20 image of a rainbow pattern with the letters of the alphabet and numbers on it in consecutive order. The dimensions of the G1240x20.jpg are the same dimensions of the faces. Although the dimensions of the G1240x20.jpg are the same as the dimensions of the faces (exactly one pixel per unit), they don't need to be. I made the map this size for ultimate clarity in this example.

   Now here's where all of our math magic comes in mighty handy.

2. Click the View Image button in the Cropping/Placement group of the Bitmap Parameters rollout.

   Try cropping that by eye! Because we are math magicians, we know all we have to do is enter our Measured Start and Percent of Path for Face Group #3.

3. In the Specify Cropping/Placement dialog box, enter these values:

   U: **0.0**

   W: **0.023**

   Close the Specify Cropping/Placement dialog box. Check Apply in the Cropping/Placement group of the Bitmap Parameters rollout. (Notice that the cropping values appear in the Cropping/Placement group as well.)

4. Assign the material to G_Object, click Show Map in Viewport, and set up the Perspective viewport so you can see Face Group #3 and Face Group #4 clearly. You should see the letter A on a nice red background on Face Group #3 (see Figure 5.31).

Figure 5.31   Shaded Perspective viewport displaying Face Group #3's texture map.

5. Save your work as **ch05-11.max**.

Exercise 5.13   Applying Material to More Straight Faces

Let's apply the material to Face Group #4.

1. With ch05-11.max loaded, open the Material Editor. Go to the root of the material and Copy (don't Instance) G_Face03 to material #4. Open material #4 and rename it **G_Face04.**

2. Go to the Diffuse map, rename it **G_Face04-dif,** and, in the Bitmap Parameters rollout, enter the following values to crop the bitmap for Face Group #4:

    U: **.023** (Measured Start)

    W: **.024** (Percent of Path)

3. Click the Show Map in Viewport button to see the texture applied to Face Group #4.

    Move on to Face Group #5.

4. Go to the root of the material and copy G_Face04 to material #5. Open material #5 and rename it **G_Face05.** Click the Diffuse button and rename the diffuse map to **G_Face05-dif.** In the Cropping/Alignment group, enter these values:

    U: **.047** (Measured Start)

    W: **.080** (Percent of Path

5. Adjust the Perspective viewport to view faces #4 and #5 and in the Material Editor click Show Map in Viewport (see Figure 5.32).

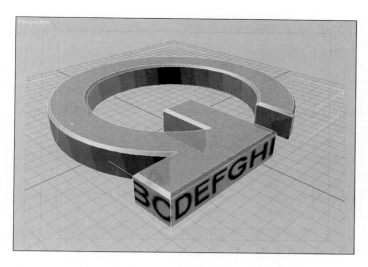

Figure 5.32   Perspective viewport with faces #4 and #5 in view.

Move forward to Face Group #6.

6. Adjust the Perspective viewport to view faces #5 and #6. In the Material Editor, enter root of the G material and copy G_Face05 to material #6. Open material #6 and rename it **G_Face06**, click on the Diffuse button, and rename the diffuse map **G_Face06-dif**. In the Cropping/Alignment group, enter the following values:

U: **.127**

W: **.064**

7. Click the Show Map in Viewport button to see the results (see Figure 5.33).

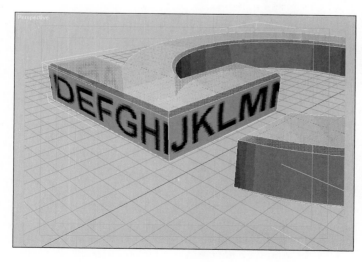

Figure 5.33   Perspective viewport with faces #5 and #6 finished.

Because we're on such a roll, let's do faces #7 and #8.

8. From the root of the G material, copy material #6 to material #7, rename the material **G_Face07.** Click the Diffuse map and rename it to **G_Face07-dif.** Enter the following values in the Cropping/Placement group:

    U: **.191**

    W: **.024**

    Click the View Material in Viewport button.

9. From the root of the G material, copy material #7 to material #8, rename the material **G_Face08**, click the Diffuse slot and rename it **G_Face08-dif.** Enter the following values in the Cropping Placement group:

    U: **.215**

    W: **.035**

    Click the View Material in Viewport button.

    Figure 5.34 shows the Perspective viewport with the G_object object so far.

Figure 5.34 G_object object's textures so far.

10. Save your work as **ch05-12.max.**

Exercise 5.14   Working with Face Group #9

Here's where the heartaches begin. "Why?" you ask. If you can think back to when we applied the texture coordinates to the faces, you will recall that we applied cylindrical mapping to the curved faces. Although the cylindrical mapping gizmos fit snugly against those faces, we must remember those faces do not create a complete circle. The cropping measurements that we have for the bitmap have the exact amount of space necessary to crop the map for the length of the faces. Applying the cropped texture to those faces would apply it on a full 360-degree rotation, causing the map to stretch larger than is intended. We need a solution, and fast!

It's not a big problem. We came this far, didn't we? What is necessary is to create a circle spline that fits against the curved faces and measure that spline to obtain the number needed to recalculate the new Percent of Path. In this way, the crop of the full 360-degrees is made possible.

1. With ch05-12.max open, go to Create/Shapes and create a circle in the Top viewport with XYZ at (**0,0,0**) and with a radius of 70; this size circle fits against the curve (see Figure 5.35).

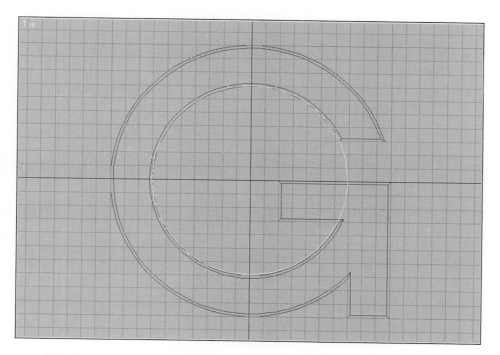

Figure 5.35   The Top viewport displaying the circle spline with a radius of 70.

2. With the circle you just created selected, click the Utilities tab and open the Measure utility. In the Splines group, you can see that the length of the spline is 439.819.

   If we divide the 360-degree measurement of the circle (439.819) by the total length of the spline (1240.427), the Percent of Path (.355) of the circle relative to the length of the total spline is calculated.

   Therefore, the Measured Start and Percent of Path calculations need reflect those in Table 5.2:

Table 5.2   Measurements for Face Group #9

Face Number	Face Length	Percent of Path	Measured Start
Face Group #9 (actual)	377.771	.305	.25
Face Group #9 (360 degree)	439.819	.355	.25

As you can see from Table 5.2, we divided the 360-degree face length (439.819) by the total length of the spline (1240.427) to achieve its percent of the 360-degree path (.355). The percent of this path (.355) was subtracted from the Measured Finish (.605) to achieve its Measured Start (.25). Let's plug in these numbers and see the result.

3. Open the Material Editor and copy material #8 to #9 open material #9 and name it **G_Face09**. Click the Diffuse tab and name the Diffuse map **G_Face09-dif**. Enter the Measured Start value (U: **.25**) and the new 360-degree face group length (W: **.355**).

4. Click the Show Map in Viewport button and check the Perspective viewport for the results (see Figure 5.36).

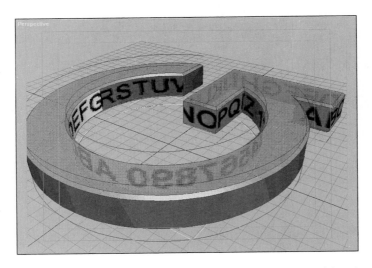

Figure 5.36   The Perspective viewport displaying Material #9 to this point.

Not quite right, is it? Here is where we must make a judgement call. Because we already know that the texture is cropped correctly to produce the correct aspect, we don't necessarily need to do more math to calculate how much offset the bitmap requires. Instead, we will tweak it until we have the map placed correctly on the object.

There are two ways to adjust the texture to its correct placement: offsetting the texture map and rotating the map gizmo. For this example, we will be offsetting the texture in the Bitmap Parameters rollout of the Material Editor. This technique is much more practical for this example because the U Offset value can be gradually shifted. Although rotating the map gizmo for Face Group #9 would work just as well, the UVW Map gizmo is in the middle of the Modifier stack. Accessing the UVW Face 9 modifier increases the chances of making a mistake in the Modifier stack, so why touch it if we can work around it?

5. Adjust the U Offset of the G_Face09-dif map until the two parts of the letter R of the texture map line up. I found a U Offset value of 0.32 to be successful (see Figure 5.37).

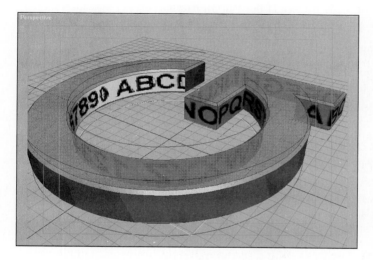

Figure 5.37   The Perspective viewport displaying the correct offset of the texture map.

6. Save your work as **ch05-13.max**.

Exercise 5.15   Adding Texture to Face Group #10

Here is the true test that will verify the calculations we made in the previous steps. We'll add the texture to Face Group #10. Hopefully, everything lines up.

1. With ch05-13.max loaded, open the Material editor and copy material #9 to #10 open material #10 and name the material **G_Face10**. Open the Diffuse map and name it **G_Face10-dif** and enter these values:

   U: **.555**

   W: **.026**

   U: Offset: **0**

2. Click the Show Map in Viewport button to show the map on Face Group #10. Way to go! The two textures match up perfectly.

3. Save your work as **ch05-14.max**.

Exercise 5.16   Applying Texture to the Outside Curve

Now it's time to apply the texture to the final face, Face Group #11. The process is similar to the process that was used to apply the texture to Face Group #9. There is only one difference between the two: The extra space we used to make up for the 360-degree rotation for Group #9 is not available to use for Face Group #11. The extra space is not available because the U value range is 0 to 1; this U value would require a value greater than 1. Therefore, we must calculate the Percent of Path of Face Group #11 and subtract that number from its finish point to acquire its Measured Start.

Let's start by calculating Face Group #11's 360-degree measurement.

1. With ch05-14.max loaded, select the circle spline that we used to measure the 360-degree measurement of Face Group #9. From the Modify panel, change the circle spline's radius to 100. Click the Utilities tab and open the Measure utility. From the Shapes group of the Measure utility, we can see that the length of this spline is 628.314. We need to work this number into our equation (see Table 5.3).

Table 5.3   Measurements for Face Group #11

Face Number	Face Length	Percent of Path	Measured Start
Face Group #11 (actual)	518.415	.418	.581
Face Group #11 (360 degree)	628.314	.507	.493

Once again, don't close the book and run away. It's much simpler than it looks. To illustrate this point, lets just plug in these numbers.

2. Open the Material Editor and copy material #10 to #11. Open material #11 and name the material **G_Face11**, open the Diffuse map and name it **G_Face11-dif**, and enter these values:

    U: **.493**

    W: **507**

    Look at the Perspective viewport and examine the results (see Figure 5.38).

    Looks great! All we have to do now is tweak the U Offset of the bitmap.

3. In the Coordinates rollout of the G_face11-dif texture, adjust the values of the U Offset until the bitmap is in the correct position. A U Offset of .627 worked well in my scene.

4. Save your work as **ch05-15.max**.

We have added precise UVW Map coordinates to our G logo object.

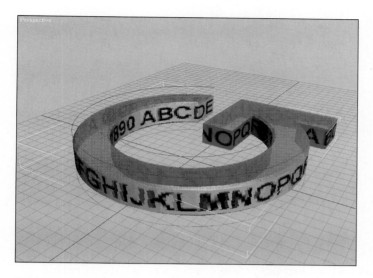

Figure 5.38   The Perspective viewport with G_face11-dif texture applied.

In Summary

In the next chapter, we will be removing the rainbow texture map from the IFL, revealing the animated production texture map. We will be finishing the scene by adding lights and secondary objects, and animating the scene. Compared to this chapter, the next chapter is a breeze.

Chapter 6

Applying Materials and Animating the Logo

How do you pull it all together once the geometry has been successfully created and the textures are ready to be applied? The next step is to add the background elements and animation to the scene. We need to keep our client's wishes in mind by featuring the logo and its special texture map.

We also have to create an environment that enhances the company's image. How do we successfully combine the prerequisite images and create the subtle nuances necessary to integrate the background?

In this chapter, we will be completing the Gravity Zone animation. We have created the main logo element and applied complex UVW Map coordinates on the logo. Now we need to adjust the material of this logo object, create the environment for the logo to live in, and animate the scene.

Finishing the Objects in the Scene

Now that we have textured the G object and we are ready to begin the animation process, we can remove the rainbow texture we used to set up the alignment of the UVW Map coordinates and bitmap cropping.

Then we will merge the G object into a fresh session of MAX. We do this for two reasons:

- To allow MAX to refresh the .ifl file. The old .ifl file usually lingers in memory until you reload the MAX file or move the timeline slider.

- To start this phase with only the item or items we need. By merging only the files we need, we help clean up our workspace, making it less confusing to work with and streamlining our workflow. We no longer need the Tape Helpers and Shapes that we used to measure the object. We also don't need the lights and cameras we used to texture the object.

Exercise 6.1   Removing the Rainbow

We will now remove the rainbow texture that we used to set up the UVW Map coordinates on our G object. To do so, we will remove the first line of the IFL, the line that loads G1240x20.jpg, by using a text editor.

1. Using WordPad or any other text editor, open plnt0000.ifl from your tutorial maps directory on your hard drive (the directory you copied the map files to in Chapter 5). When loading the file, you may need to choose Files of Type/All Documents to find files with the .ifl extension.

2. Select and delete the first line from the list (G1240x20.jpg) as shown in Figure 6.1.

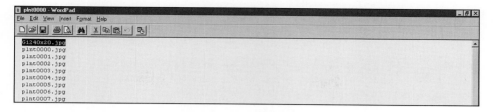

Figure 6.1   Select the G1240x20.jpg line in the IFL and delete it.

3. Save **plnt0000.ifl**, replacing the original file on your hard drive.

4. Close the text editor and open a fresh session of MAX, or choose File, Reset.

5. Choose File, Merge, select ch05-15.max from the Merge File dialog box and click Open. In the Merge – ch05-15.max dialog box, select G_object and click OK to merge the object into the fresh scene. In the shaded Perspective viewport, you should see the planetary symbol texture on the UVW Mapped sides of the G_object (see Figure 6.2).

Figure 6.2   Shaded Perspective view with correctly textured G object.

6. Save this file as **ch06-01.max**.

The rainbow texture has been successfully removed from the IFL. The remaining images in the .ifl file create the loopable 60-frame animation of the planetary symbols. If you would like to see this 60-frame animation, load and play tx1-anim.avi, found in the ch06\images directory of the accompanying CD. Because the first (frame 0) and last frames (frame 60) are identical, frame 60 was not rendered; this creates a seamless loop.

To examine the .max file that created this animation, check out PlanetObjects 01MT01.max, in the ch06\maps directory of the accompanying CD:

Note

The Tx1-anim.avi file, which is found in the ch06\images directory, is an accurate representation of the rendered frames of the PlanetObjects01MT01.max file.

- The rendered frames of PlanetObjects01MT01.max were used to create the texture surrounding the G object. The output of the PlanetObjects01MT01.max animation is 620×70 (roughly 9:1), so the image needed to be tiled so that it matched the aspect of G1240x20.jpg (62:1).

- To adjust the image aspect, the rendered frames of PlanetObjects01MT01.max were loaded into a fresh session of MAX as the Rendering/Environment Environment Map with Screen coordinates. U Tile set to 7, tiling the image seven times across the U axis, matching the aspect of the G1240x20.jpg (62:1).

- This scene was then rendered at a resolution of 8680x140 (62:1) to create the plnt.jpg image sequence.

Creating the Primary Animation

Now that we have removed the rainbow texture from the G object's diffuse .ifl file, we can start preparing the scene for animation. It is important to pre-visualize the animation before beginning the animation process. I always keep a toy box near my workstation filled with all shapes and sizes of toys. I grab a toy or two and begin to rough out the animation, as if I were a puppeteer. This helps me to gain an understanding of how the animation will flow. Knowing how the scene is going to move helps me align the axis of objects and decide what type of Helper object hierarchies to create.

We know that we want to feature the side of the G object, showing off the complex texture coordinates we created. The G object will be lying flat on its back and the camera will slowly truck around the side of the object. After the side of the G object has been established, the G object will slowly rotate forward, standing up, finishing the logo animation. Knowing the path of the animation before keying the scene will save you time; you eliminate trial and error in MAX.

Exercise 6.2   Centering the G Object for Animation

I have found that it is always best to center the primary object in world space. Doing so makes setting up the camera and lights easier. Because the G object is the primary object in this animation, let's place the pivot point of the G object at the center of the G object itself and then center the G object in world space.

1. Make sure the G_object is selected, open the Hierarchy panel and, in the Adjust Pivot rollout, activate Affect Pivot Only. In the Alignment group, click Center to Object to move the pivot point to the center of the object. Deactivate Affect Pivot Only.

2. Activate the Select and Move tool and right-click the Select and Move tool to open the Transform Type-In. Move the G_object to the Absolute:World coordinates XYZ: [**0,0,0**]. Close the Transform Type-In dialog box.

Now the G_object is centered in world space. Let's begin to animate this object now.

Exercise 6.3   Animating the G object

Gravity Zone specifically requested that the planetary symbols are clear and apparent during the animation. We have made the decision to showcase these symbols during the beginning of the animation. We must be sure to give plenty of time for the symbols to be established so they are not lost in pre-roll. We also want the symbols to play on the screen long enough to set the mood for the animation.

The G object is currently lying on its back in world space. This position is ideal because we want to truck around the side of the object before it stands up and reaches its final resolve in the animation. We will simply allow the G object to peacefully rest there while we truck the camera around it. After the side of the object has been established, we will rotate the object to stand it up.

1. Right-click the Play Animation icon to open the Time Configuration dialog box. Set the Animation Length to **300** and click OK to close the dialog box.

2. Open the Track View and expand the G_object\Transform track. Activate the Add Keys button and, in the G_object\Transform\Rotation track, click to add keys at frames 60 and 210 (see Figure 6.3).

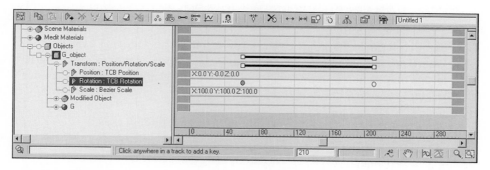

Figure 6.3   Track View open with G_object\Transform\Rotation keys added at frames 60 and 210.

3. Make sure you are using the default TCB Rotation controller by right-clicking the Filters icon and activating Controller Types. Each animated track now shows the type of controller assigned to the track. If the controller type for G_object\Rotation is not TCB Rotation, use Assign Controller to assign a TCB Rotation controller to the track.

4. Right-click the key at frame 60 to open the G_object\Rotation dialog box. Set Ease From: to **25** and click the arrow pointing to the right in the top left of the dialog box to move to key #2.

5. Advance the time slider to frame 210 before completing the next step because we will be adding the rotation information for the key at frame 210. Advancing to frame 210 will allow you to see the object rotating as you change the Angle value.

6. In the G_object\Rotation dialog box for frame #2 (Frame 210), enter the values shown in Figure 6.4 and close the dialog box.

   X: **1**

   Angle: **90** (to rotate the G_object 90 degrees to stand it up)

   Ease To: **25**

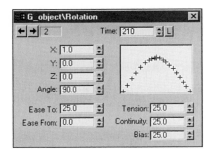

Figure 6.4   The correct settings for Key #2 in the G_object\Rotation dialog box.

Note

Because X equals 1, the object will rotate about its local X-axis. The angle is the amount of rotation about that axis, where positive rotations go in the counter-clockwise direction.

7. Right-click on the Perspective viewport's name, set the rendering level to Wireframe and play the animation. The G_object remains stationary on its back for the first 60 frames and then rotates upward and gently eases into its upward position at frame 210.

This completes the animation for the G object: a graceful, smooth move.

Exercise 6.4   Planning the Camera Move and Creating the Hierarchy

As we learned earlier, we will be slowly trucking the camera around the edge of the G object. After the logo is formed, it needs to remain the focus of the scene, maintaining its integrity. To maintain the integrity of the logo, we need to create a continuing visual interest once it has resolved. Ways to preserve the integrity of the logo could be a moving highlight, or an animated reflection map. In this case it's a slow truck around the logo object.

When the animation has resolved, the camera will continue a slow, almost impercepti-ble, truck around this G object. Trucking the camera slowly around an object when the animation resolves adds drama and pad to the animation, avoiding the appearance of a still image. It is important to remember that the logo is most important to the client.

To create this move easily, we will implement two dummy helpers linked to the camera in order to create the graceful and dramatic rotation.

The parent dummy will rotate slowly at a constant speed throughout the duration of the animation. The sibling dummy will rotate more quickly, allowing the camera to truck around the G object before and during its upward rotation. When the G object has reached its resolve, the sibling dummy will stop and ride the rotation of the parent dummy.

1. Activate Snap, open Create/Helpers, click Dummy, and, in the Top viewport, click and drag to create a dummy helper at XYZ [**0,0,0**]. The size of the dummy is unimportant: I made mine the same size as the G_object (see Figure 6.5). Leave the name Dummy01. This dummy will be the slowly rotating parent.

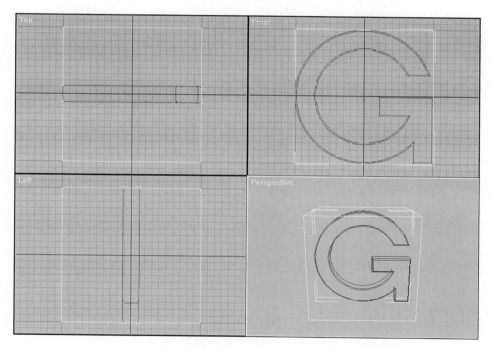

Figure 6.5   Create a dummy helper at XYZ [0,0,0].

2. Create another dummy in the Top viewport at XYZ [**0,0,0**] and make it slightly smaller than the Dummy01 (see Figure 6.6). Leave the name Dummy02. This dummy helper will be the rotating sibling one that allows the camera to truck around the side of the G_object.

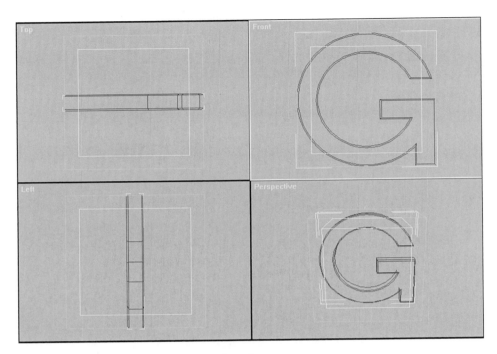

Figure 6.6   Create a dummy helper at XYZ [0,0,0].

3. To create the camera we will need for this animation, open the Create/Cameras panel, click Free, and click in the Front viewport to create a Free Camera. Move the Camera to XYZ [**0,–550,0**]. Activate the Perspective viewport and press C to change the view to Camera.

   Now let's build the hierarchy we need to execute the desired camera move.

4. Activate Select and Link, and then link Camera01 to Dummy02 and link Dummy02 to Dummy01.

Because we created this hierarchy, Dummy02 and the Camera are rotated whenever Dummy01 is rotated. When Dummy02 is rotated, the camera rotates with it.

Exercise 6.5   Animating the Camera Hierarchy

Earlier it was mentioned that Dummy01 will be rotating slowly at a constant speed, allowing the Camera to truck continuously around the logo, even after it resolves. Dummy02 is linked to Dummy01 and will rotate with Dummy01. Before animating this hierarchy, we must rotate Dummy01 to the position where the Camera01 truck will begin.

1. Using Select and Rotate, select Dummy01 in the Top viewport and rotate it –190 degrees using the Top viewport's Z view coordinates. This rotates the camera to its starting position (see Figure 6.7).

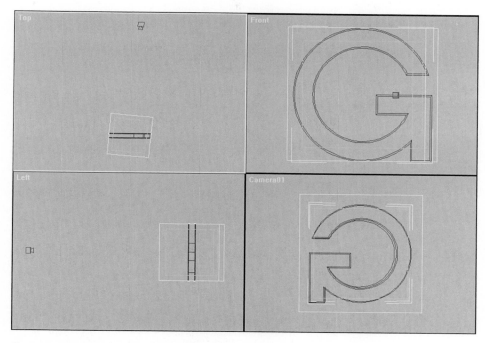

Figure 6.7 The correct rotation from Dummy01.

2. To animate Dummy01, open the Track View and expand the Dummy01\Transform tracks. Activate Add Keys and click to add a key at frame 0 and 30 in the Dummy01\Transform\Rotation track. Right-click the key at frame 30 to open the Dummy01\Rotation dialog box. Make Z: **1** and Angle: **5**, as shown in Figure 6.8. Close the dialog box.

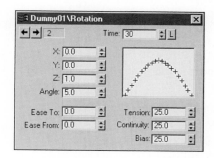

Figure 6.8 The correct settings for the Dummy01\Rotation key at frame 30.

3. Play the animation to examine the slow rotation of Dummy01 between frames 0 and 30. When the timeline gets to frame 30, the rotation stops; we need to continue it throughout the animation.

4. To continue the Dummy01 rotation, click on the Dummy01\Transform\Rotation track's name to select it and click the Parameter Curve Out-of-Range Types. Click the Relative Repeat Out and click OK to close the dialog box (see Figure 6.9).

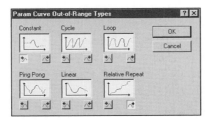

Figure 6.9   The correct settings in the Parameter Curve Out-of-Range Types dialog box.

Relative Repeat Out instructs MAX to continue the rotation at its current speed throughout the length of the animation.

5. Play the animation and you will notice the Dummy01 object rotates evenly over the course of the animation.

   Dummy01 is rotating during the entire animation. However, it is not rotating quickly enough to be looking at the front of the G_object at frame 210—when the G_object reaches its final position. Alas! This is why we have added Dummy02 into the hierarchy. We need to animate the rotation of Dummy02 through frames 0–210, and then the animated "truck" will have the camera hitting its mark at frame 210.

6. Advance to frame 210 of the animation and select Dummy02. Activate the Animate button and, using the Select and Rotate tool, rotate Dummy02 150 degrees using the Top viewport's Z view coordinates (see Figure 6.10). This will position the Camera directly in front of the G_object at frame 210.

7. Turn off the Animate button and play the animation to view the results.

   Dummy01 rotates at steady slow steady rate continuously throughout the animation. Dummy02 Rotates quickly through frames 0–210 then abruptly stops. Because Dummy02 is linked to Dummy01 the rotation continues at Dummy01's slow steady rate.

   We need to tone down the abrupt stop at frame 210 to ease the Dummy02 rotation to a stop.

8. Open the Track View (if it isn't already) and right-click the key at 210 in the Dummy02\Transform\Rotation track to open the Dummy02\Rotation dialog box. Enter an Ease To value of **25** and click OK to exit.

9. Play the animation again.

   Dummy02's rotation now slowly eases into its final keyframe, making the stop of its rotation blend seamlessly into the rotation of Dummy01, the desired result.

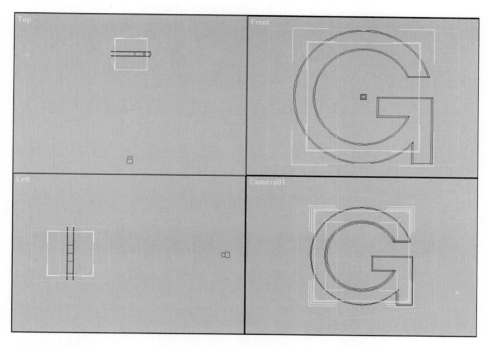

Figure 6.10   The correct rotation for Dummy02 at frame 210.

Exercise 6.6   Finishing the Camera Animation

We are almost finished assigning the primary keys in the animation of the camera. However, there are a few things that we still need to tend to. Let's move the camera closer to the G object during the beginning of the animation so that our audience can see all the hard work we put into texturing it. Then let's have the camera slowly move away as the G object resolves. We probably should make sure that the G object is higher in the screen when the animation resolves so that we have enough room to place the title "Gravity Zone" under it. This is going to be easy.

Let's dolly the camera closer to the G object so it is closer to the G object during the beginning of the animation.

1. Open the Track View and expand the Transform tracks for Camera01. Because the camera is the correct viewing distance from the G_object at 210, activate Add Keys and click frame 210 in the Camera\Transform\Position Track to add a key. Since we are going to want it to ease into that keyframe, right-click the new key, change the In tangent type to Slow (see Figure 6.11), and close the Camera01\Position dialog box.

    Now we must dolly the Camera closer to the G_object, bringing it in for the opening close-up.

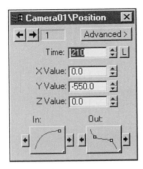

Figure 6.11   The correct settings for the Camera01\Position dialog box.

2. Advance to frame 0 of the animation and activate the Animate button. Highlight the Camera01 viewport and activate the Dolly Camera tool. Dolly the camera toward the G_object until its edges move outside the viewport (see Figure 6.12).

3. Turn off the Animate button and play the animation.

   The dolly looks pretty good. However, it would look better if the dolly of the camera were delayed so the camera stays closer to the G_object longer, and then pulled away for the logo to resolve. Let's fix that right now.

4. Open the Track View and locate the Camera01\Transform\Position track. Move the key from frame 0 to frame 60, and right-click the key to open the Camera01\Position dialog box. Change the Out tangent type to Slow (shown in Figure 6.13) and exit the dialog box. (Changing the Out tangent to Slow will ease the camera dolly away from the G_object.) Play the animation and view the results.

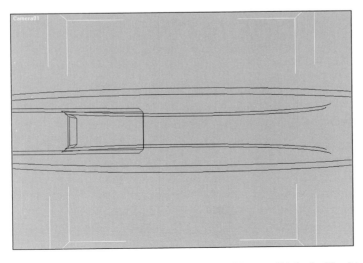

Figure 6.12   Dolly the camera towards the G_object until it looks like this.

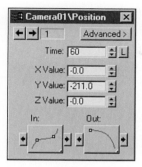

Figure 6.13   The correct settings for the Camera01\Position dialog box.

Note

We didn't originally assign the key at frame 60 because an unnecessary key at frame 0 would have been created. This unnecessary key would figure into the smoothing of the motion and negatively affect the motion. Creating a key at frame 0 when we want a key at frame 60 forces us to remember to move it to 60.

Looks fantastic! All that is left is to move the G_object higher in the screen to allow space for the Gravity Zone text.

5. Right-click the Camera01's viewport name and activate Show Safe Frame.

Note

Safe Frame is a tool to aid you with correctly composing your image. Although it is a term that originated with animations created for television, Safe Frame is handy when composing an image for any media or non 4:3 aspect output images. When Activated, Safe Frame displays three rectangular shaped guides in the viewport:

● *Live Area.* This yellow rectangle is a representation of what will render, according to the Output Size assigned to the Render Scene dialog box.

● *Action Safe.* This green rectangle represents the area of the image where important action can take place in the animation.

● *Title Safe.* This cyan rectangle represents the area of the image where it is pleasing to include title or logo elements in the animation. The term Title Safe, or Safe Title, is used in the television industry because older televisions often didn't display the entire image. The Title Safe area helps broadcast designers to ensure that important information will be visible on every television.

Safe Frames can be configured in the Safe Frames tab of the Viewport Configuration dialog box.

6. Select Dummy01, advance to frame 210, and activate the Animate button. Using the View coordinate system, activate Restrict to Y and move Dummy01 downward in the Front viewport until the top of the G_object almost touches the cyan Safe Frame box (see Figure 6.14). Turn off the Animate button and play the animation.

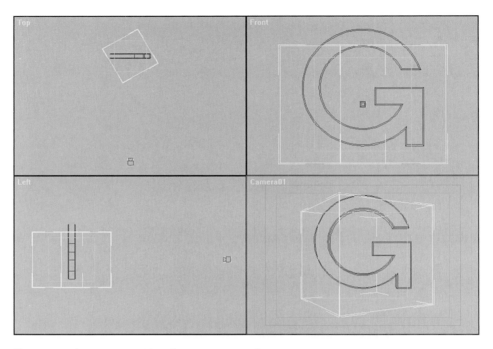

Figure 6.14   The correct position for Dummy01 at frame 210.

The G_object certainly moves upward in the Camera viewport, but does so way too early. Let's take care of that right now.

7. Open the Track View, if it isn't already, and locate the Dummy01\Transform\Position track. Move the key at frame 0 to frame 60. Right-click this key to open the Dummy01\Position dialog box, change the Out tangent type to Slow, and leave the dialog box open. Click the arrow pointing to the right to change the active key to key #2. Change key number 2's In tangent type to Slow. Now the position will ease in and out smoothly. Close the Dummy01\Position dialog box and the Track View. Play the animation.

Exactly what the doctor—I mean Gravity Zone—ordered. The camera slowly trucks around the side of the G_object, allowing us to view the planetary symbols mapped on it, and then the camera pulls back to view the big letter G in all its glory. The camera continues to truck slowly around the G_object, adding drama and interest. We have now completed the primary animation of the logo object and the camera in the scene. It's time to save our hard work.

8. Save your work as **ch06-02.max**.

Adding Secondary Objects and Animation to the Scene

Now that the animation of the primary object is complete, we will create secondary objects, animation, and texture; and then light the scene. Before we do so, let's better understand how to establish a mood.

When creating animations, the importance of color and motion cannot be overemphasized. Correct use of color and motion will make a simple animation appear complex and beautiful. Improper use of color and motion could make the most complex scene ineffective.

It is very helpful to look at 2D or 3D animated features to find colors to create a mood. Larger animation production companies know the suggestive power of color and spend a great deal of time planning the colors used in each scene. They have become masters at using color to invoke mood, constantly discovering new ways to invoke mood through color. Carefully watch these movies and be aware of the colors used. Remember the mood and the colors and use their careful research to your advantage.

The motion of the secondary objects should compliment the primary objects, enhancing the desired mood. We don't want to create any objects that will overpower or take away from the logo element in our scene. Rather, secondary objects should compliment the logo, distract from it. Because the logo is a warm color (orange) we should keep the background cool colors to compliment the logo and add overall contrast. The moon is round, echoing the roundness of the G logo, creating a visual link to the moving background images of the clouds and sky changing from day to night.

Exercise 6.7   Adding the Moon

If you recall, the inventive promotion people at Gravity Zone requested that the moon should be incorporated into the animation to emphasize Gravity Zone's connection to the people of earth. We should add that now.

1. With ch06-02.max open, open the Create/Geometry panel. Click Sphere and, in the Keyboard Entry rollout, create a sphere with a Radius of 335 at X,Y,Z [**0,2000,–1000**]. Name this object **moon**.

   We have decided to center the moon behind the G_object when the logo resolves at frame 210, creating a sense of completion to the logo. I usually add some type of "stinger" to a logo when it resolves. The stinger lets the viewers know "This is the finale!" Sometimes it's a subtle lens flare; sometimes it's a particle effect. For this animation, it's as simple as centering the moon with the logo. Let's key that now.

2. Advance to frame 210 and activate the Animate button. Click Restrict to Y and move the moon object upward in the Front viewport until it is centered behind the G_object in the Camera viewport (see Figure 6.15).

3. Turn off Animate and play the animation.

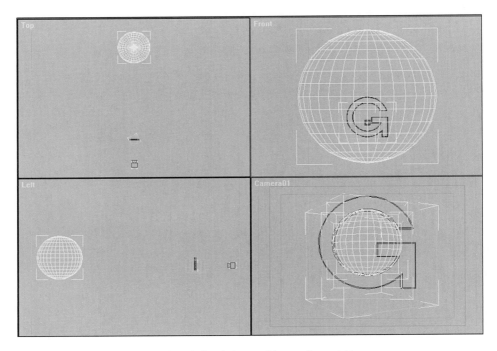

Figure 6.15   Center the moon object behind the G_object at frame 210.

The moon now rises in the scene, but stops abruptly at frame 210. We need to continue the moon's momentum throughout the animation.

4. Open the Track View and expand the Moon\Transform tracks. Select the Position track's title and click the Parameter Curve Out-of-Range Types button. In the Parameter Curve Out-of-Range Types dialog box click the button pointing to the right under Relative Repeat. Click OK to close the dialog box and close the Track View. Play the animation to view the results.

Great job! We have just completed animating all of the objects in this scene. Don't get too excited, however; there is still more work ahead. We need to add lights to the scene, and then we can move on to finalizing the textures and setting the mood with a cool environment.

Exercise 6.8   Shedding Light on the Scene

Gravity Zone has requested that their animation be dramatic and eye-catching. We have successfully created a complex textured logo object and choreographed a dazzling camera move. Let's add a few lights to the scene that will justify all of our hard work.

Let's start by creating a light that will create dramatically light the moon.

1. Open the Create/Lights panel and create an Omni light at XYZ [**–3000,2800,–1400**] (see Figure 6.16) and set the color to RGB (**105,120,120**), a pale blue color. Name this light **OmniMoon**.

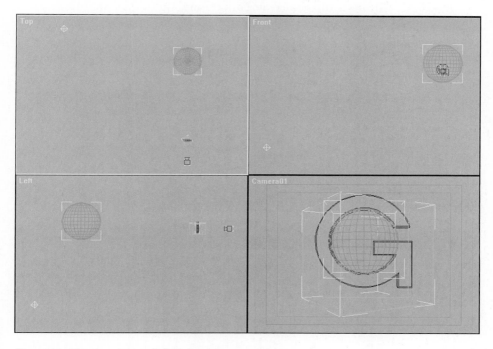

Figure 6.16   The OmniMoon light in its correct position.

2. To make the diffuse edge sharper and more dramatic on the moon, set Contrast to **100**.

3. Because this light should illuminate only the moon, we need to create an Include list. Click the Exclude button, and in the Exclude/Include dialog box, select moon and click the arrow pointing to the right. Activate Include and click OK to exit the dialog box.

   Now let's move on to lighting the G_object. We will place the Key light in the center of the world's XY coordinate system so the G_object catches a dramatic highlight as it resolves. The key light is going to provide another "stinger" to the G_object. This light, because of its position in the scene, will add a bright highlight on the readable face of the G_object as it reaches its final position in the scene.

4. Create an Omni light with these values:

   XYZ: [**0,–1000,0**]

   RGB: (**180,180,180**)

   Contrast: **0**

5. Name this light **OmniLogoKey** and create an Include list including G_object.

We will add a fill light to the scene now. This light will act as the fill light during the beginning of the animation and the backlight when the logo resolves. After you create the light, examine its position and you will see how this is accomplished.

6. Create an Omni light at XYZ [**–600,700,0**] and set color values to RGB (**100,100,100**). Name this light **OmniLogoFill** and create an Include list including the G_object.

Notice that, at frame 0, the OmniLogoFill light is acting as a fill light (see Figure 6.17). The light is on the same side of the G_object as the camera. By the time the animation reaches frame 210 (shown in Figure 6.18), the light is on the opposite side of the G_object and is acting as a backlight.

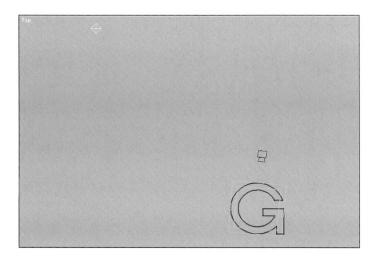

Figure 6.17   OmniLogoFill is acting as the fill light at frame 0.

7. Save your work as **ch06-03.max**.

We are now finished with creating the vital pieces of the scene. All that is left to do is finish off the texture of the G object, texture the moon, and create the environment for the animation to take place in.

Figure 6.18   OmniLogoFill is acting as the backlight at frame 210.

Using the Material Editor

In this section, we will be finishing the materials for all of the objects in the scene. We must finish the materials on the G object and create the lunar surface of the moon.

Exercise 6.9   Finishing the G_object's Materials

Because we have already completed most of the G object's materials, this shouldn't take long. All that is left to do is create a material for the readable face and bevel for the G object.

1. With ch06-03.max loaded, open the Material Editor.

   Because we merged the G_object into the scene, its material is no longer in a Material Preview slot. Let's go get it.

2. Select the first Material slot and click Get Material to open the Material/Map Browser. Choose Browse From: Scene, double-click the G material from the list to load it into the slot, and close the browser.

3. To edit the material on the readable face of the G_object, click the Material 1 slot in the Basic Parameters rollout to open the material. Change the following settings:

   Shader: **Metal**

   Self-Illumination: **0**

   Opacity: **50**

   Specular Level: **86**

   Glossiness: **65**

   These settings will produce a soft metallic material that is ideal for our object.

For the bevel of the G_object, we will apply a bright and reflective metallic material. This will help outline the G_object. Because of the high reflective quality of the material, the edges will always appear to be bright even when no lights are shining on it.

4. In the Material Editor, click the Go Forward to Sibling button to move to Material #2 of the G material. Use these settings:

> Shading: **Metal**
>
> Diffuse Color: RGB (**230,210,200**)
>
> Self-Illumination: **0**
>
> Specular Level: **91**
>
> Glossiness: **54**

These settings result in a dull silver metallic material.

5. To make the material appear bright, we will add a Reflection Map. Open the Maps rollout, click the Reflection Map slot, and choose Bitmap from the Material/Map Browser. In the Select Bitmap Image File dialog box, which automatically opens, choose refmap.gif from the tutorial maps directory on your hard drive (the directory you copied the maps to in Chapter 5) and click Open to exit the Select Bitmap Image File dialog box. Name this map **G-Face02-rfl** and change Blur Offset to **.05** to soften the image up a bit.

6. Click Go To Parent to return to the Basic Parameters of Material #2. In the Maps rollout, change Reflection to **75** to make the reflection less harsh.

Now it's time to add a material to the moon object.

7. Activate the second material preview slot in the Material Editor and name this Material **Moon**. Use these settings:

> Shading: **Phong**
>
> Specular Level: **19**
>
> Glossiness: **15**

Uncheck Color in Self-Illumination and set the value to **15.** Open the Extended Parameters rollout and activate Falloff: Out and enter Amt: **25.** The falloff amount will soften the edge of the moon.

8. Open the Maps rollout, click the Diffuse Color map button, choose Bitmap from the Material/Map Browser, and load Moon.jpg from the tutorial maps directory on your hard drive. Name this Map **Moon-dif.** Click Go To Parent and, in the Maps rollout, drag the Moon-dif map to the Bump map slot and select Copy from Copy [Instance] Map dialog box.

9. Click the Bump Map button to open it, name this map **Moon-bmp** and, in the Coordinates rollout, change Blur to **4.** This will soften the bumps of the bump map.

10. Apply the Moon material to the Moon object in the scene. To do this, you can drag the Moon material preview slot to the Moon object in any viewport and release the mouse.

11. Save your work as **ch06-04.max**.

Adding the Environment and Background

Gravity Zone requested that their logo be floating in a sky environment that changes from a cheery blue sky to a clear, peaceful night sky. This will emphasize that they are working for us day and night and that their company reaches far beyond the reaches of earth.

Exercise 6.10   Adding the Day/Night Background

We will first create the day sky and then create the keys to turn it into night.

1. With ch06-04.max loaded, open the Material Editor and open the Rendering/Environment dialog box.

2. In the Environment dialog box click the Environment Map button and choose Composite from the Material/Map browser. Drag the Composite map from the Environment dialog box and drop it in the third material preview slot. Choose Instance from the Copy [Instance] Map dialog box. Close the Environment dialog box and in the Material Editor, name this map **Environment**.

3. In the Composite map, click the Map 1 button and choose Gradient from the Material/Map Browser. Name Map 1 **Sky** and, in the Coordinates rollout, choose Environ/Screen.

4. Change the colors in the Gradient Parameters rollout to create a nice mid-day sky color, using these values:

    Color #1: RGB (**30,55,100**)

    Color #2: RGB (**35,105,170**)

    Color #3: RGB (**45,165,170**)

5. Let's add keys to hold the day sky color until frame 130. Open the Track View, expand the Environment Texture Map track, and then expand the Map 1: Sky track. Activate Add Keys and click to add keys for Color 1, Color 2, and Color 3 at frame 130 (see Figure 6.19).

6. Now we are able to add the keys to create the night sky. Activate Add Keys and create keys at Frame 210 for Color 1, Color 2, and Color 3 (see Figure 6.20).

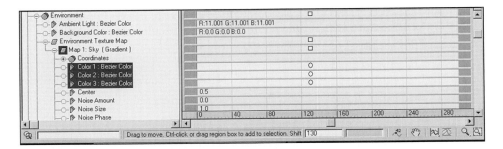

Figure 6.19   Activate Add Keys and create keys for Color 1, Color 2, and Color 3 at frame 130.

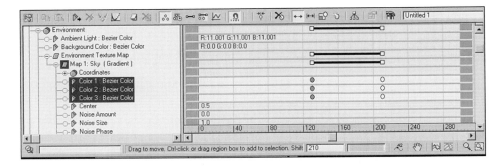

Figure 6.20   Color Keys added at frame 210.

7. Change the color of the keys at 210 to create the night sky. Use these values:

   Color 1: RGB (**0,0,10**)

   Color 2: RGB (**10,10,55**)

   Color 3: RGB (**90,5,90**)

Exercise 6.11   Adding the Stars

Now it's time to add some beautiful stars into the scene.

1. To add stars in the background, close the Track View and click the Go To Parent button to return to the root of the Environment map. Click the Map 2 button and select Mask from the Material/Map Browser. Name the Mask map **Stars**.

2. Let's first add the star's color. Click the Map button and select Gradient from the Material/Map Browser. Name this map **StarColor** and, in the Coordinates rollout, choose Environ/Screen. In the Gradient Parameters rollout, use these values:

   Color #1: RGB (**25,155,190**)

   Color #2: RGB (**35,105,170**)

   Color #3: RGB (**45,155,170**)

The Color #3 color matches the day sky color, so the stars will not be obvious on the bottom of the screen during the beginning of the animation. Stars will be apparent in the top of the screen during the beginning of the animation. This adds drama.

3. Now we will add the star mask, to cut the star pattern into the sky. Click the Go To Parent button to return to the Stars map. Click the Mask button and, from the Material/Map Browser, choose Bitmap. Choose Stars.gif from the tutorial Maps directory you copied to your hard drive. Name this map **StarMask**.

4. From the Coordinates rollout, choose Environ/Spherical Environment. Using the Spherical Environment will allow the stars to move in conjunction with the camera.

Note

When creating a starfield background using a bitmap, you must be very careful with the resolution. If the bitmap is large and the stars are small, the MAX filtering of the star bitmap causes the stars' intensity to vary on each rendered frame, which results in flickering stars.

5. Close the Material Editor and save your work as **ch06-05.max**.

This completes the sky environment background.

Exercise 6.12   Creating Puffy Clouds

Let's add clouds to the scene to cheer up the scene even more. Instead of using bitmap clouds as an environment, we will be using Environmental Fog. We do this for several reasons. Clouds created with Environmental Fog are "real" in the scene and will respond to the motion of the camera more realistically than a bitmap of clouds. Because of their position, when the camera moves through the scene the clouds will move at a different rate than the stars and will add depth to the rendered scene. The Environmental Fog clouds will appear behind the logo and in front of the logo as well. Let's get started.

1. With ch06-05.max loaded, open the Create/Helpers tab. Change the Standard type to Atmospheric Apparatus. Create a CylGizmo with the values shown in Figure 6.21:

  Radius: **1000**

  Height: **2000**

  Absolute/World: XYZ [**0,0,–1000**]

  The CylGizmo object is surrounding the G_object, but not the moon, much like the earth's atmosphere. Let's apply the Volume Fog to the CylGizmo.

2. Open the Rendering/Environment dialog box. From the Atmosphere rollout, click Add. Choose Volume Fog from the Add Atmospheric Effect dialog box and click OK to exit. From the Volume Fog Parameters rollout of the Environment dialog box, click Pick Gizmo, and then click CylGizmo01 to activate the Atmospheric Apparatus.

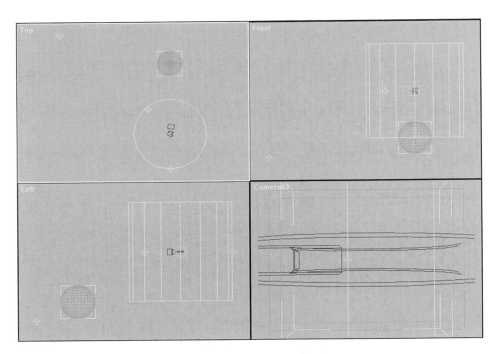

Figure 6.21   Correct size and position for the CylGizmo in the viewports.

3. In the Volume group of the Volume Fog Parameters rollout, change Color to RGB (**150,250,240**) to create a bright teal color. Then make these changes:

   Density: **3**

   Step Size: **4**

   MAX Steps: **30**

4. In the Noise group of the Volume Fog Parameters rollout, set Low to **.25** and Size to **200** (see Figure 6.22). Close the Environment dialog box.

Figure 6.22   The correct settings for Volume Fog.

5. Let's animate the clouds' color so that they darken as day turns to night. Open the Track View and expand the Environment/Volume Fog track. Activate Add Keys and click to add a key for Fog Color at frame 130 (see Figure 6.23).

Figure 6.23 Use Add Keys to create a key at frame 130 for Fog Color.

6. To darken the clouds as the animation progresses into night, use the Add Keys tool to add a Fog Color key at frame 210. Right-click the key at 210 and change the color to RGB (**120,0,130**), a purple color (see Figure 6.24).

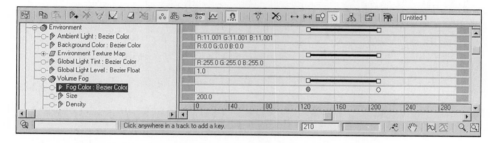

Figure 6.24 Use a Fog Color Key at frame 210 to make the clouds darken.

7. Close the Track View and save your work as **ch06-06.max**.

We are now ready to create a Video Post queue to add the Gravity Zone text.

Video Post Compositing

A first attempt at compositing in Video Post can be very intimidating. Without a doubt, mastering the use of Video Post takes time and practice. Video Post is much easier to use when you know exactly what you want to do and plan the Video Post events before plugging them in. Visualize the events, describe them on paper, and check for errors before building the queue. After the queue is properly planned, insert the events and render test frames of the critical periods in the queue.

We will be using Video Post compositing to add the Gravity Zone text to the animation. After the G object resolves at frame 210, we will use a 1-second dissolve to add this text under the G object. The Gravity Zone text, shown in Figure 6.25, is a 320×240 .tga file that was created in Photoshop. The file consists of white text on a black background; it also contains alpha channel information for the text. We will use Video Post to key out the black of this image and dissolve the white text over the animation.

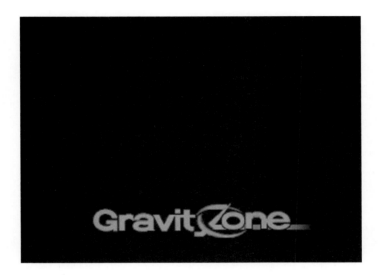

Figure 6.25   Title.tga.

Before we can build the queue in Video Post, however, we must first examine this Video Post task in detail:

- *Frames 0–209.* The rendered MAX scene.
- *Frames 210–240.* The Gravity Zone text dissolves over the MAX scene (remember, at Frame 210 the G object resolves).
- *Frames 241–300.* The Gravity Zone text remains keyed over the MAX scene at 100% intensity.

It helps to create a timeline on paper for quick reference when working in Video Post. Figure 6.26 shows a good example of a reference timeline.

		text dissolves	
Notes	rendered MAX scene	over the MAX scene	text "keyed over" the MAX scene
Frames	0 209	210 240	241 300

Figure 6.26   An example of a timeline used for reference when working with Video Post.

Now we need to decide which type of events we will need to create the Video Post queue. We'll need these five events: we will need:

- *Scene Input Event: Frames 0–300.* This event will render the scene.
- *Image Input Event: Frames 210–300.* This event will load Title.tga into the queue.
- *Alpha Compositor Event: Frames 210–300.* This event will composite Title.tga over the scene.
- *Cross Fade Transition: Frames 210–240.* This event will dissolve Title.tga over the scene.
- *Image Output Event: Frames 0–300.* This event will save the rendered frames.

We now know the timeline of the animation and the events that we will need during the construction of the queue. In the next section, we will build the queue and render a few tests.

Exercise 6.13   Creating the Queue

Creating the queue is not always as straightforward as one would like. Some of the Video Post events are very limited with their capabilities. I frequently have to pull out some tricks to finish the job correctly. We will encounter the limitations of the events as we finish this animation and discover new techniques to get the job done.

One thing is for certain: We will need Camera01 to render in the queue. Because the camera is the lowest level in the composite, we can add it first.

1. With ch06-06.max loaded, open the Video Post dialog box.
2. Click the Add Scene Event button, and, in the Add Scene Event dialog box, click OK to exit, adding the Camera01 event to This the queue (see Figure 6.27).

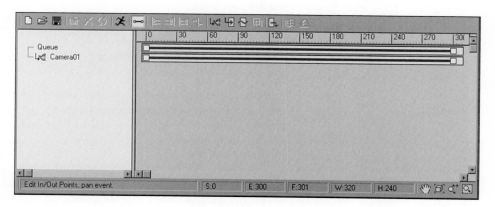

Figure 6.27   Camera01 Scene Event in the Video Post queue.

Now that the camera is in place from frames 0–300, it's time to add the Title.tga that dissolves over Camera01.

3. Click the Image Input Event button to open the Add Image Input Event dialog box. Choose Title.tga from the ch06\maps directory of the accompanying CD. In the Video Post Parameters dialog box, enter a VP Start Time value of **210** and a VP End Time value of **240** (the length of the cross fade). Click OK to close the dialog box. The Title.tga event is added to the queue (see Figure 6.28).

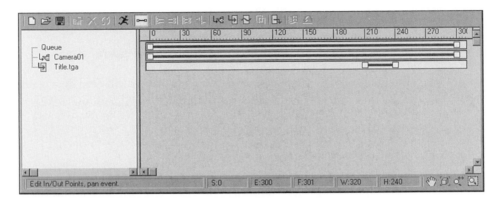

Figure 6.28   Title.tga is added to the Video Post queue.

We will be using a Cross Fade Transition event to dissolve Title.tga over Camera01. Sounds simple, but it isn't. The Cross Fade Transition event cross fades between two images over its active time segment. If we cross faded between Camera01 and Title.tga throughout frames 210–240, we wouldn't get the intended result. What would happens is that, at frame 210, a cross fade between Camera01 and Title.tga would occur, which means at frame 240 we would see only Title.tga—white text on a black background.

To fix this problem, we need to be creative. We need to cross fade a black image to the Title.tga image during frames 210–240 to create the fade on. Then we need an Alpha Compositor to composite the cross fade from black to Title.tga over Camera01. Let's add the black image to the queue.

4. Click the Add Image Input Event button to open the Add Image Input Event dialog box. Choose black.tga (a 5×5 black image with an empty alpha channel), and, in the Video Post Parameters group, enter a VP Start Time value of **210** and a VP End Time value of **240**. Click OK to close the dialog box. The black.tga event is added to the queue (see Figure 6.29).

Now we will add the Cross Fade Transition event to the queue.

5. Using Ctrl+click, select both the Title.tga and black.tga event titles (see Figure 6.30).

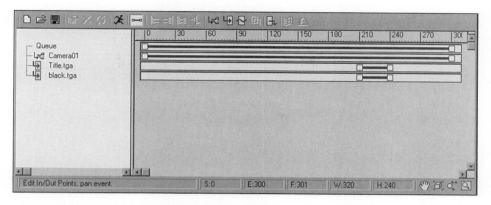

Figure 6.29 Black.tga added to the Video Post queue.

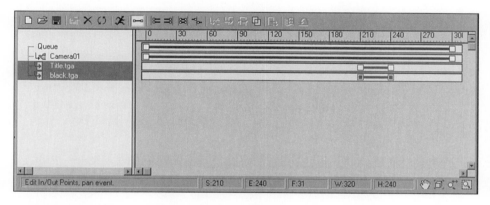

Figure 6.30 Select both the Title.tga and black.tga event titles.

6. Click the Add Image Layer Event button. In the Add Image Layer Event dialog box, choose Layer Plug-In: Cross Fade Transition. Notice the VP Start (210) and End (240) times are correct. Click OK to exit the dialog box.

   The Cross Fade Transition event now cross fades from black.tga to Title.tga between the frames of 210 and 240. Let's render test frames to make sure.

7. Click the Execute Sequence button to open the Execute Video Post dialog box. To render frame 210, choose Single and enter **210.** Set the Output size to **320×240** and click Render to render frame 210. You will see Camera01 render, and then the virtual frame buffer will display the Title.tga. This is because it is being composted over Camera01.

   Something is wrong here, though. The cross fade should be from black.tga to Title.tga; currently, it's cross fading Title.tga to black.tga. We need to swap the order of the events.

8. To swap the order of the Title.tga and black.tga, select both of their names and click the Swap Events button (see Figure 6.31).

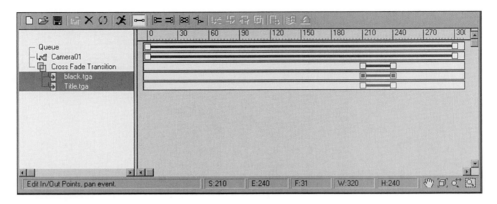

Figure 6.31   The black.tga event is now on top of Title.tga.

9. Click Execute Sequence and render frame 210. Camera01 will render in the virtual frame buffer, and then the screen will abruptly change to black (black.tga).

    The black image at frame 210 is exactly what we wanted to happen. To ensure that the cross fade is fading to Title.tga, we will render frame 240 and view the result.

10. Click the Execute Sequence button to open the Execute Video Post dialog box. Enter a Single value of **240** and click Render to render the frame. Frame 240 of Camera01 now renders and the virtual frame buffer abruptly changes to Title.tga. Everything is coming along great.

    Because the cross fade transition ends at frame 240, so will the Title.tga image coming from the cross fade. We need to add another Image Input Event to extend Title.tga through frames 241–300.

11. Unselect the selected events and click Add Image Input Event. Choose Title.tga and set VP Start Time to 241 and VP End Time to 300. Click OK to exit the dialog box. Another Title.tga event has been added to the queue (see Figure 6.32).

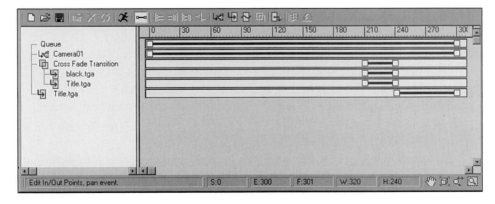

Figure 6.32   Another Title.tga event has been added.

Now we need to attach the Cross Fade Transition (frames 210–240) to the Title.tga image input event (frames 241–300) to form a continuous set of images that we can alpha composite with the scene render. We will do this by adding a Simple Additive Compositor event to the Cross Fade Transition and the second Title.tga. The Simple Additive Compositor simply adds its two input events together. Because in this case the VP time ranges of the input events don't overlap, each input event is effectively added to a black image over their VP time ranges. The result is that the Cross Fade Transition event output is the output of the Simple Additive Compositor for frames 210–240, and Title.tga is the output for frames 241–300.

12. Using Ctrl+click, select the Cross Fade Transition event and the second Title.tga event (see Figure 6.33). Click Add Image Layer Event and in the resulting dialog box choose Filter Plug-In: Simple Additive Compositor. Notice the Video Post Start (210) and End (300) times are correct.

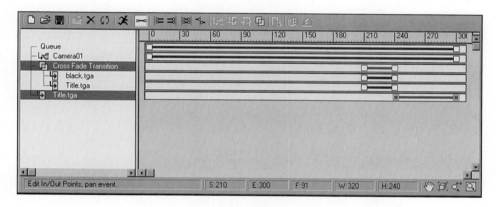

Figure 6.33   Select the Cross Fade Transition event and the second Title.tga event.

All we need to do now is composite the Simple Additive Compositor over Camera01. To do so, we will use the Alpha Compositor event.

13. To add the Alpha Compositor event, select the Camera01 event and the Simple Additive Compositor event (see Figure 6.34) and click Add Image Filter Event. In the Add Image Filter Event dialog box, choose Filter Plug-In Alpha Compositor and click OK to exit the dialog box. The resulting queue should look like Figure 6.35.

There is only one event to add to complete the queue: the Image Output Event. Let's add it.

14. Deselect all the tracks in the queue and click Add Image Output Event. In the resulting dialog box, navigate to your output directory (ch06\images), enter the name **Gravity.avi,** and click OK to exit the dialog box.

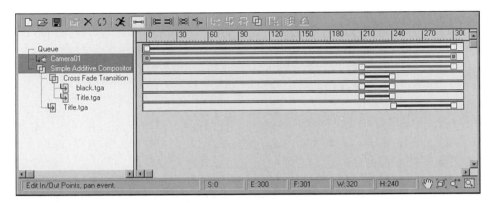

Figure 6.34   Select the Camera01 event and the Simple Additive Compositor event.

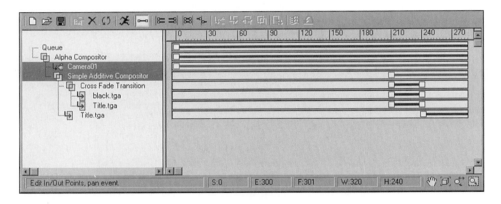

Figure 6.35   The Video Post queue with the Alpha Compositor event added.

15. Save your work as **ch06-07.max.**

16. Render the Video Post queue by clicking Execute Sequence, and, in the Execute Video Post dialog box, choose the Range 0–300 and the Output Size (320×240), and click Render to render the queue. Figure 6.36 shows the final rendered logo.

View the animation when the queue finishes rendering. The camera trucks around the edge of the G object, showcasing the planetary symbols. The logo rotates upwards and after it reaches its final position the Gravity Zone text dissolves over the animation.

In Summary

Great work. You completed this project—just in time for the next one.

Figure 6.36 The final rendered Gravity Zone logo.

Camera starts above
scene and slowly
orbits counter-clockwise
and downward.

Camera orbit continues.
Bright lens flare appears
from center of logo.

Camera orbit continues.
Lens flares emit
from beacon objects
surrounding the base
object. A glow appears
around V logo.

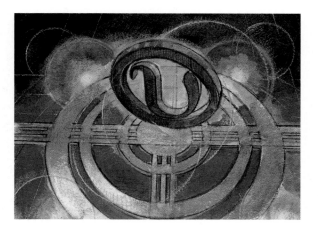

Project III
The V

Camera orbit continues. Bright highlight calls attention to V logo.

designed by Victor Newman

Chapter 7

Modeling and Animating the V

In the fast-paced world of computer animation, employers are looking for animators who are flexible and can visualize animations on paper before the animation process even begins.

Storyboards are frequently created to help accurately plan and visualize key moments in an animation. The project that we are about to create is intended to simulate the actual working environment in the computer animation field.

In this chapter, we will examine a storyboard, build the models, and animate the scene. The integrity and feel of the storyboard is of maximum importance. Following this project will give you an understanding of how to plan an animation in order to achieve the greatest result.

Introducing the Project

We just landed a fantastic job and have been handed our first big project. The art director has provided us with a detailed storyboard, which illustrates critical aspects such as motion and effects. It is our job to utilize our skills as animators to put this storyboard into motion. We will utilize every trick in our animation arsenal, including some Video Post mastery. Can you handle it? Sure you can. You just need to dissect the elements.

Let's take a look at the storyboard in Figure 7.1. Notice these features:

- The animation in the scene looks straightforward. Nothing is really moving in the scene, but the camera starts with a high pedestal (*pedestal* is a term that refers to the height of the camera head on a tripod), and then it pedestals down as the camera trucks to the left.
- The lighting is very dramatic and creates a high contrast image.
- The objects in Panel #1 and Panel #2 are in exactly the same position. This is not because the designer was lazy, this was done intentionally to emphasize pad and to illustrate how the lens flare effects establish themselves.
- The background environment is distant and dark.

Those are the most obvious aspects of the storyboard. We know the animation of the scene is simple and straightforward, so we can probably get away without creating motion tests of the scene. Because we don't need to create motion tests, we will concern ourselves with creating the geometry.

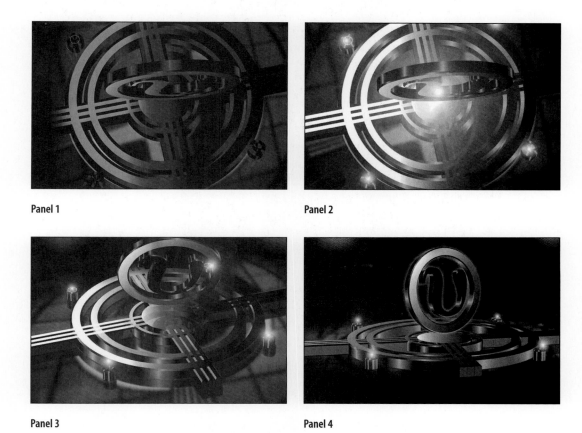

Panel 1

Panel 2

Panel 3

Panel 4

Figure 7.1   The storyboard you just received.

Building the Base Object

We will start the modeling process by building the Base object. As you can see from the storyboard, the Base object is a very prominent object throughout the animation. Because the Base object is so large and stationary, we will build it first. Doing so allows us to get a feel for scale in the scene, giving us a gauge by which to model the rest of the scene.

The storyboard clearly illustrates the shape of the Base object, which is composed of concentric circles with two crosspiece beams passing through the centers of the circles, much like a target crosshair. Close examination of the storyboard shows that the length of the crosspiece aligned in Z world space is shorter than the length of the crosspiece aligned in X world space. It is also notable that the crosspieces consist of three beams each.

Exercise 7.1   Creating the Shapes for the Base Object

We will begin the modeling process by creating the concentric circle shapes, which we will bevel to create the Base object.

1. Open a fresh session of MAX.

2. Activate the Create/Shapes panel and maximize the Top viewport. Using Keyboard Entry, create a circle with a radius of **40** at XYZ **[0,0,0]** (see Figure 7.2).

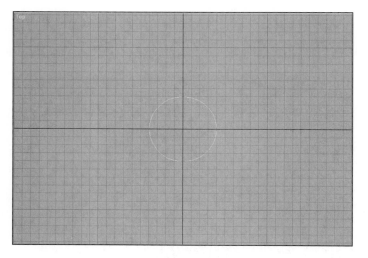

Figure 7.2   The circle shape with a radius of 40, created at XYZ [0,0,0] in the Top viewport.

3. Create six more circle shapes in the Top viewport at XYZ **[0,0,0]** with radii of **50, 65, 100, 120, 130,** and **160** (see Figure 7.3).

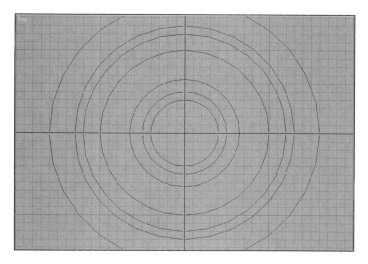

Figure 7.3   The correct size and quantity of circle shapes in the Top viewport.

The concentric circle shapes are in their correct positions. Now we will create the crosspiece shapes that intersect the circles. First we will create the longer crosspieces, which are aligned with the world space X-axis.

4. In the Top viewport, use Create, Shapes to create a rectangle using these values:

   Length: **10**

   Width: **700**

   XYZ: [**0,0,0**]

   Corner Radius: **0**

   Figure 7.4 shows the rectangle you just created.

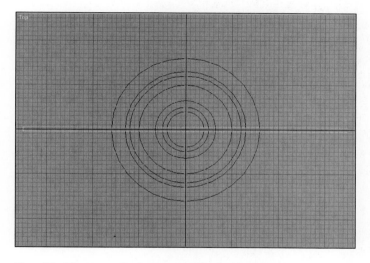

Figure 7.4   The rectangle shape created in the Top viewport.

5. With the newly created rectangle still selected, choose Edit, Clone (from the toolbar) to copy the rectangle, and then use Transform Type-In to move it to XYZ [**0,–12,0**].

6. Choose Edit, Clone again to copy the selected rectangle once more, and then move it to XYZ [**0,12,0**] (see Figure 7.5).

   To create the crosspieces that are aligned with the Z world axis, we will copy the rectangles we have already created and adjust their sizes.

7. Select all three rectangle shapes, activate Select and Rotate (use Selection Center), press and hold down the Shift key, and rotate the rectangles 90 degrees. In the Clone Options dialog box, make sure Copy is active and click OK to copy the rectangle shapes (see Figure 7.6).

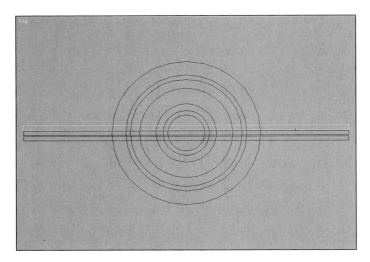

Figure 7.5   The Top viewport with three rectangle shapes in the correct positions (Show Grid is deactivated for clarity).

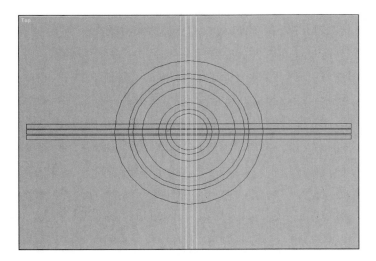

Figure 7.6   Use Select and Rotate while holding down the Shift key to rotate and copy the rectangles.

Next, we need to adjust the size of the rectangles we just copied.

8. Select each one separately and, in the Modify panel, enter a Width of **380** (see Figure 7.7).

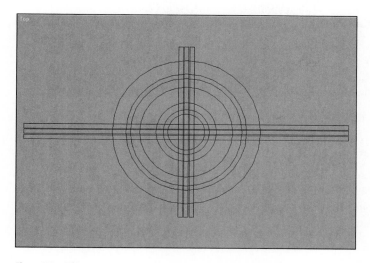

Figure 7.7   The correct position and size for all of the shapes necessary to build the Base object.

9. Save your work as **ch07-01.max**.

Exercise 7.2   Combining the Shapes

As we learned in the first project when modeling the Hidden Eyes logo, Boolean operations expedite tedious spline creation. For this logo, we will use Boolean operations to join the circle and rectangle shapes we just created into one shape that we can use to bevel. This beveled object will become the Base object in our scene.

Before we can apply Boolean operations to the shapes, we must combine them into one shape. To do so, we will need to apply an Edit Spline modifier to a shape and attach the remaining shapes to it.

1. With ch07-01.max open, select Circle01 and apply an Edit Spline modifier to it. In the Geometry rollout, click Attach Mult. to open the Attach Multiple dialog box (see Figure 7.8).

2. Click Invert to select all the shapes, and then click Attach to join all the shapes into one.

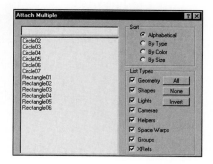

Figure 7.8   The Attach Multiple dialog box.

The shapes are now attached to create one shape. Looking at the shape, we can see that segments of the shape overlap one another. If we were to apply a Bevel modifier to the shape with overlapping segments, the beveled object would appear. The overlapping segments of this shape, when beveled, would create overlapping faces, opening the door for complications later in the rendering stages. When faces on objects are overlapping, smoothing groups are ineffective, which makes edges visible.

Exercise 7.3   Applying Boolean Operations

In order to remove these overlapping segments, we need to apply Boolean operations to them, joining the shapes into one solid shape. Doing so will create a beveled object with no overlapping faces, which means the object will be more streamlined and will render without errors on its surface.

1. In the Edit Spline modifier, activate Sub-Object/Spline and select the innermost circle spline (see Figure 7.9).

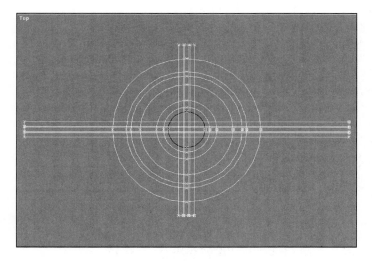

Figure 7.9 Select the innermost circle spline.

2. In the Geometry rollout, activate Boolean/Union and click each of the rectangle splines to unite them with the innermost circle spline (see Figure 7.10).

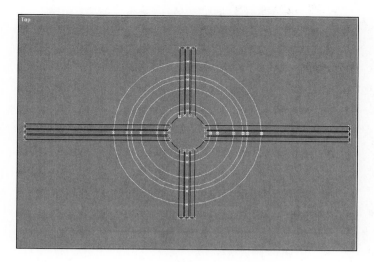

Figure 7.10 The rectangle shapes are united to the innermost circle spline using Boolean/Union.

3. Right-click to turn off Boolean. Then select the next circle spline from the inside (see Figure 7.11), activate Boolean/Subtraction, and click the crosspiece spline.

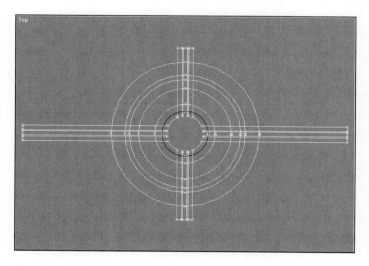

Figure 7.11 Select this circle spline.

Subtracting the crosspiece from the circle spline produced the desired result; however, as you can see in Figure 7.12, the crosspiece is now gone! We need to create a duplicate of the crosspiece, so we can subtract the duplicate from the circle and keep the original to complete the Base shape.

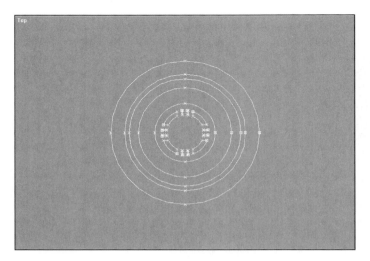

Figure 7.12   The result of subtracting the crosspiece from the circle spline.

4. Choose Edit, Undo Boolean to return the shapes to their original states in step 3.

5. To create the duplicate of the crosspiece, activate the Select and Rotate tool and Angle Snap. Press and hold down the Shift key, rotate the crosspiece 5 degrees, and rotate it −5 degrees to place it precisely back on the original crosspiece spline.

Warning

When duplicating splines in the Sub-Object/Spline level of the Edit Spline modifier, be sure to copy the spline only as many times as you need. Accidentally copying the spline too many times and leaving the duplicates in the shape can create unpredictable extrude/bevel results.

6. Select the circle spline (indicated in Figure 7.11), activate Boolean/Subtraction, and click on the crosspiece spline (see Figure 7.13).

   The Boolean operation is successful. Notice that the original crosspiece spline is still present in the shape. When we cloned the spline by holding down the Shift key and rotating the spline back on itself, we created two identical crosspiece splines precisely on top of one another. The Boolean operation used only one of the crosspiece splines, leaving the other behind so we can continue joining the shapes.

7. Select the third circle spline from the inside (see Figure 7.14), activate Boolean/Union, and click the crosspiece spline (see Figure 7.15).

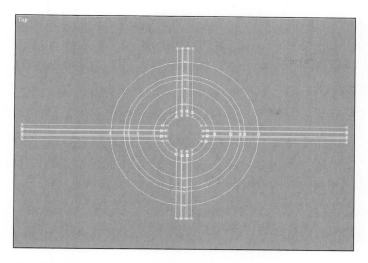

Figure 7.13 The result of the Boolean/Subtraction operation.

 Note

If the Boolean operation does not unite the two splines, try rotating the circle a fraction of a percent. This will move the orientation of the vertices of the circle shape and help the Boolean unite the splines. Make sure the vertices of the circle are in the interior of one of the crosshair splines; otherwise, unnecessary vertices will be created.

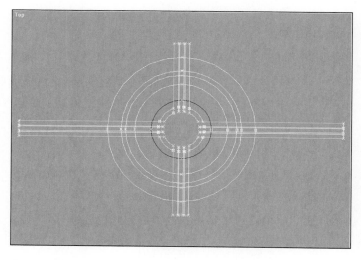

Figure 7.14 Select this spline.

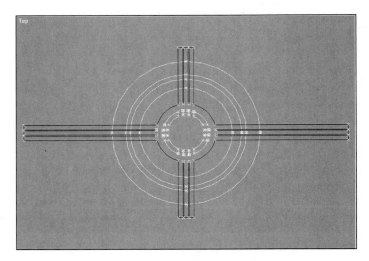

Figure 7.15   The result of the Boolean/Union operation.

We need to duplicate the crosspiece shape again so we can subtract the crosspiece from the next circle shape.

8. With the crosspiece spline selected (as shown in Figure 7.16), press and hold down the Shift key and use Select and Rotate to rotate the crosspiece spline 5 degrees and then immediately rotate it –5 degrees back to its original position. Release the mouse button to copy it.

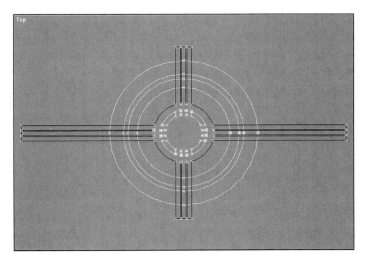

Figure 7.16   Select this crosspiece shape.

9. Select the next circle spline (see Figure 7.17), activate Boolean/Subtraction, and click the crosspiece spline (see Figure 7.18).

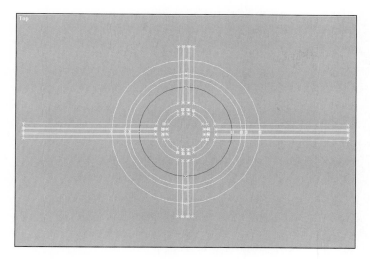

Figure 7.17   Select this circle spline.

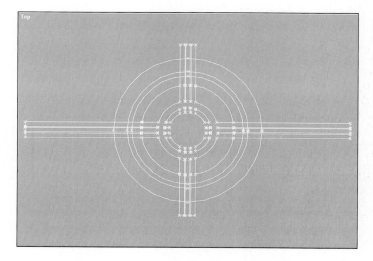

Figure 7.18   The result of the Boolean/Subtraction operation.

10. Select the next circle spline (see Figure 7.19), activate Boolean/Union, and click the crosspiece spline to unite them (see Figure 7.20).

   We need to duplicate the crosspiece spline one last time so we can subtract it from the next circle spline.

11. With the crosspiece spline selected, press and hold the Shift key and use Select and Rotate to rotate the object 5 degrees and then, without releasing the mouse, rotate it back –5 degrees precisely on top of the original.

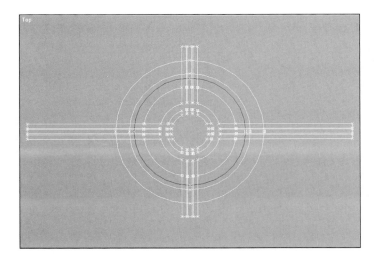

Figure 7.19   Select this spline.

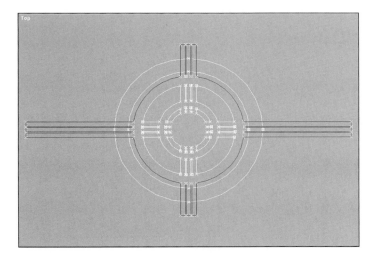

Figure 7.20   The result of the Boolean/Union operation.

12. Select the next circle spline (shown in Figure 7.21), activate Boolean/Subtraction, and click the crosspiece spline to subtract it.

13. Select the outermost circle spline (see Figure 7.22), activate Boolean/Union, and click the crosspiece spline to unite them (see Figure.23).

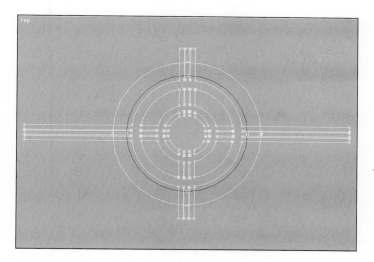

Figure 7.21 Select this circle spline.

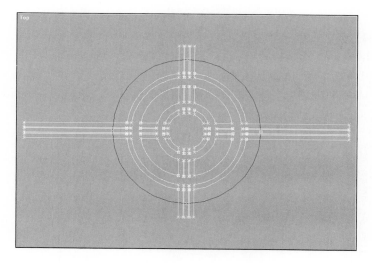

Figure 7.22 Select this spline.

14. Save your work as **ch07-02.max**.

This completes the Boolean operations necessary to create the Base object for the scene.

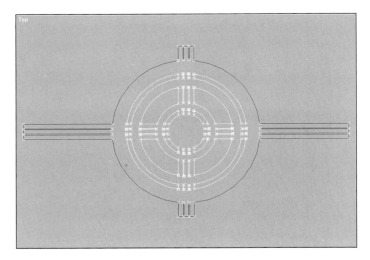

Figure 7.23   The completed Base object shape.

Exercise 7.4   Preparing the Base Shape for Beveling

Using Boolean operations, we have created the correct shape for the Base object. To optimize the shape for beveling, we will adjust the shape's vertices and add more steps.

1. With ch07-02.max loaded, select the Base object shape and name it **Base**.
2. Activate Sub-Object/Vertex and select the vertices shown in Figure 7.24.

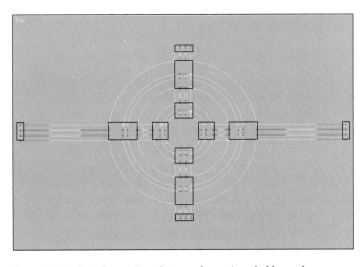

Figure 7.24   Select the vertices that are shown in ruled boxes here.

Notice that these vertices have Bézier Corner type applied. These vertices create primarily square splines. Because they have Bézier Corner type applied, when the Bevel modifier is applied, multiple faces will be created along their associated segments based on the Steps value of the shape, even though Optimize is active. To prevent the unnecessary faces created from these vertices, we will change their type from Bézier Corner to Corner. The Corner vertex type instructs the Extrude and Bevel modifiers to create only one polygon between the two vertices, creating fewer overall faces.

3. Right-click one of the selected vertices and change the type to Corner. Deactivate Sub-Object. We are now guaranteed that these vertices will not create unnecessary faces.

   Before we bevel this shape, let's collapse the stack and add more steps to the shape. Adding steps will make the circles smoother.

4. Click the Edit Stack button to open the Edit Modifier Stack dialog box.

5. Click Collapse All and click Yes in the resulting dialog box. Click OK to close the Edit Modifier Stack dialog box.

6. In the General rollout, enter a Steps value of **20** and make sure Optimize is checked.

7. Save your work as **ch07-03.max**.

Now we are ready to bevel the shape to create the Base object.

Exercise 7.5   Beveling the Base Object and Preparing It for Materials

We have carefully created the Base shape and adjusted its vertices for beveling. We can now bevel the shape and prepare the resulting object for materials.

1. With ch07-03.max open, select the Base shape.

2. Minimize the Top viewport and apply a Bevel modifier to the Base shape from the Modify panel. In the Bevel Values rollout, enter these values:

   Start Outline: **0**

Level 1:	Height: **10**
	Outline: **0**
Level 2:	Height: **2**
	Outline: **-2**

3. Adjust the Perspective viewport to view the Base object (see Figure 7.25).

   Now we will prepare the Base object for its materials. We will assign a different Material ID to the top faces of the base, the bevel, and the extruded side. We will also delete the bottom faces because they will not be displayed in the render.

4. Apply an Edit Mesh modifier to the Base object and activate Sub-Object/Polygon.

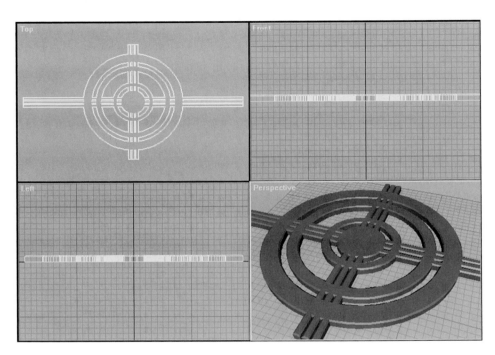

Figure 7.25   The beveled Base object.

> 5. Maximize the Left viewport. Using Rectangular Selection region (Window Selection), select the bottom faces as shown in Figure 7.26, and press the Delete key to delete them.

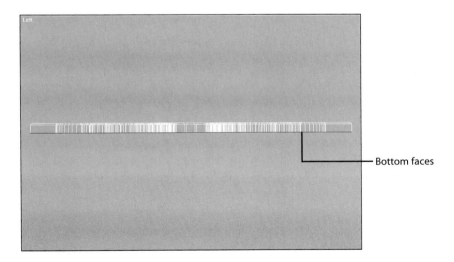

Bottom faces

Figure 7.26   Select the bottom faces.

6. Use Edit, Select Invert to select every polygon of the Base object (see Figure 7.27).

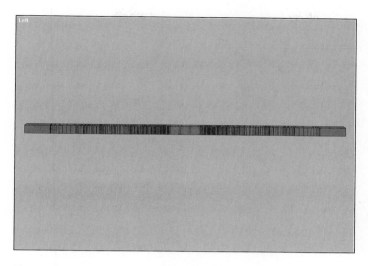

Figure 7.27   Every polygon of the Base object is selected.

7. In the Surface Properties rollout, enter a Material ID of **3**. This will be the Material ID for the extruded side of the Base object.

8. Use Rectangular Selection Region to select the polygons that create the bevel and top of the Base object (see Figure 7.28). Enter a Material ID of **2** for these polygons.

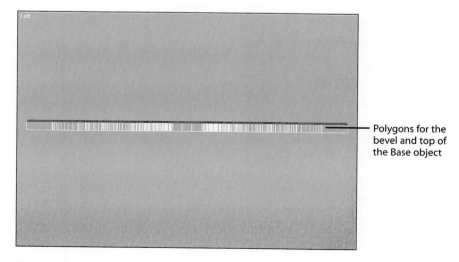

Polygons for the bevel and top of the Base object

Figure 7.28   Select these polygons.

9. Using Rectangular Selection Region, select the top polygon of the Base object (see Figure 7.29) and enter a Material ID of **1.**

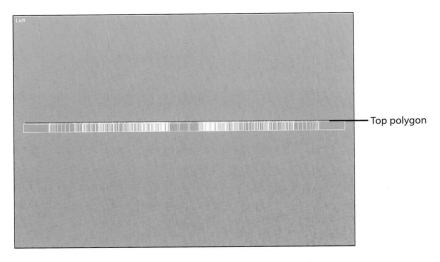

Figure 7.29   Select these polygons and enter the Material ID of 1.

10. Deactivate Sub-Object and save your work as **ch07-04.max.**

This completes the creation of the Base object.

Creating the Light Beacons

In the storyboard, we can see four identical light beacon objects positioned around the outside of the concentric circles. They are cylindrical objects with a bevel on the top edge, a flat surface on top, and an interior bevel. A lofted shape would usually be used to create an object of this type because of the simplicity of the cross section of the object.

Instead of creating the beacons using a loft, we will implement a different technique: *box modeling*. Box modeling originated in the gaming industry when modelers were searching for an easier way to create low-polygon models. Generally, the modeler would start with a box primitive, apply an Edit Mesh modifier, and begin to extrude faces, transforming them as necessary to create the desired object. Since then, it has become a very mainstream modeling technique for animators in all aspects of the field.

Right-Click Menus in 3D Studio MAX help to simplify the box modeling process. They provide shortcuts to common procedures such as Sub-Object bevel and extrude. In this section, we will create a cylinder primitive and use Right-Click Menus to add the bevels, creating the beacon objects in the storyboard.

Exercise 7.6   Creating the Beacon Objects

1. With ch07-04.max open, minimize the Left viewport. Open the Create/Geometry panel and create a cylinder using these values:

   Radius: **12**

   Height: **10**

   Height Segments: **1**

   XYZ: [**−122,−122,0**]

   Figure 7.30 shows the cylinder. Name this object **Beacon01**.

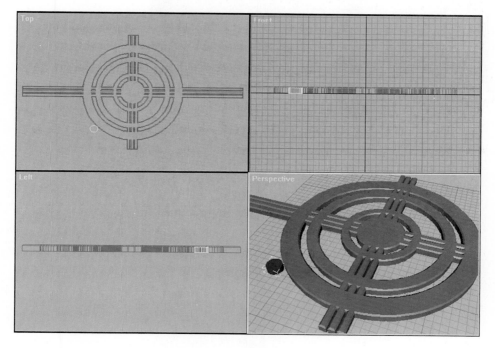

Figure 7.30   The cylinder object created at XYZ [−122,−122,0].

Because we will not see the bottom of this object in the animation, let's delete the bottom faces.

2. Apply an Edit Mesh modifier to the Beacon01 object. Activate Sub-Object/ Polygon and select the bottom polygon of the Beacon01 object (see Figure 7.31). Press the Delete key to delete the polygon, and then choose Yes in the resulting dialog box.

   Now we will create a beveled edge on top of the Beacon01 object.

3. With Sub-Object/Polygon active, select the top polygon of the Beacon01 object (see Figure 7.32). Click Zoom Extents All Selected to view Beacon01 closely in all the viewports.

Figure 7.31   Select and delete this polygon.

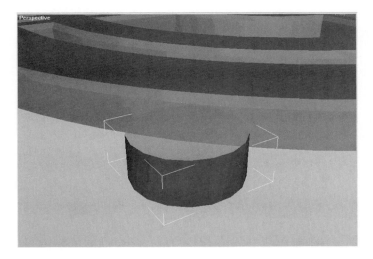

Figure 7.32   Select this polygon.

4. Press the spacebar to activate Lock Selection Set. Right-click in the Left viewport and choose Chamfer/Bevel, Bevel Polygon from the Right-Click Menu. The pointer will change to the Bevel pointer. Click and slowly drag the mouse upward, creating a new top polygon roughly two units higher than the original; the new face should be approximately the height of the Base object's highest face (see Figure 7.33). When you release the mouse button, Bevel Polygon is active. Slowly move the mouse down, designating a bevel of approximately two units (see Figure 7.34).

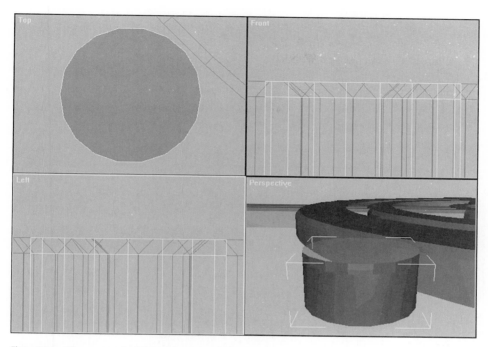

Figure 7.33   The correct height of the extruded face.

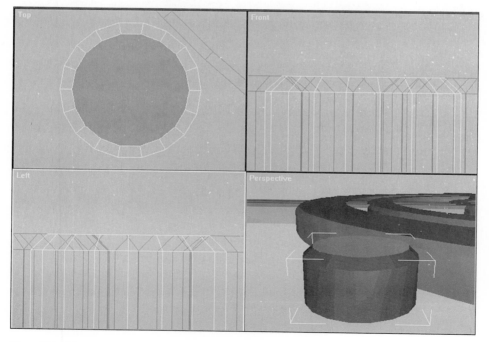

Figure 7.34   The completed bevel.

To create the flat surface, which will be the top of the Beacon01 object, we will apply another Bevel, but a little differently.

5. Right-click and choose Chamfer/Bevel, Bevel Polygon from the Right-Click Menu. Click+drag upward until you see the newly created face; then move the newly created face back down to be placed exactly on the original face (see Figure 7.35) and release the mouse button. When you release the button, Bevel becomes active. Move the mouse approximately three units downward to create an inset (see Figure 7.36).

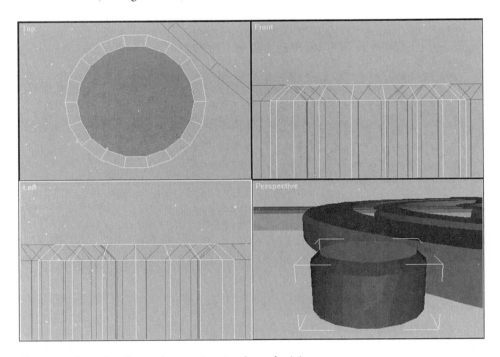

Figure 7.35   Extrude a face and return it to its place of origin.

We will create one last bevel for the interior of the Beacon01 object.

6. Right-click and choose Chamfer/Bevel, Bevel Polygon from the right-click menu. Place the mouse over the selected face in any viewport and drag upward to create an extrude about five units high (see Figure 7.37). Release the mouse button. With Bevel active, move the mouse downward to create a bevel of approximately five units (see Figure 7.38).

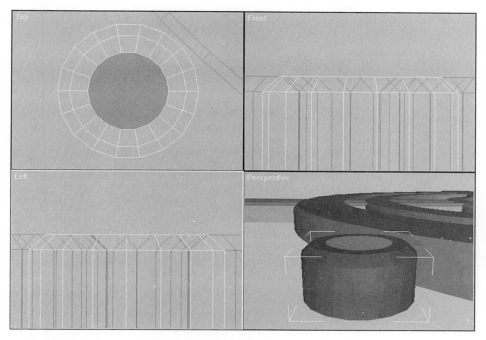

Figure 7.36   Create an inset of three units using Bevel.

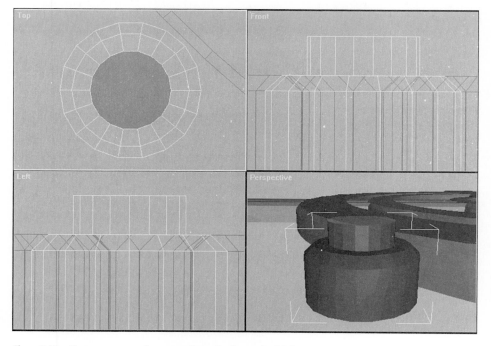

Figure 7.37   Create an extrude approximately five units high.

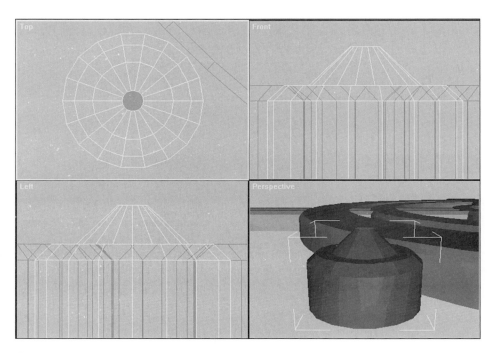

Figure 7.38   Create a bevel of approximately five units.

7. Activate the Select and Move tool. Constrain to Y View coordinates and, in the Left viewport, move the selected polygon down approximately eight units to create a bevel inset (see Figure 7.39).

   Notice that the newly created faces of the Beacon01 object are not smoothed. We will fix that right now.

8. Deactivate Lock Selection Set and select all the polygons of the Beacon01 object using Rectangular Selection Region (see Figure 7.40).

9. In the Surface Properties rollout, click Auto Smooth (it should have a value of 30 by default). Deactivate Sub-Object mode. Notice in the shaded Perspective view that the polygons of the Beacon01 object are correctly smoothed by the Auto Smooth function. The Auto Smooth function applies identical smoothing groups to faces whose angles do not exceed the Auto Smooth value.

   We are now finished modeling the first Beacon object, but there are four in total around the Base object. We will create the remaining three Beacon objects by instancing the one we just modeled.

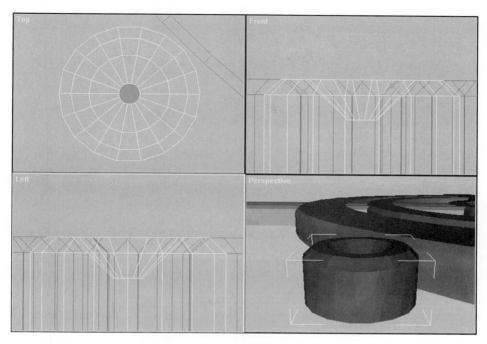

Figure 7.39   Move the top polygon down 8 units to create a bevel inset.

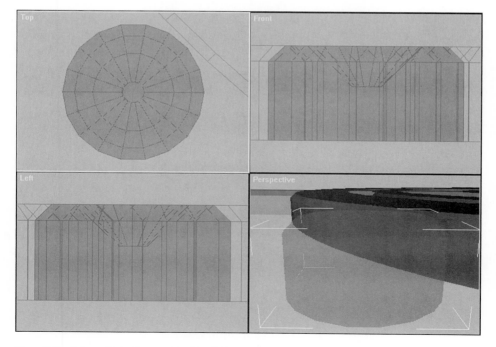

Figure 7.40   Select all the Beacon01 object's faces.

Note

To easily position the instanced beacon objects, we will use a little trick. Because the position of each beacon object is symmetrical from the center of the Base object, we will move the Beacon01's pivot axis to XYZ [0,0,0] and rotate the object to create the instanced beacon objects.

10. With Beacon01 selected, click the Hierarchy tab. In the Adjust Pivot rollout, activate Affect Pivot Only. For a clearer view, click Zoom Extents All. Open the Move Transform Type-In dialog box, enter the coordinates XYZ [**0,0,0**] for the pivot, and then deactivate Affect Pivot Only.

11. To instance the Beacon01 object in its correct positions, activate Angle Snap and the Select and Rotate tool. In the Top viewport, hold down the Shift key and rotate the Beacon01 object 90 degrees about its View Z-axis. In the Clone Options dialog box, choose Instance and enter Number of Copies: **3**. Click OK to exit the dialog box and create the instanced geometry (see Figure 7.41).

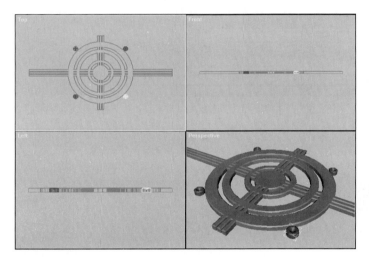

Figure 7.41   The completed Base object and four beacon objects.

12. Save your work as **ch07-05.max**.

This completes the modeling of the beacon objects. In the next section, we will create the logo object.

Building the Logo Object

Here is where we can have a little fun. This is the last project of the book and it's going to look cool when it's finished, so we should get to design our own logo to animate in this scene. You can design a personalized logo for yourself or a business or something neat to impress your friends.

Before you fire up MAX and create your logo, you should know that a few restrictions apply. Follow the next few steps and you will be on your way!

Exercise 7.7   Creating the Logo Shape

The animation we are creating is built to accommodate the size of the logo that is illustrated in the storyboard. If you decide to design your own logo, you will need to conform your logo size to the size of the logo in the storyboard. To give you a "canvas" size to create your logo in, we will create a rectangle shape in the Top viewport.

1. With ch07-05.max open, maximize the Top viewport.

2. From the Create/Shapes panel, create a Rectangle at XYZ [**0,0,0**] with a Length and Width of **130**. This creates a square that is about the same size as the interior "ring" of the Base object (see Figure 7.42). Name this shape *ReferenceSquare. This will be the "canvas" size for your logo design.

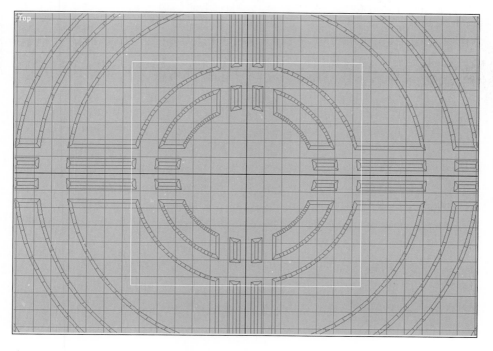

Figure 7.42 The correct size and position for *ReferenceSquare.

Now we can hide the base and beacon objects. Doing so will give you a clean workspace to design your logo in.

3. Open the Display panel and click Hide by Name. In the Hide Objects dialog box, select the Base and the Beacon objects. Click Hide to exit the dialog box and hide the objects.

If you want to have a little fun by creating your own logo shape, follow the next section. If you don't want to create your own logo, skip ahead to the next exercise, "Using the Provided Logo."

Exercise 7.8   Creating Your Own Logo

As long as your logo shape fits in the area of the *ReferenceSquare shape, you will be able to continue this tutorial and use your own design.

1. Create your own logo in the Top viewport, centering it inside of the *ReferenceSquare shape. Make sure the logo fills the *ReferenceSquare as much as possible. Keep these points in mind as you work:

   - The Bevel on the logo object will have a –2 outline; make sure your logo can accommodate it without creating overlapping faces.
   - Look for tight corners and fix them using the techniques you learned in the earlier projects.
   - Your logo shape's pivot must be placed at XYZ [0,0,0] before you can continue.

2. Save your work as **ch07-06.max**.

When you finish creating your own logo shape, you can move to the exercise titled "Beveling the Logo" and continue from there.

Exercise 7.9   Using the Provided Logo

You don't have to create your own logo for this lesson; you can use the one provided for you. Also, you can re-create the one used in this lesson or modify the logo shape included in this lesson. Just remember that the entire logo must fit in the area designated by the *ReferenceSquare shape.

1. To use the logo provided in this lesson, choose File, Merge and select logoshape.max. In the Merge – logoshape.max dialog box, select Logo. Click OK to close the dialog box and merge the shape into the scene (see Figure 7.43). Note that the Logo shape fits precisely inside the *ReferenceSquare object.

Figure 7.43   The Logo shape merged into the scene.

2. Save your work as **ch07-06.max**.

We now have a great logo shape that we can bevel to create a logo object for our scene.

Exercise 7.10   Beveling the Logo

Now that we have a slick logo shape, it is time to apply a bevel to it.

1. With ch07-06.max (the saved logo file) loaded, select the Logo shape.

2. Open the Modify panel and apply a Bevel modifier. Enter these settings:

Start Outline: **–2**

Level 1:

       Height: **2**

       Outline: **2**

Level 2:

       Height: **10**

       Outline: **0**

Level 3:

       Height: **2**

       Outline: **–2**

The resulting object should look like Figure 7.44.

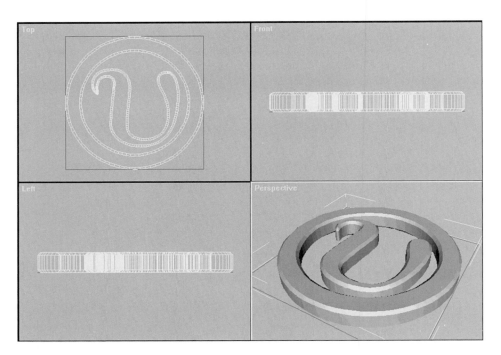

Figure 7.44   The completed logo object.

If you created your own logo shape, make sure the logo looks correct in the shaded Perspective view. If you encounter any problems with missing faces, go back and fix the spline, looking for any of the problems we discussed in regard to the first project of the book.

An optional challenge for you is to make a rounded bevel for the Logo object. You learned how to easily create a rounded bevel in the first project when you created the Hidden Eyes logo. Here is a checklist to keep in mind if you accept this challenge:

- Using the beveled logo as a reference, create the Bevel Profile shape by tracing the right side of the beveled logo in the Front viewport.
- Set the Steps value to **3** for the Bevel Profile shape.
- Delete the Bevel modifier from the Logo object and apply the Bevel Profile modifier to the Logo while the Logo is still lying flat in the Top viewport.
- To follow the tutorial easily, make sure the logo object is named Logo.

Whether or not you accept this challenge, you can move to the next section to complete the lesson. For those of you who accept the challenge and successfully create the rounded bevel, congratulations!

Exercise 7.11   Applying Material IDs to the Logo Object

We will prepare the logo object for materials now. To do so, we must first apply an Edit Mesh modifier to the Logo object so we can assign Material IDs.

1. With Logo selected, apply an Edit Mesh modifier to the logo. Activate Sub-Object/Polygon.

   We will now select the polygons of the logo and apply the appropriate Materials IDs to them. We will follow the convention we have used in the previous tutorials: ID:**1** for the readable face, ID:**2** for the bevel, and ID:**3** for the extruded side.

2. Use Edit, Select Invert to select all the polygons (see Figure 7.45) and apply Material ID:**3** to them.

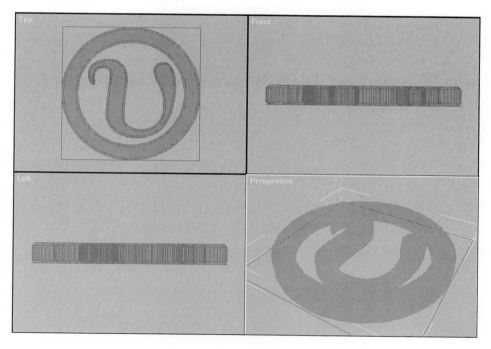

Figure 7.45   Use Edit, Select Invert to select these polygons and apply Material ID:3.

3. Using Rectangular Selection Region, select the polygons indicated in Figure 7.46 and apply Material ID:**2** to them.

4. Select the polygons indicated in Figure 7.47 (the top and bottom faces) and apply Material ID:**1** to them.

5. Deactivate Sub-Object and save your work as **ch07-07.max**.

We have now created all of the objects we will need to animate the scene.

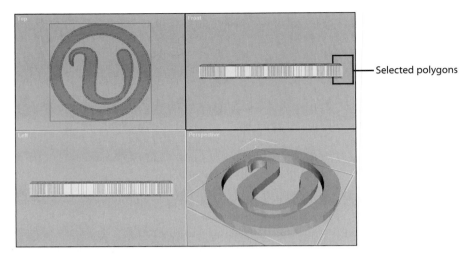

Selected polygons

Figure 7.46   Select these polygons and apply Material ID:2.

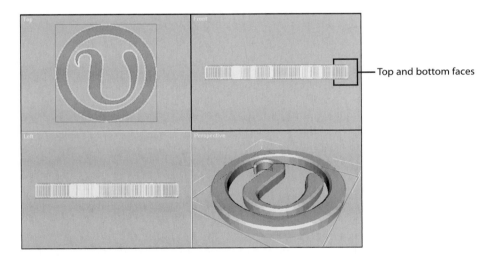

Top and bottom faces

Figure 7.47   Select these polygons and apply Material ID:1.

Animating the Scene

Right about now you are probably asking yourself, "What about the materials?" We will apply the materials to the objects after we animate the scene. Why? Examine the storyboard images, and you will notice that the light on the objects is critical to the success of the animation. Specular highlights are carefully placed on the objects in this animation. It is complicated to add materials when the scene is not lit and animated because we need to set up the lighting and the motion that place the highlights as they are represented in the storyboard. After you have captured the essence of the storyboard, the materials can be applied.

Animating and lighting the scene before adding the materials allows us to more accurately create the materials. This is because we can render actual test frames from the animation as we apply textures. Doing this will save time by preventing us from having to create the materials twice.

With that said, let's animate the scene!

Exercise 7.12   Positioning the Logo Object

If you haven't noticed yet, our logo object is still lying on its back in the scene. We will need to stand it up and place it accurately in the scene. Before we can accurately position the logo in the scene, however, we need to unhide the Base and Beacon objects.

1. With ch07-07.max loaded, click Unhide All in the Display panel to unhide the Base and Beacon objects (see Figure 7.48).

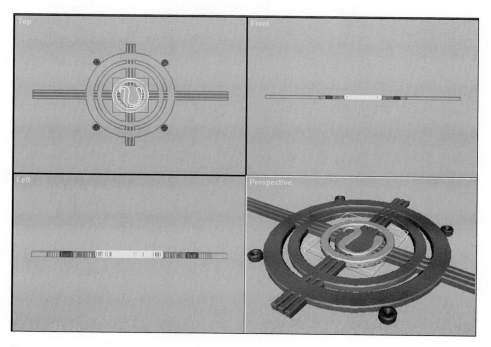

Figure 7.48   The scene with the Base and Beacon objects visible.

Now we must position the Logo object where it will appear in the scene.

2. Make sure the Logo object is selected and activate Select and Rotate. Then, in the Left viewport, rotate the logo object –90 degrees on its View Z-axis to stand it upright (see Figure 7.49).

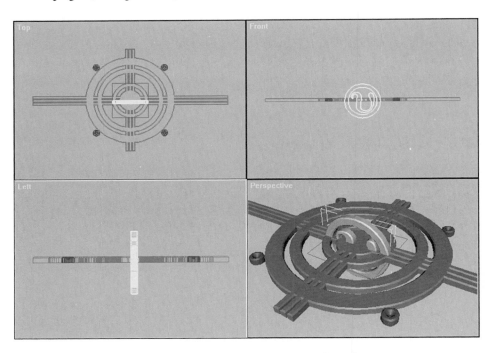

Figure 7.49   Stand the logo upright by rotating it –90 degrees in the Left viewport.

Now we need to raise the object above the Base object.

3. Using Move Transform Type-In, move the Logo object to XYZ [**0,0,100**] (see Figure 7.50).

We need to adjust the pivot of the logo object so it is centered in the logo on all axes.

4. In the Hierarchy panel, activate Affect Pivot Only. Using Move Transform Type-In, move the pivot to Y: **–7.** Deactivate Affect Pivot Only. Then with the Move Transform Type-In still open, move the logo to XYZ [**0,0,100**] (see Figure 7.51). Now the logo is centered to the Base object.

5. Save your work as **ch07-08.max**.

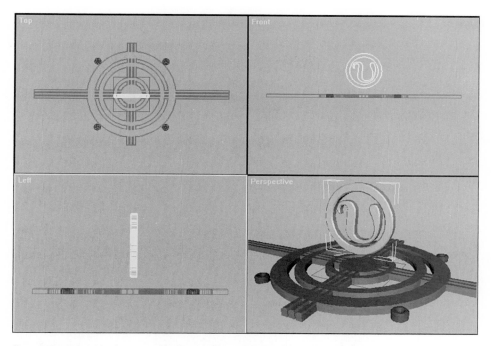

Figure 7.50 Move the logo to XYZ [0,0,100] to place it above the Base object.

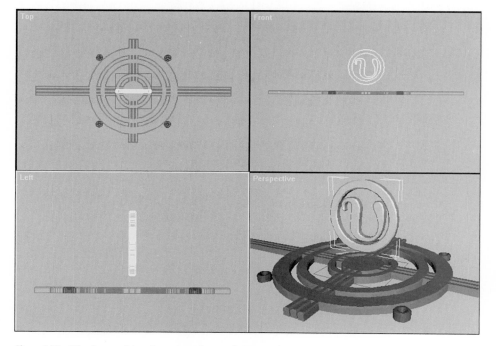

Figure 7.51 The Logo object is centered over the Base object.

Exercise 7.13   Creating a Camera/Dummy Relationship

Now that the objects are in the correct position in the scene, we can create a camera/dummy relationship and create its key frames.

1. With ch07-08.max loaded, open the Create/Cameras panel and create a Free camera with Lens:35mm in the Front viewport at XYZ [**0,–400,0**]. Change the Perspective viewport to the Camera01 viewport by pressing the C key on the keyboard (see Figure 7.52).

   Now we will create two dummy helpers to control the animation of the camera.

2. Open the Create/Helpers panel and create two Dummy helpers at XYZ [0,0,0] in the Top viewport. Make the second one slightly smaller than the first (see Figure 7.53).

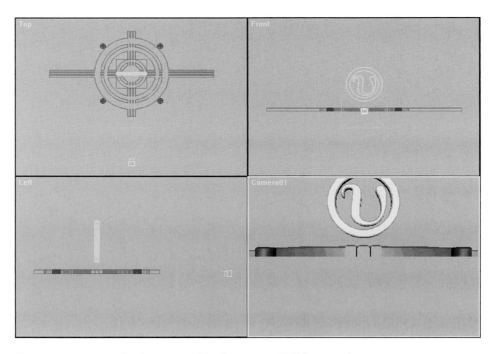

Figure 7.52   Camera01 has been created in the scene at XYZ [0,–400,0].

   Now let's create the Camera/Dummy hierarchy.

3. Select Camera01 and, using Select and Link, link the Camera to Dummy02. Link Dummy02 to Dummy01. We will use the two dummy objects to control the two axes the camera will travel.

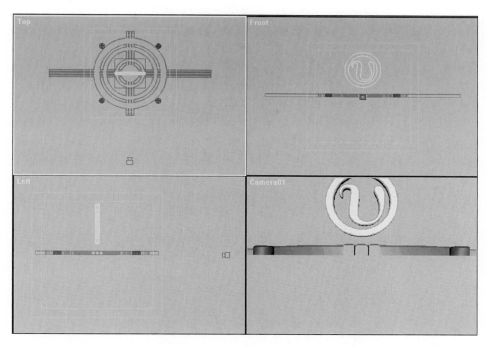

Figure 7.53   Create two Dummy helpers at XYZ [0,0,0], making the second one smaller than the first.

Exercise 7.14   Animating the Camera Relationship

Let's begin to animate the camera relationship. We know that the Camera must be at a high pedestal to look down on the logo object. The camera then orbits downward to view the logo from a lower angle. Let's animate that motion first. But before we do, let's align the camera for an approximate final frame, so it is viewing the scene from a somewhat centered point of view.

1. Using Select and Move constrained to Y, move Dummy01 upward approximately 60 units in the Left viewport (see Figure 7.54).

   Now we are ready to animate.

2. Make sure you are on frame 0 and activate the Animate button. Using Select and Rotate constrained to Z View axis, rotate Dummy02 75 degrees in the Left viewport (see Figure 7.55). The camera is now looking down on the Logo object at frame 0.

   We need to adjust the length of the animation before we can add the final rotation key for Dummy02.

3. Right-click the Play button to open the Time Configuration dialog box, change the Length to **300**, and click OK to exit the dialog box.

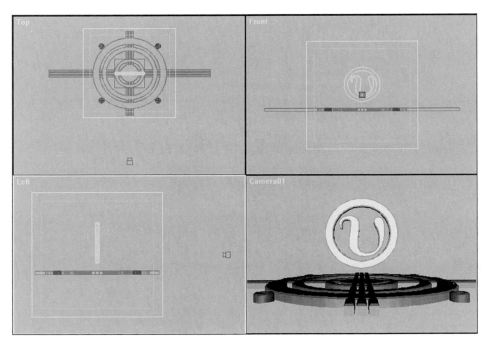

Figure 7.54   Move Dummy01 upward approximately 60 units in the Left viewport.

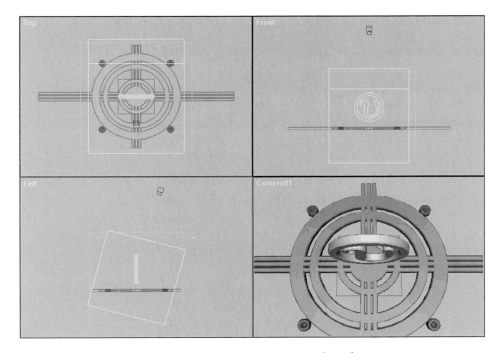

Figure 7.55   Rotate Dummy02 75 degrees using View Z-axis in the Left viewport.

4. Click Go To End to advance to frame 300. Using Select and Rotate constrained to Z, rotate Dummy02 –60 degrees in the Left viewport (see Figure 7.56).

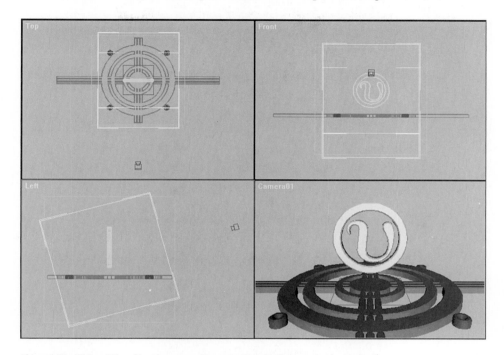

Figure 7.56   Using View Z-axis, rotate Dummy02 –60 degrees in the Left viewport.

Now we will animate Dummy01 to create the truck around the logo.

5. Return to frame 0. Using Select and Rotate constrained to View Z-axis, rotate Dummy01 30 degrees in the Top viewport (see Figure 7.57).

Let's create the rotation key for Dummy01 at frame 300.

6. Activate the Animate button and advance to frame 300. Using Select and Rotate constrained to View Z-axis, rotate Dummy01 –60 degrees in the Top viewport (see Figure 7.58).

7. Deactivate the Animate button and view the animation.

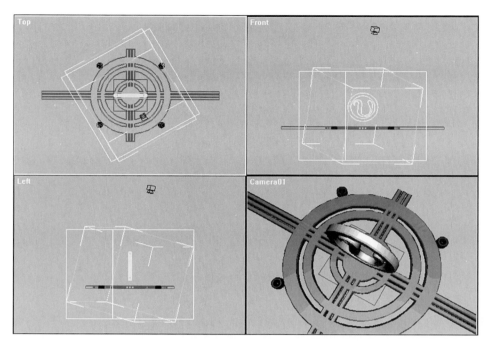

Figure 7.57 Using View Z-axis, rotate Dummy01 30 degrees in the Top viewport.

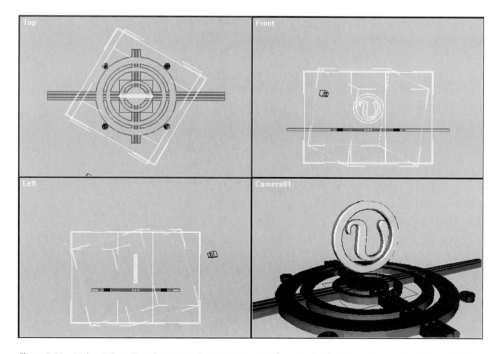

Figure 7.58 Using View Z-axis, rotate Dummy01 –60 degrees in the Top viewport at frame 300.

Exercise 7.15 Adjusting the Camera/Dummy Animation

The camera at frame 0 is above the logo object looking downward. As the animation plays, the camera begins to pedestal down and trucks to the left. The animation of the camera is very nice; however, we need to add pre-roll and pad to the animation. By adding pre-roll, we will make the camera remain above the logo until frame 60, when it begins to move downward. We will also add pad to the animation, making the logo reach its lowest point by frame 240, which leaves 60 frames of animation for pad.

1. Select Dummy02, right-click its key in the Trackbar, and select Dummy02:Rotation to open the Dummy02\Rotation dialog box. Change the Time value to **60** and enter an Ease From value of **25** to make the rotation ease from the keyframe (see Figure 7.59).

   Now we will add pad.

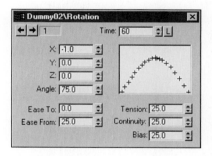

Figure 7.59 The Dummy02\Rotation dialog box for key 1 at frame 60.

2. With the Dummy02\Rotation dialog box open, click the arrow pointing to the right to move to key 2. Enter Time: **240** to move the key from 300 to 240. Enter an Ease To value of **25** to make the rotation ease into the key (see Figure 7.60). Close the Dummy02\Rotation dialog.

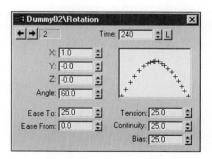

Figure 7.60 The Dummy02\Rotation dialog box for key 2 at frame 240.

3. Play the animation and study the changes you made. Looks pretty good, but the move would be much more dynamic if the camera were closer to the Logo object in the beginning of the animation. Let's do that now.

4. Activate the Animate button and return to frame 0. With the Camera01 viewport active, use the Dolly Camera tool to dolly the camera closer to the logo object; the outermost ring of the Base object should barely touch the top of the viewport (see Figure 7.61).

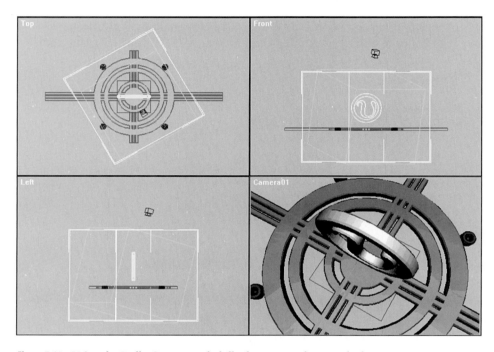

Figure 7.61   Using the Dolly Camera tool, dolly the camera closer to the logo.

5. Advance to frame 240 and use the Dolly Camera tool to dolly the camera away from the Logo object. The outermost ring of the Base object should be just above the bottom of the Camera01 viewport (see Figure 7.62).

The Logo and Base objects are not centered in the Camera01 viewport at frame 240. While the Animate button is active, we can fix that.

6. Using Select and Move constrained to View Y, move Dummy01 downward in the Left viewport approximately 15 units until the Logo and Base objects are centered in the Camera01 viewport (see Figure 7.63). Then play the animation.

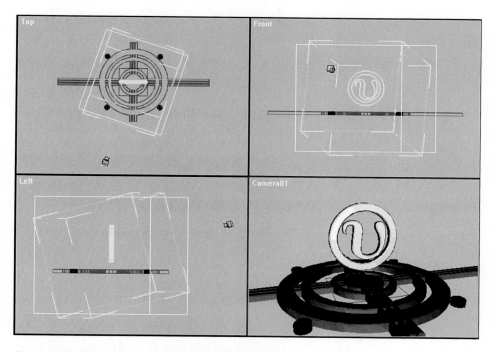

Figure 7.62 Use the Dolly Camera tool to dolly the camera away from the logo.

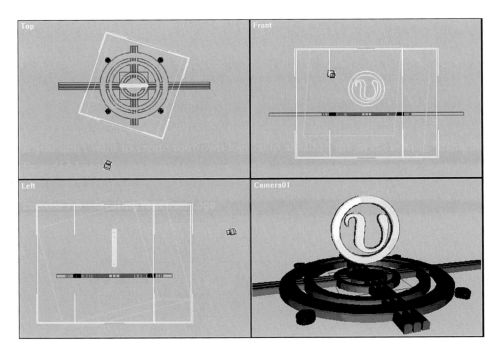

Figure 7.63 Move Dummy01 downward in the Left viewport to center the Logo and Base objects in the Camera01 viewport.

Exercise 7.16   Animating the Logo Object

The animation of the camera is complete. Before we save our scene and begin to texture and light the scene, let's give the Logo object a slight rotation throughout the animation, mimicking the storyboard. The rotation of the logo should counter the rotation of the camera as it trucks through the scene; this will create an interesting contrast throughout the animation.

1. With the Animate button still active, return to frame 0. Using Select and Rotate constrained to View Z, rotate the Logo object –25 degrees in the Top viewport (see Figure 7.64).

2. To add the Logo's final rotation key, advance to frame 300 and, using Select and Rotate constrained to View Z-axis, rotate the Logo object 25 degrees in the Top viewport (see Figure 7.65). Deactivate the Animate button and view the animation.

3. Save your work as **ch07-09.max**.

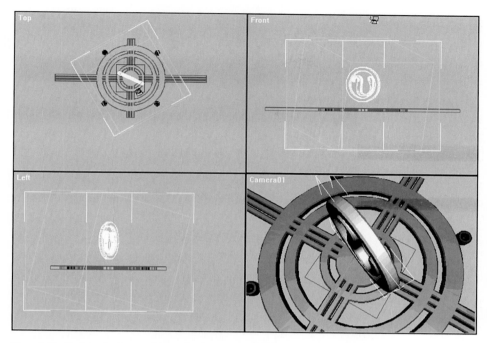

Figure 7.64   Rotate the Logo object –25 degrees in the Top viewport at frame 0.

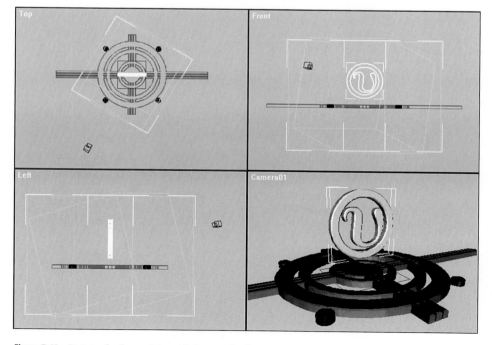

Figure 7.65   Rotate the logo object 25 degrees in the Top viewport at frame 300.

In Summary

We have successfully modeled the Base, Beacon, and Logo objects and prepared their faces for materials. A camera/dummy hierarchy was created in the scene and successfully animated with pre-roll and pad. At the beginning of the animation, the camera is to the right of the logo and looks downward. As the animation progresses, the camera gently lowers as it trucks to the left of the scene. A slight animated rotation of the logo was created to counter the rotation of the camera.

This scene is an excellent starting point for an effective animation. In the next lesson, we will light the scene, making sure to position the specular highlights on the objects as they are illustrated in the storyboard. After the scene is lit, we will apply materials and finish off the environment of the scene.

Chapter 8

Building the Environment

So far, so good. You have created the models and animated them, duplicating the essence of the storyboard. Think the hard part is over? Perhaps it is, but the road ahead could be very bumpy if the correct route isn't planned before finishing the animation.

Even though the animation phase is complete, we still have lights, materials, and effects to plan for. These are the aspects of the animation that will make or break the quality of the animation.

People working in the computer animation business are often categorized as "creative" types. Although this is true, 3D animation involves much more than being creative; it requires technical and mechanical skills. Along with these skills, the 3D animator must have a problem-solving mentality. 3D animation requires a perfect union of the right and left brain. The animator must preplan every step of the production, assuring reasonable polygon count and knowing everything is going to look great after a 30-hour (or more) render.

When you are handed a storyboard that someone else has designed, it usually indicates that the client has given the green light for production. When the animation is complete, it should capture the vital aspects of the storyboard and look better.

Working with someone else's storyboard essentially removes you from the creative process and places you in a position of replicating someone else's artist vision. You are now 10% artist and 90% highly trained technician. There is no "I can't do that!" or even better, "The software can't do that!" Everything is possible; the software is limited only by the user's imagination.

Planning the Lights and Materials

Now that the objects have been built and the scene has been animated, we can place the lights in the scene to create the specular highlights on the objects in the scene. Let's take one more look at the storyboard (see Figure 8.1).

Looking at all four panels, we can see a very important highlight on the left side of the Base object. The highlight is prominent throughout the animation. Because of the camera truck around the base object, we probably need more than one light, or one light with animated position, to maintain the highlight.

Examining the logo element throughout the progression of the storyboard, we can see that the logo is in darkness through the first two panels (with the exception of the highlight on the left). On Panel 4, we can see that the logo has a more prominent highlight. Personally, I interpret this highlight as something that moves onto the logo as the animation resolves.

Notice that there are several highlights along the bevels of both the base and logo objects; many lights will be required to achieve this effect. Being a render-conscious animator, you should attempt to produce the highlights on the bevels without using lights.

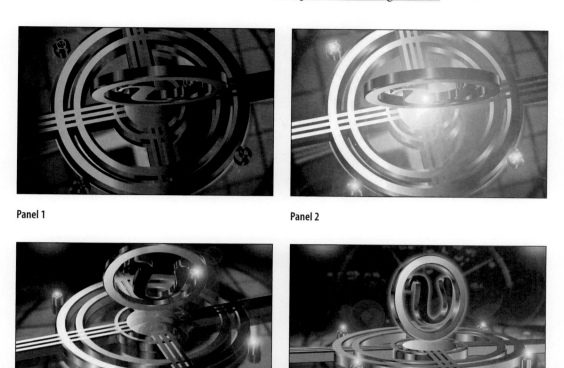

Panel 1

Panel 2

Panel 3

Panel 4

Figure 8.1   The four panels in the storyboard.

Lighting the Scene

As we have learned in previous projects, lighting is one of the most vital elements in the scene. Incorrect lighting can destroy hours of hard work by ruining the contrast in the scene, adding too many highlights and increasing rendering time. Always try to illuminate your scene using Three-Point Lighting. If you absolutely cannot illuminate the scene correctly by using three lights, add special lights only where necessary.

Let's begin to light the scene by creating our preliminary Key, Fill, and Back lights.

Exercise 8.1   Setting Up the Key Light

The Key light is the most important light in the scene. Its purpose is to illuminate the most important object(s) in the scene. By examining the storyboard, we have learned that the logo element is the most important object in the scene. The sequence of events that the storyboard illustrates shows the logo in darkness during the beginning of the animation, where all of the cool lens effects are establishing. As the animation reaches its resolve, the logo enters the light, receiving a bright highlight. Let's place the Key light to create that highlight.

1. Load ch07-09.max, the last file we created in Chapter 7.

2. Advance to frame 240, where the logo reaches its resolve. Using Zoom All and Pan, adjust your viewports to see the world space in front of the Logo object (see Figure 8.2).

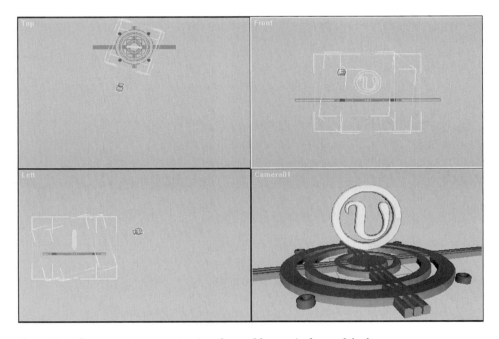

Figure 8.2   Adjust your viewports to view the world space in front of the logo.

While lighting the scenes in the previous projects, we learned that in order to create a highlight on an object the light must bounce directly off the face of the object into the camera lens, much like a mirror.

3. Examine the position and rotation of the Logo object and the position of the camera to decide where to position an Omni light to place the highlight directly on the Logo object at frame 240.

4. Open the Create/Lights panel and create an Omni light in the scene to place the highlight on the Logo object. Name this light **Omni-Key**. In my scene, I found an XYZ placement of [**75,–770,30**] to be ideal (see Figure 8.3).

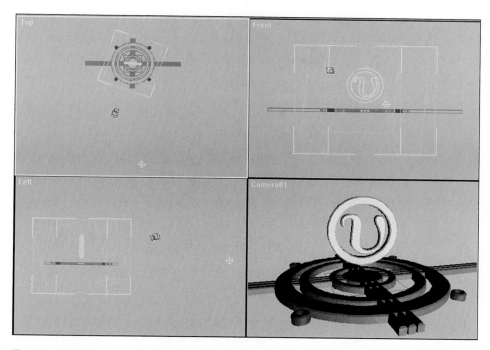

Figure 8.3 Position the Omni-Key light to place a highlight directly on the Logo object at frame 240.

5. Play the animation or just shuttle the time slider through the animation to view the effect the Omni-Key light has in the scene. The Logo object does not have a highlight on it between frames 0 and 160. After frame 160, the highlight begins to appear on the upper-right corner of the Logo object and, by frame 240, the highlight is placed exactly in the center of the Logo object. After frame 240, the highlight begins to travel leftward off the Logo object.

6. Examine the storyboard one more time to see if we are following suit. Notice in the first two panels of the animation the highlight is placed to the left of the logo. The highlight in our animation is on the upper-right of the logo from frames 160 forward. Are we wrong? The answer is, "not exactly."

Several things cause anomalies such as this. When designers create a storyboard, the resulting panels illustrate the overall effect and mood of the animation. They have to ensure the quality of the images, so the client says "Yeah, that's what we wanted!" Because this storyboard was created in a 2D-paint program, the designers don't have full capabilities to determine the influence of light in the 3D scene. Therefore, the designers do their best to illustrate the mood of the lighting in the scene.

Examining the storyboard, we have decided that the most important purpose of the Key light is to illuminate the Logo object when the logo resolves. We have completed this task, and the designer should be happy. To replicate the storyboard exactly would require us to animate the Key light, opening the door for unpredictable results (such as erratic movement of the highlight on the Logo object due to the movement of the light, logo, and camera).

A judgment call needs to be made. Do we animate the light, or do we leave it as is? In this example, there probably won't be too much repercussion over the highlight appearing in the upper-right as opposed to the left. We decide to leave it as is because the position of the highlight in this animation is not a vital compositional aspect in the scene.

Exercise 8.2   Placing the Fill Light

Now that the Key light is positioned correctly in the scene, it is time to decide where to place the Fill light in the scene. By definition, the Fill light should softly light areas of the scene that are left in shadow from the Key light. Although the Key light is not casting shadows, it isn't illuminating the top of the Base object at all.

The Fill light needs to pick up where the Key light leaves off—by illuminating the Base object and adding some highlights to the bevel and extruded side of the Logo object. We can see a prominent highlight on the Base and Logo object on the first panel of the storyboard. We decided that the animation would have more punch if the logo remained in darkness until the Key light highlight made its appearance at frame 160. Because of this, we must make sure that the Base object has a prominent highlight to provide contrast to the beginning of the animation, preventing the animation from becoming too dark and uninteresting.

With that decided, we must place a highlight on the Base object at frame 0 in the animation.

1. Return to frame 0 of the animation, and adjust your viewports to examine the position of the camera and Base objects (see Figure 8.4).

    At frame 0, the camera is high above the scene, which means that the Fill light must also be placed directly above the scene in order to create a highlight on the Base object. Remember that the highlight on the Base object is to appear on the left side of the Base object.

2. Examine the scene and predict where your Fill light placement should be; the light needs to reflect directly off the top surface of the Base object into the camera lens. As we look at the scene at frame one, it is obvious that the Fill light should be high and to the left of the scene.

3. From the Create/Lights panel, create an Omni light in the scene to create a highlight on the top surface of the Base object at frame 0. A position of XYZ [−330,70,580] should work well (see Figure 8.5). Name this light **Omni-Fill** and set the light's color to RGB (**150,150,150**); the Fill light should always be less intense than the Key light.

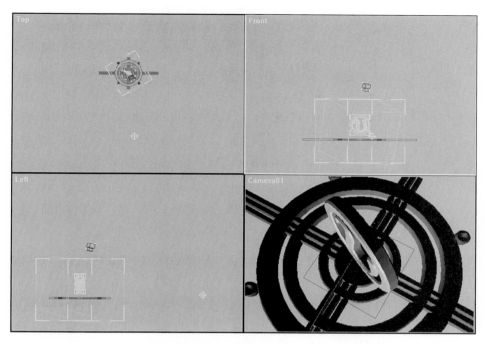

Figure 8.4 Adjust your viewports to view the position of the camera and Base objects.

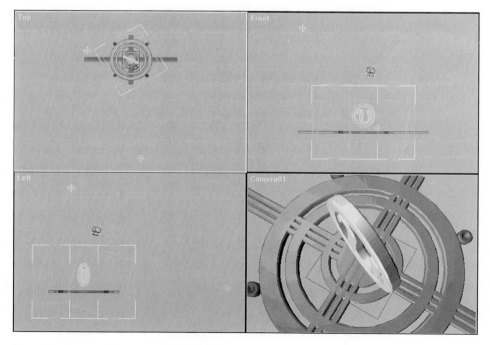

Figure 8.5 Correct placement of the Fill light.

4. Shuttle through the frames of the animation and examine the position of the highlight on the Base object. The highlight remains on the left side of the Base object until frame 170, where the highlight moves off the lower-left of the Base object. The highlight moves off of the Base object because of the lower position of the camera. The camera pedestals down to look at the logo.

Let's examine the influence of the highlights created by both the Key and Fill lights at this point. The Key light begins to cast a prominent highlight on the Logo object at frame 160. The highlight created by the Fill light on the Base object ends at frame 170. The result is overlapping action, which is good. As the highlight diminishes on the Base object, the highlight on the Logo object begins to intensify. This forces the viewer to say "I can't see the base object, but look at that logo!" Because of the overlapping action, the animation never goes stale and continues the visual flow.

Exercise 8.3   Positioning the Back Light

The purpose of the Back light is to light the scene from behind. This creates a halo on the top of the objects in the scene, defining edges and creating depth. Looking at the storyboard, we can see a highlight on the Base object that is created by a Back light. We also need a Back light to create interesting highlights on the extruded side and bevel of the Logo object. We can create a Back light that will serve all of those purposes.

1. Advance to frame 240, the frame at which the animation resolves.

There is a bright highlight that is cast by the Key light on the Logo object; however, no highlight is being created on the Base object at this point. We don't want the Base object to be lost in the animation, but we also don't want it to be illuminated more brightly than the Logo object. Remember that the Back light is usually the lowest-intensity light in the scene.

2. To help visualize where to place the Back light, adjust your viewports to see the area behind the Logo and Base objects (see Figure 8.6).

We must now decide where to place the Back light in the scene. We know that the light must bounce off the surface of an object directly into the lens of the camera in order to produce a highlight. We will position the Back light behind the objects in the scene at frame 240 to create a highlight in the center of the Base object. Placing the highlight in the center of the Base object gives the highlight plenty of time to move to the left as the camera trucks around the scene.

3. From the Create/Lights panel, create an Omni light high and behind the scene to produce a highlight in the center of the Base object (see Figure 8.7). A position of XYZ [**315,1030,640**] should work well. Name this light **Omni-Back** and change its color to RGB (**100,100,100**).

4. Play the animation and view the affect the Omni-Back light has in the scene. Because of the low intensity of the light, it may be hard to see the highlight.

5. Change the Multiplier value to **5** so you can see the highlight in the viewport. (Remember to change the multiplier back to **1** when you are finished!)

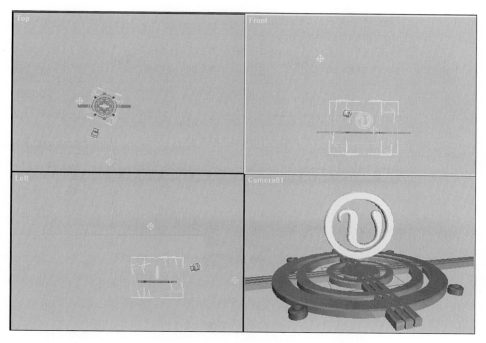

Figure 8.6 Adjust the viewports to view the area behind the Logo and Base objects.

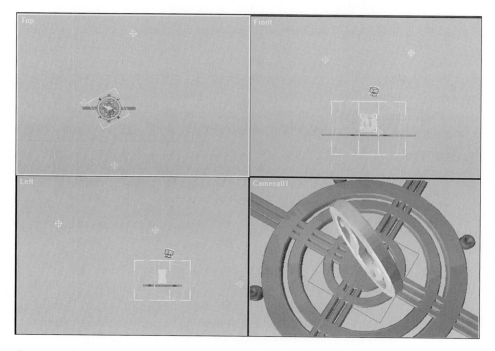

Figure 8.7 The highlight is in the center of the Base object.

The highlight makes its predominant appearance at roughly frame 180, where it creates a strong vertical highlight through the center of the Base object. As the animation plays forward, the highlight slowly moves to the left—exactly the effect we predicted and desired.

Another thing to keep in mind is the overlapping action created here. The highlight created by the Fill light on the Base object ends at frame 170. This is countered by the overlapping action of the highlight appearing on the logo at frame 160. As a final sting, the Back light creates a subtle highlight on the Base object at frame 180.

6. Save your work as **ch08-01.max**.

By examining the storyboard and using a little brainpower, we have illuminated the scene correctly. The lights in the scene not only correctly illuminate the scene, but also provide effect and action through the moving highlights. The highlights created by the lights also produce interest in the scene through overlapping action that is choreographed to call attention to the logo when the animation resolves.

Adding the Materials

We will now add the materials to the 3D scene. While doing so, we can add our personal touch to the outcome of the output images. Examine the storyboard to get a "feel" for the scene. The objects consist of blue polished metal, which create sharp, bright highlights when illuminated directly by the lights in the scene. It is our job, when adding materials to the scene, to ensure that every object looks even better than the storyboard.

To do so, we need to look at the objects to see where we can add a subtle color change or material effect. As we apply the materials, we will dissect the appearance of the material and its purpose in the scene.

The Base Object

By examining the storyboard, we can quickly guess what type of materials to add to the Base object. The Base object has three Material IDs: one for the top surface, one for the bevel, and one for the extruded edge. Because the Base object has these material channels applied, we can assign custom materials to each surface. We will use these Material IDs to achieve the maximum result.

Exercise 8.4   Creating the Material for the Top Face

We will create a material for the top surface of the Base object first. This is because the top surface is the most prominent surface of the Base object, and we need to ensure that the appearance of the highlight is correct.

1. With ch08-01.max loaded, open the Display panel and hide the lights and helpers. We don't need to see them anymore. Click Zoom Extents All and return to frame 0.

   Before we create the material, let's adjust the background color to a mid-level gray. This is done to give us a comparison of the contrast in the image.

2. Open the Rendering/Environment dialog box and change the Background Color to RGB (**125,125,125**).

3. Open the Material Editor and make sure that the first material preview slot is selected. Name this material **Base** and apply it to the Base object.

4. Render frame 0 to view the highlight that the Fill light is currently creating on the Base object (see Figure 8.8).

   The result is not quite what we were expecting. Keep in mind that the current material shader is Blinn, and the default setting doesn't produce a very sharp highlight. It is at this point that we must decide what type of shader to apply to the top face.

Figure 8.8 Frame 0 rendered in order to view the Base object material.

The material should resemble polished metal, so the obvious choice is the Metal shader. However, the Metal shader is not the best choice for this situation. The shader of choice for the top surface of the Base object would be the Multi-Layer shader. Because the highlights on the objects play a critical role in the animation, they should be as interesting as possible. The Multi-Layer shader provides two specular highlight colors and settings to create more interesting highlights than the Metal shader.

5. Before applying the Multi-Layer shader, let's change the material Type to Multi-Sub object, to make use of the multiple Material IDs on the object. Click the Standard button and from the Material/Map Browser, choose Multi/Sub-Object, and click OK to close the Browser. In the Replace Material dialog box, choose Discard Old Material? and click OK to apply the Multi-Sub Object material.

6. Click the Set Number button and change the Number of Materials to **3** to accommodate the three Material IDs on the Base object. Click the first material button and change its name to **Base-Face.**

7. Change the Shader to **Multi-Layer.** To make the material blue, set Ambient to RGB (**16,2,16**) and Diffuse to RGB (**53,84,172**).

8. To create a sharper, bright highlight, use these settings in the First Specular Layer group:

   Color: RGB (**98,212,229**)

   Level: **200**

   Glossiness: **68**

9. Render frame 0 through the Camera01 view to see the result (see Figure 8.9).

Figure 8.9   Frame 0 Rendered at this point.

The highlight looks pretty good; it is a bit smaller than it should be, but we still have another Specular level to add. What we should be concerned with now is the contrast between the highlight and the Diffuse level of the material. Examine Panel 1 of the storyboard closely. The Diffuse color of the unlit area of the Base object is almost black; the Diffuse color in our test rendering is dark blue. Let's adjust that now.

10. Change the Diffuse level of the material to **40**. Render a test frame and examine the result.

Because we dropped the Diffuse level of the material, the area of the Base object that doesn't receive a specular highlight is much darker, producing the desired result.

Now let's utilize the Second Specular Layer and add a slightly different color to add visual interest. We will want this highlight to be darker and much wider.

11. To add visual interest, enter these settings:

Color: RGB (**175,51,201**)

Level: **100**

Glossiness: **50**

12. Render a test frame and examine the result.

The second Specular level widened the highlight and added another color to the highlight, producing a subtle and interesting effect. So far this material is looking great!

To add a little more punch to the material, we will add a reflection map, so the Logo object reflects onto the Base object. We will use a Flat Mirror reflection because it provides the highest quality result with the lowest rendering time. The Flat Mirror reflection type works only when it is applied to a group of coplanar faces. If it is applied to a group of curved faces, it will not yield a reflection.

13. Open the Maps rollout of the Base-Face material. Click the Reflection button to open the Material/Map Browser. Choose Flat Mirror and click OK to exit the Browser. Name this map **Base-Face-rfl**.

14. To soften the reflection, leave Apply Blur checked and change Blur to **4.0**. This will produce a soft defocus in the reflection.

We want only the Logo object in the scene to reflect on the Base object, not the environment surrounding it.

15. To ensure that the environment does not reflect on the material, uncheck Use Environment Map.

16. Click Return to Parent and render frame 0 (see Figure 8.10).

What happened to our beautiful material?! What made it turn white? Remember when we unchecked Use Environment Map? That option doesn't mention Use Background Color. In step 2 of this exercise, we changed the Background Color to a mid-level gray to help us view the contrast of our image. Unfortunately, unchecking Use Environment Map refers only to the Environment Map, not the Background Color. To accurately view the Flat Mirror reflection, we need to change our Environment Color back to black.

Figure 8.10   Test frame rendered with Flat Mirror reflection applied.

17. Open the Rendering/Environment dialog box and change the background color back to black RGB (**0,0,0**). Render frame 0 again.

    That looks much better. However, the reflection is awfully bright. Let's adjust the reflection value to make the reflection less noticeable.

18. In the Maps rollout of the Base-Face material, change the Reflection value to **9**. Render a test frame to view the result (see Figure 8.11). Save your work as **ch08-02.max**.

Figure 8.11   Base-Face flat mirror reflection with a value of 9.

The reflection now appears as though it belongs there. The first of three Base object materials is complete. Next, we will create the bevel material for the Base object.

Exercise 8.5   Creating the Material for the Bevel

When we were examining the storyboard for light placement earlier, we noticed that the bevels had an incredible amount of specular highlights on them. We didn't want to create additional lights to produce this effect because the lighting in the scene would have become washed out and would have lacked contrast. Because of this, we must be inventive in the Material Editor to simulate the specular highlights on the bevel. Before we devise the solution to create the highlights, let's create the material.

1. With ch08-02.max loaded, open the Material Editor and open sub-material 2 of the Base material. Name this material **Base-Bevel**.

   Much like the Base-Face material, the bevel needs to have the appearance of polished metal. Even though there are more highlights on the bevels, their appearance isn't as critical to the rendered image as the highlights on the top face of the Base object. For this reason, we can use a Metal Shader and achieve the desired results. Let's create the material.

2. To create the blue metal material, use these settings:

   Shader: **Metal**

   Ambient Color: RGB (**3,1,11**)

   Diffuse Color: RGB (**27,79,128**)

   Specular Level: **80**

   Glossiness: **70**

   Render frame 0 from the Camera01 viewport.

   As we guessed, the blue metal material isn't catching as many highlights as the storyboard illustrates. We will simulate the highlights by using a reflection map. Images used as reflection maps are applied to the material in a self-illuminating nature.

Note

Reflection maps should not to be confused with self-illumination maps. Although both maps can increase the luminance of a material, the reflection map and the self-illumination map are completely different. A *reflection map* applies the map in an additive nature, adding its color over the original color of the material. A *self-illumination map* uses the luminance value of the map and increases the illumination of the material's diffuse color.

We will be using a simple .jpg image applied to a Spherical Environment to simulate the highlights on the bevel. Figure 8.12 shows the image we will be using as the reflection map.

Figure 8.12   Bevelrfl.jpg.

The Spherical Environment will apply this map to a virtual sphere surrounding the scene. The vertical cyan stripes in the image will remain vertical and will act as long strips of vertical light. Therefore, vertical strips of light will surround the scene. A reflection is created much like the influence of light. The reflected image must bounce directly off the face and into the camera lens. Let's apply the reflection map and view the result.

3. Open the Maps rollout of the Base-Bevel material. Click the Reflection button to open the Material/Map Browser. Select Bitmap and click OK to close the Browser. In the Select Bitmap Image File dialog box, choose bevelrfl.jpg from the ch08\maps directory of the accompanying CD. Click Open to close the Select Bitmap Image File dialog box and apply the reflection map. Name this map **Base-Bevel-rfl**. To soften the reflection, enter a Blur offset of **.005**. Render frame 0 and view the result (see Figure 8.13).

Figure 8.13   Base-Bevel material with reflection map applied.

With the reflection map added to the material, we now have soft highlights surrounding the bevel.

Exercise 8.6   Instancing the Material for the Extruded Side

A close examination of the storyboard will show that there isn't much difference between the bevel material and the material on the extruded side of the Base object. Because they are the same, we can instance the bevel material [material 2] to the extruded side material [material 3].

1. With ch08-03.max loaded, open the Material Editor and return to the root of the Base material. To copy Material 2 to Material 3, drag the Material 2 button and drop it on the Material 3 button. In the Instance (Copy) Material dialog box, choose Instance and click OK to close the dialog box.

2. Render frame 0 and view the result (see Figure 8.14).

   The highlights on the extruded side appear random and bright, exactly the same way they appear on the bevel of the Base object. We are now finished creating the Base material.

3. Save your work as **ch08-03.max**.

Figure 8.14   Frame 0 rendered, illustrating the finished Base material.

The Logo Object

Before creating the material for the Logo object, we should certainly look at the storyboard. A close examination tells us that the logo material is the same as the Base material. It would be logical to think "I can just apply the Base material to the Logo, right?" Although you could certainly do that, we will copy the material, rename it, and modify the material a bit to make it appear to be different.

Exercise 8.7   Applying the Logo Material

Let's change the material a bit because we want our output image to have enough variance to add interest. The colors in this animation are all very dark and very blue. Slightly changing the color value of the logo material will make it stand out from the color of the base object.

1. With ch08-03 loaded, open the Material Editor and copy the Base material preview slot to the second preview slot. Rename the material **Logo** and apply it to the Logo object.

2. Advance to frame 160 and render the camera viewport.

   Because the two materials are identical, the image produced is dull and uninteresting. It needs something to make the logo "pop out" at the viewer. Examining the color relationship in the storyboard reveals that there are two main colors in the animation: blue and orange. We will be adding the glow around the logo and the lens flares later in production; they will certainly help by creating some color contrast in the image. But we should be able to change the materials a bit and not wander too dangerously far from what the storyboard illustrates.

   We will start by removing the purple from the specular highlight of the logo.

3. Click the first sub-material button in the Logo material to open its settings and change its name to **Logo-Face.** Change the Second Specular Layer Color to RGB **(0,136,240)**. This changes the purple color to a light blue.

   Adding the purple color to the Base object was our creative decision. Leaving the purple color on the Logo object would probably be a dangerous move for us. The client may think the color on the storyboard suits their logo best. Usually clients are so caught up in making sure their logo looks great, they often overlook the fact that we added a little color to the rest of the scene.

   The Base object is more purple than it is blue, creating the illusion that the Base object is further away in space because the purple is darker than the blue color of the highlight on the Logo object. A subtle change in color hue allows us to create depth without having to the make the unimportant images too dark.

   Because we are currently matching the storyboard to the logo element and we want the logo to match the storyboard as closely as possible, we should change the Diffuse Level of the Logo material to make the diffuse areas of the logo darker.

4. Change the Diffuse Level to **20**. Render frame 160 once more to examine the change.

   That looks much better. Now let's place our attention on the bevel and extruded side of the logo. The first thing that stands out is that the reflection map is too noticeable and bright. Let's fix that now.

5. Click Go Forward to Sibling to enter the settings for the second sub-material. Rename this material **Logo-Bevel**.

6. In the Maps rollout of the Logo-Bevel material, change the Reflection amount to **75**. Render a test frame to see the result.

That looks better, but something is wrong with the reflections. The Base object is lying in XZ space, requiring the reflection highlight bands of the reflection map to travel vertically. The Logo object is upright in XY space, requiring the highlight bands to travel horizontally. It's easy to change.

7. Click the Reflection map button to open its settings. Rename the map **Logo-Bevel-rfl**. To make the highlight bands of the image travel horizontally, enter a W value of **90** in the Coordinates rollout. Render another frame to view the result (see Figure 8.15).

Figure 8.15   Logo-Bevel-rfl map rotated W: 90.

Rotating the bitmap to create horizontal bands created more highlights around the Logo object. This finishes the material for the Logo object.

8. Save your work as **ch08-04.max**.

Exercise 8.8   Applying the Base Material to the Beacon Objects

Looking at the beacon objects, we can see that their material is exactly the same as the material that is applied to the bevel and extruded side of the Base object. We will simply apply the Base material to the beacon objects. However, before we do so we have to set the Material ID of all the faces of the beacon objects to 2.

1. With ch08-04.max loaded, select any beacon object, and, in the Modify panel, activate Sub-Object Polygon. All of the polygons of the beacon object should still be selected from when we applied the Smoothing groups to the object. If all of the faces are not selected, use Edit, Select All to select them.

2. In the Surface Properties rollout, change the Material ID to **2**—clicking the up spinner button should do the trick. Because the four beacon objects are instances, the Material ID will be applied to all four. Deactivate Sub-Object.

3. Open the Material Editor and apply the Base material to the four beacon objects. Close the Material Editor and render frame 200 to see the material on the beacon objects (see Figure 8.16).

Figure 8.16   Frame 200 rendered displaying the Base material on the beacon objects.

4. Save your work as **ch08-05.max**.

All of the primary objects in the scene are now textured. In the next section, we will create the environment in which the scene will live.

Building the Environment

Now that the primary objects have been modeled, animated, lit, and textured, we can start to plan the environment. Examine the storyboard one more time (refer to Figure 8.1).

The environment looks pretty complicated. We need to dissect it, simplifying its creation. The primary concern is that where the floor meets the "walls"—the seam where the two meet—is not visible. Make a mental note of that; it will probably work to our advantage.

Panel 1 and Panel 2 clearly illustrate a black grid pattern on the floor. There are also black concentric circles mimicking the shape of the Base object. The grid and concentric circles seem to be coplanar, so we can create a bitmap duplicating this and apply it to a simple floor object. We now know how we will create the grid and concentric circles, but what is the blue stuff behind it?

On the storyboard, all we can see is blue behind the grid floor pattern. We can certainly re-create that easily. What can we put in there that would add to the visual impact of the scene without being distracting? Let's drop a noise texture in there to simulate a slow-moving electric current. That seems to tie in with the hi-tech look of the animation.

We have now planned what the floor is going to be, but we still haven't figured out how it's going to join with the "walls". To solidify our plan of attack, we need to decide how to create the "walls." Panel 4 illustrates what the walls should look like. The "walls" don't seem to be walls at all; the corners and ceiling are not visible. The walls are more of back-ground accent than a primary element. Because there are no visible joints where the background meets the floor, we can probably create the background with bitmaps used in the Environment Background, Spherical Environment.

If we keep the bottom of the Environment Background black and the edge of the floor object black, a seam will not be noticeable. Another reason to create the background using the Environment Background is that it will render much faster than geometry would.

There we have it. Our plan of attack on the environment is complete. Let's create the floor object and texture it. Once we have the floor object created, we can create the Environment Background and ensure no seams are visible.

The Floor

Since we made all of our decisions on how we were going to create the environment that our current scene would live in, the first step in creating this environment would be the floor. We decided that the floor will have the grid pattern and concentric circles. To tie the floor to the Environment Background, the edges need to be black so that no seam is visible.

Exercise 8.9   Modeling the Floor Object

Let's begin the modeling process for the floor. We should keep the floor object simple since the entire floor object will be created using texture maps. Remember the *ReferenceSquare object that we created as a template for the logo's size? Because it's already in the scene, we can use that to create the floor object.

1. With ch08-05.max loaded, select the *ReferenceSquare object.

    We need to make the square larger so that it looks more like a floor.

2. In the Modify panel, open the Parameters rollout and change the Length to **600** and Width to **600** to make the rectangle shape larger (see Figure 8.17).

    The rectangle shape now surrounds most of the Base object. We need to change this shape into a mesh object so we can apply textures.

3. From the Modify panel, apply a Mesh Select modifier and rename the object **Floor**. The rectangle shape is now an object, thanks to the Mesh Select modifier. In the shaded Camera01 viewport, you should see the shaded Floor object (see Figure 8.18).

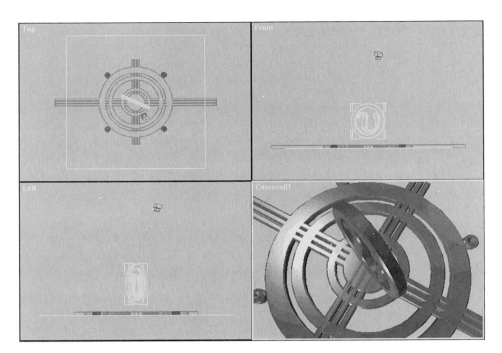

Figure 8.17   The *ReferenceSquare object with a Length and Width of 600.

Figure 8.18   The Floor object is now visible in the shaded Camera01 viewport.

Because we will be applying textures to the object, we need to apply UVW mapping coordinates.

4. Apply a UVW Map modifier. The UVW Map gizmo will be applied precisely to the size we need (see Figure 8.19).

The floor object is finished. We will depend on the Material Editor to make this floor object sing.

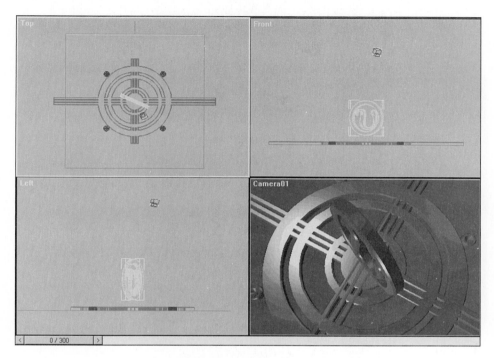

Figure 8.19 The UVW Map gizmo automatically sizes to fit the floor.

Exercise 8.10   Creating the Electric Effect

Because we have pre-planned, we know exactly what we need to do to texture the Floor object. Let's start out by adding the electric noise effect.

1. Open the Material Editor, activate the third material preview slot, and name this material **Floor**.

   Because we will be using texture maps, the Ambient and Diffuse colors do not matter.

2. We don't want the floor object to receive highlights from the lights in our scene, so enter the Specular Level of **0** and Glossiness of **0**.

   Because we have full control over the appearance of the floor, we will self-illuminate it.

3. Enter Self-Illumination of **100** and uncheck Color.

4. Open the Maps rollout and click the Diffuse Color button to open the Material/Map Browser. Choose Noise and click OK to close the Browser. Name this map **Floor-dif**.

5. To make the noise map look like dark blue electricity, open the Noise Parameters rollout and change the Noise Type to Turbulence. Apply the Floor texture to the Floor object and render frame 150 through the Camera01 viewport (see Figure 8.20).

   Doesn't look much like electricity, does it? It looks like little puffs of smoke. Let's swap the black and white color to invert the color placement to see if that improves it some.

Figure 8.20   The Floor material rendered at frame 150.

6. Click the Swap button to swap the colors and render frame 150 again (see Figure 8.21). That looks better, but the electric effect looks too soft. We need to make it more crisp.

7. Change the High value to .4. Render frame 150 again and view the effect.
   Let's increase the size of the effect.

8. To make the noise effect larger, change the Size value to **35**. Render a test frame at frame 150 to see how it looks.
   The noise map looks great; we just need to make it blue.

9. To make the noise blue, make Color 1 RGB (**89,85,170**) and Color 2 RGB (**84,15,113**). Render frame 150 to see the result (see Figure 8.22).
   Now we need to animate this noise effect so the electricity churns mysteriously.

10. To animate the noise map, activate the Animate button at frame 150 and enter Phase of .5. Deactivate the Animate button.

11. To preview the effect, click the Make Preview button in the Material Editor. In the Create Material Preview dialog box, activate Custom Range and set the range from **0** to **150**. Click OK to make the preview. When the preview is finished rendering, view the result.
   Looks like the churning is a little slow. We will need to quicken it up a tad.

Figure 8.21   Floor-dif with the noise color channels swapped.

Figure 8.22   The blue electricity noise effect.

12. Drag the key in the Trackbar to frame 30 (you can see its location displayed as you are dragging the key in the lower left display). Create another material preview for frames 0–150. When the preview is finished rendering, play the preview to see the result.

The speed of the churning looks great until the preview gets to frame 30, where the churning comes to a screeching halt. It is no longer churning because there are no more keys after frame 30 to animate the Phase parameter. We will fix that now.

13. Open the Track View and expand the Scene Materials track. Expand the Floor\Maps\Diffuse Color track and locate the Phase track (see Figure 8.23).

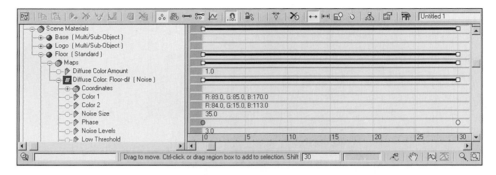

Figure 8.23   The Track View with Scene Materials\Floor\Maps\Diffuse Color track expanded.

14. Select the Phase title and click the Parameter Out-of-Range Types button. In the Param Curve Out-of-Range Types dialog box, click the Out button (the arrow pointing to the right) under Relative Repeat (see Figure 8.24). Click OK to close the dialog box and close the Track View.

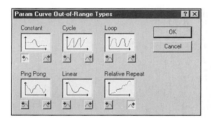

Figure 8.24   The correct settings in the Param Curve Out-of-Range Types dialog box.

Setting Relative Repeat Out instructs MAX to continue the animation at its current rate beyond the last keyframe in the track. Let's create another material preview to see the result.

15. In the Material Editor, click the Make Preview button, and, in the Create Material Preview dialog box, click OK to make a preview for frames 0–150.

16. Save your work as **ch08-06.max**.

The Phase parameter is now animated beyond frame 30 through to the end of the animation. It is a wise practice to animate textures using Param Curve Out-of-Range Types Relative Repeat because if you needed to add extra frames to the end of the animation, the material would continue to animate during those added frames.

Exercise 8.11   Blending the Floor to the Black Background

Our electric noise effect looks great. However, when we were rendering frame 150 for our test frames, the edge of the floor was visible. Earlier, we decided the joint where the floor met the environment needed to be black. We will disguise the edge of the floor by making it black right now.

1. With ch08-06.max loaded, open the Material Editor and open the Diffuse Color map Floor-dif.

    To disguise the edge of the floor, we will use a gradient map.

2. Click the Type:Noise button to open the Material/Map Browser. Choose Gradient and click OK to close the Browser. In the Replace Map dialog box, choose Keep Old Map As Sub-Map? and click OK to close the dialog box.

3. Render frame 150 from the Camera01 viewport and see the result of the change (see Figure 8.25).

Figure 8.25   Frame 150 rendered with Gradient map applied to the Floor.

Didn't seem to help too much. The Noise map we created now gradates to white. That doesn't seem to disguise the edge of the floor too well. Let's change the Gradient Type to Radial and view how that works out.

4. In the Gradient Parameters rollout, change the Gradient type to Radial and render frame 150 to view the result.

Tip

To view the material preview better, you can change the preview type from a sphere to a cube. To do so, click the Sample Type button and choose the cube from the fly-out. This will give you a better view of how the material will be applied.

That's closer to what we want. We will need to get the electric noise map out of the color 1 slot, however, because currently it's in the only place we don't want it to be.

5. Drag the Floor-dif map button from Color 1 to Color 2's map button. In the Copy (Instance) Map dialog box, choose Swap. This will swap the map slots, placing the black Color 1 color where the noise map was. Render frame 150 again to view the result.

Now that looks good! We can no longer see where the Floor object meets the black background. Now we have to place our attention on the white spot in the center of the gradient. To remove the white center, we will simply copy the Color 2 map button to the Color 3 map button.

6. Drag the Color 2 map button and drop it on the Color 3 map button. In the Copy (Instance) Map dialog box, choose copy and click OK to close the dialog box. Render frame 150 to view the change).

All right. That looks great, but there always seems to be a "but." We could probably add more depth to the floor by darkening the colors of the Color 2 noise map. Doing so will not only add depth but also will create a smoother gradation from the center to the black on the edge.

7. Click the Color 2 map button and rename this map **Floor-dif-dark**. Change the Color 1 to RGB (**68,65,130**) and Color 2 to RGB (**63,11,85**). Render frame 150 to view the change (see Figure 8.26).

Figure 8.26   The finished gradient map.

The gradation from the electric center to the black edge is much smoother. It looks fantastic! All we need to do now is to apply the grid and concentric circle pattern to the floor to finish the diffuse map.

Exercise 8.12   Adding the Grid and Concentric Circles to the Floor

Now that we have finished the hard part of the floor material, we need to add the grid and concentric circle pattern. It's very simple; we will create a composite material and use a bitmap to composite a black grid pattern over the noise.

1. From the Floor-dif-dark map, click Go to Parent once to return to the Floor-dif gradient map. To change the type of the map from Gradient to Composite, click the Type:Gradient button to open the Material/Map Browser. In the Material/Map Browser, choose Composite and click OK to exit the Browser. In the Replace Map dialog box, choose Keep Old Map As Sub-Map? and click OK to close the dialog box. The Material Editor now displays the Composite Parameters for the map (see Figure 8.27).

2. Name this map **Floor-dif-cmp**.

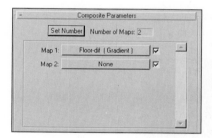

Figure 8.27   The Composite Parameters.

To composite one map over another, you must give the Material Editor information on how to composite the maps. We created a simple grid pattern with concentric circles in a paint program and saved it as floorgrid.jpg (see Figure 8.28). The white area of the bitmap needs to be black when we composite it over the gradient map of the Floor material. To do this, we will use a Mask material and apply the floorgrid.jpg as the mask. This will instruct MAX to apply black to the material where there is white in the floorgrid.jpg.

Let's add the Mask map to finish the material.

3. Click the Map 2 button to open the Material/Map Browser. Choose Mask and click OK to close the Browser. Name this map **Floor-dif-cmp-msk**. Click the Mask button to open the Material/Map Browser, choose Bitmap and click OK to close the Browser. In the Select Bitmap Image File dialog box, choose floorgrid.jpg from the ch08\maps directory of the included CD. Click Open to load the image and then close the dialog box. Name this map **Floor-dif-cmp-msk-msk**. Render frame 150 to view the result (see Figure 8.29).

Because we didn't assign a Map yet for the Mask map, the Material applied white as the default. That's okay; rendering the frame gave us an opportunity to see how crisp the grid pattern looks. Let's defocus it a bit.

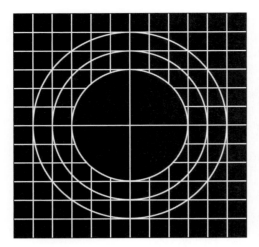

Figure 8.28   Floorgrid.jpg.

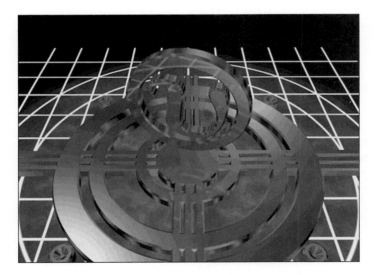

Figure 8.29   The Floor material with floorgrid.jpg applied as the mask.

4. To defocus the grid pattern, enter a Blur of **4** in the Coordinates rollout of the map. Render frame 150 and view the result (see Figure 8.30).

   Now we will fill the Mask map with a color map. All we need is something to generate the color black; any of the procedural maps in the Material Editor that allow us to enter a color value will do the trick.

5. Click Go to Parent to return the Mask map. Click the Map button to open the Material/Map Browser. Choose Checker and click OK to exit the Browser. Name this map **Floor-dif-cmp-msk-map**.

Because the Checker map is currently generating a black-and-white checker pattern, we need to remove the white color.

Figure 8.30   The grid pattern is now defocused.

6. Drag the Color 1 black color swatch over the Color 2 white color swatch and release the mouse button. From the Copy or Swap colors dialog box, choose Copy. Render frame 150 to see the result (see Figure 8.31).

Figure 8.31   The finished Floor diffuse map.

Exercise 8.13   Adding the Reflection

The floor looks fantastic. However, because we are not going to be rendering shadows in the scene, it would probably be best to add a slight reflection to the floor. Doing so will fill in for the lack of shadows and make the Base object appear to be attached to the floor.

1. Advance to frame 225 and render the frame through the Camera01 viewport.

    The floor doesn't seem to be attached to the Base object. Adding a reflection to the Floor material will make the Base object appear to be placed on it.

2. In the Material Editor, navigate to the root of the Floor material. In the Maps rollout, click the Reflection button to open the Material/Map Browser. Choose Flat Mirror and click OK to exit the Browser.

3. Name this map **Floor-rfl**, change Blur to **5**, uncheck Use Environment Map, and check Apply to Faces with ID (the Mesh Select modifier we applied to the floor automatically assigns a Material ID value of 1). Render frame 225 once more to see the difference the reflection makes.

    Instantly, the Base object appears to be resting on a highly polished floor. However, the reflection is too bright. It's an easy fix.

4. Click Go to Parent to return to the root of the Floor material. In the Maps rollout, change the Reflection value to **45**. Render frame 225 again and examine the changes (see Figure 8.32).

Figure 8.32   Floor materials reflection map value set to 45.

    The reflection is subtle and just enough to make the Base object appear to be resting on it. It's time to save our work and begin to create the background environment for the scene.

5. Save your work as **ch08-07.max**.

The Background Environment

With the floor complete, we need only to place the background environment maps into place before the scene is finished. Earlier we were examining the storyboards and decided to use bitmaps to create the background environment for the scene. To determine which maps are required, we need to examine the storyboard closely. The only panel of the story-board that illustrates the background environment clearly is Panel 4 (refer to Figure 8.1).

Examining Panel 4, two elements in the background become apparent: an arch with high-tech patterns inside, and glowing lights that appear to be shining through a honey-comb pattern. Knowing this, we have created two bitmap textures: hitech.jpg (shown in Figure 8.33) and hivelite.jpg (shown in Figure 8.34).

Figure 8.33   Hitech.jpg.

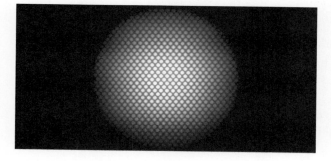

Figure 8.34   Hivelight.jpg.

Hitech.jpg re-creates the arch with the hi-tech texture inside. Notice the bottom of Hitech.jpg gradates to black on the bottom of the image. This is to help conceal the joint where the Environment map will meet the floor. Hivelight.jpg replicates the glowing light through a honeycomb pattern.

Let's start applying the Environment maps and finish the scene.

Exercise 8.14   Applying the Hi-Tech Arch Texture

We will start with the hi-tech arch texture. We will apply this map to the environment, much like we applied the grid pattern to the floor, with a Mask map.

1. With ch08-07.max loaded, open the Rendering/Environment dialog box. In the Background group of the dialog box, click the Environment Map button to open the Material/Map Browser. Choose Mask and click OK to exit the Browser. Drag the Environment Map button into the first material preview slot in the second row in the Material Editor. From the Instance (Copy) Map dialog box, choose Instance and click OK. Name this map **Env**.

   Looking at the storyboard, we can see the color for the arch is pale orange. Let's apply the orange color to the Map button now.

2. Click the Maps button to open the Material/Map Browser. Choose Checker and click OK to exit the Browser. In both the Color 1 and Color 2 values enter RGB (**130,99,54**). The map is now a solid orange color. Name this map **Env-Arc-Map**. Click the Go to Parent button to return to the root of the map.

   Now we will add the Mask map.

3. Click the Mask button to open the Material/Map Browser. Choose Bitmap and click OK to exit the Browser. In the Select Bitmap Image File dialog box, choose hitech.jpg from the ch08\maps directory of the accompanying CD. Click Open to load the bitmap. Name this map **Env-Arc-Msk**.

4. In the Coordinates rollout, change Mapping to Environ Mapping/Spherical Environment. This will map the bitmap on an imaginary sphere surrounding the scene, so it will move when the camera moves.

5. Render frame 240, the frame where the logo resolves, through the Camera01 viewport (see Figure 8.35).

   Doesn't look right, does it? We can certainly see that it has been applied; it just needs adjustment. This takes practice because we can't accurately see anywhere in real-time. The Material Editor preview will be our guide.

   Right now the bitmap is applied once to the entire "sphere." We need to tile the bitmap in all directions to make it smaller. Then we need to offset it so it is placed where we need it to be.

Figure 8.35   Frame 240 rendered.

6. In the Coordinates rollout, enter U Tiling of **8** and V Tiling of **7**. Render frame 240 again (see Figure 8.36).

Figure 8.36   Frame 240 with Background Environment map tiled.

Looks much better. We need to center the image by offsetting it, and we can turn off V Tiling because we need only one vertical strip of the image.

7. To turn off V Tiling, uncheck Tile in the V row of the Coordinates rollout. Now there is only one vertical strip in the environment.

Now we need to adjust the U Offset of the map to center it to the logo at frame 240. Changing the U Offset moves the map left or right depending on whether a positive or negative value is used.

8. Because the map needs to move to the left, start by entering a small negative U Offset value to move it slightly. Then render the frame to see where it is and make educated guesses, entering new values until the map is centered. A U Offset value of –.05 works well in my scene.

   The map seems a little too high. Let's drop it down a bit using the V Offset value. Positive values move it upward; negative values move it downward. Once again, practice makes perfect when working with the offset values.

9. Start with a V Offset value of –.01 and render a test frame. For me, that value just so happened to be exactly what I was looking for.

   A close examination at the render shows that the floor is overlapping the bitmap. But it is very hard to see. We would rather the bitmap be centered to the logo and barely see the overlap, as opposed to not having the map centered. The chances of someone catching the seam in the rendering are slim, especially when they don't know how the scene was constructed.

   The arc looks a little bright. Let's lessen its intensity.

10. Open the Output rollout of the Env-Arc-Msk map (the hitech.jpg bitmap). Enter an Output Amount value of .5. This instructs the Material Editor to apply the luminance of the bitmap at half its intensity. Render frame 240 to see the result (see Figure 8.37).

Figure 8.37   The Env-Arc-Msk with an Output Amount of .5 dims the Environment map.

We are now finished creating the arc environment map. All we need to do is apply the honeycomb lights.

Exercise 8.15   Applying the Honeycomb Lights

Earlier, we decided the honeycomb lights would be created using a bitmap as an environment map, much like the arc was created. We already created the bitmap of the honeycomb lights; all we need to do is apply it to the scene.

1. In the Material Editor, navigate to the root of the Env material. We need to create a composite map to add the honeycomb light map to the Environment Background. Click the Type:Mask button to open the Material/Map Browser. Choose Composite and click OK to close the browser. In the Replace Map dialog box, choose Keep Old Map As Sub-Map? and click OK.

2. To add another Mask map, click the Map 2 button to open the Material/Map Browser. Choose Mask and click OK to close the Browser. Name this map **Env-lite-msk**.

    We need to fill the Map channel with a bright orange color to simulate the color of the honeycomb lights.

3. Click the Map button to open the Material/Map Browser. Choose Checker and click OK to exit the Browser.

4. Change both the Color 1 and Color 2 color to RGB (**231,114,0**). This fills the map with an orange color. Name this map **Env-lite-msk-map**. Click Go to Parent to return to the Env-lite-msk map.

    We need to apply the honeycomb light bitmap now.

5. Click the Mask button to open the Material/Map Browser. Choose Bitmap and click OK to close the Browser. In the Select Bitmap Image File dialog box, choose hivelite.jpg from the ch08\maps directory of the accompanying CD, click Open to load the bitmap and close the dialog box. Name this map **Env-lite-msk-msk**. Set mapping to Environ Mapping:Spherical Environment.

    Much like the arc bitmap we applied to the Environment Background, we will need to Tile and Offset the bitmap to create the correct effect.

6. Experiment with the Tiling and Offset values to place the highlights on the side of the arc as Figure 8.38 illustrates. Remember to uncheck V Tiling so the tiled map creates one horizontal strip around the environment.

    U Offset: **.015**

    U Tiling: **8**

    V Offset: **.03**

    V Tiling: **9**

These settings work well in my scene.

Figure 8.38   The honeycomb lights in the correct position.

To add drama to the scene, we could slowly oscillate the intensity of the lights.

7. To animate this effect, advance to frame 30 and activate the Animate button. Open the Output rollout and enter an Output Amount of **.7**. Advance to frame 60 and return the Output Amount to **1**. Deactivate the Animate button.

To loop this effect throughout the animation, we need to apply a Loop Parameter Out-of-Curve Type to the Output Amount.

8. Open the Track View and expand the Environment\Environment Texture Map\Map 2\Mask\Output track. Select the Output Amount title and click the Parameter Out-of-Range button to open its dialog box. Click Loop Out and click OK to exit the dialog box. Close the Track View and the Material Editor.

9. Save your work as **ch08-08.max**.

The honeycomb light effect in the Environment Background now slowly oscillates throughout the animation. We have completed the scene. All that is left is to add the glow around the logo and the lens flares.

Attempting to Use Lens Effects

We will be using Lens Effects in the Video Post dialog box to add the glow around the logo and the lens flares into the scene. The Lens Effects are very powerful, yet limited, post-rendering effects. Shortly, we will learn the greatest limitation of Lens Effects.

We will attempt to place a Lens Effects Glow around the Logo object. Before we can start, we need to adjust an object properties setting of the Logo object. Lens Effects applies its effects to the rendered image when Video Post is finished rendering the frame. In order for it to apply the effect to the Logo object, we need to give the Logo object a unique Object ID so the Lens Effects filter can locate the pixels that form the logo. We will learn more about Lens Effects in the next chapter. For now, let's set up the scene.

Exercise 8.16   Setting Up the Scene

Before we can apply the Lens Effects Glow filter, we need to apply an Object ID to the Logo object.

1. With ch08-08.max loaded, select the Logo object and right-click it to bring up the right-click menu. Select Properties to open the Object Properties dialog box. In the G-Buffer group of the dialog box, enter Object Channel of **1** and click OK to exit the dialog box.

   When we apply Lens Effects, we will tell it to look for Object ID 1 to find the pixels of the Logo object.

   We will now create a Video Post queue to set up the Glow effect.

2. Advance to frame 200. Use Rendering/Video Post to open the Video Post dialog box.

3. To add Camera01 to the queue, click Add Scene Event. Accept the default values by clicking OK to close the Add Scene Event dialog box.

   Now we will add a Lens Effects Glow event.

4. Click the Add Image Filter Event button to open the Add Image Filter Event dialog box. From the Filter Plug-In list, choose Lens Effects Glow and click OK to close the dialog box. The Video Post queue should look like Figure 8.39.

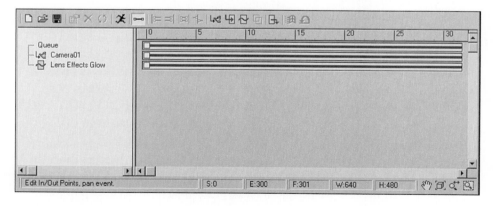

Figure 8.39   The Video Post dialog box with a Camera01 event and a Lens Effects Glow event.

5. To configure the Lens Effects Glow event, double-click the Lens Effects Glow event to open the Edit Filter Event dialog box. Click Setup to enter the Lens Effects Glow dialog box. Activate VP Queue and Preview to preview the scene (see Figure 8.40).

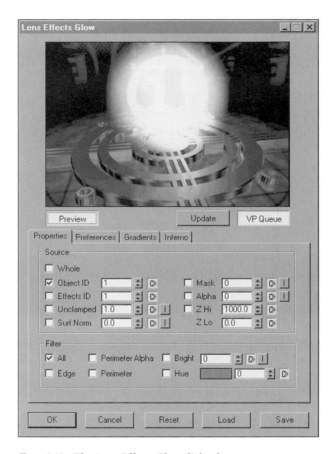

Figure 8.40   The Lens Effects Glow dialog box.

The glow is applied to the entire logo object. We want the effect to appear only around the perimeter of the logo object. We need to change the Filter of the Lens Effects Glow.

6. In the Filter group of the dialog box, check Perimeter Alpha (Figure 8.41).

Notice the glow effect using Perimeter Alpha has an anti-alising problem where the Logo object overlaps the Base object and the floor. This is because when the alpha of two objects overlaps in the rendering, Video Post can't determine the object's edge. Because the perimeter alpha of the logo object is not available where the logo overlaps the other objects in the scene, Lens Effects uses G-Buffer image data. The Object ID channel is returning the Object ID of the face fragment at the center of the pixel.

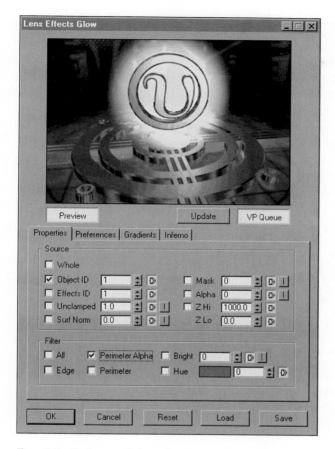

Figure 8.41   Perimeter Alpha active.

Currently, there is no true fix to this problem. We will have to render the scene without the effects and apply the Lens Effects with a second pass over the rendered scene.

Rendering the Scene

Because the Video Post dialog box is open, we will utilize it to render the scene. This way, we could render the animation as two separate output images: as high-quality .tga files, and as an .avi enabling us to preview the animation, when it finishes rendering.

Exercise 8.17: Rendering without Lens Effects Filters

1. With the Video Post dialog box open, select the Lens Effects Glow track and delete it. Click the Add Image Output Event button to open its dialog box. Navigate to your output directory ch08\images and enter the name **back.tga**. To add a second output image event, click the Add Image Output Event. In the resulting dialog box, navigate to your ch08\images directory and enter the name **back.avi**. Now when the queue is rendered, it will save as two separate file types: one, the high-quality .tga files we will use as the background for the second pass and two, the .avi that we could preview our animation with.

   Because of the often unpredictable nature of Lens Effects filters, I have found it to be a smart working practice to render all of my scenes without the Lens Effect filter and apply the Lens Effects with a second pass over the rendering. This way, if the Lens Effects produce an undesirable effect or the parameters of Lens Effects have been animated incorrectly the 3D scene does not need to be re-rendered, saving valuable time.

2. Save the scene as **ch08-09.max**. In the Video Post dialog box, click Execute Sequence to render the queue. Set Output size to **320×200** and click Execute to render the queue.

In Summary

When the animation finishes, view the back.avi file the queue created. Looks very cool! All of your hard work has paid off. In the next chapter, we will learn more about Lens Effects and apply them to the scene.

Chapter 9

Applying Lens Effects Glow to the V

A correctly configured Lens Effects Glow can make all the difference in the world in the appeal of your animation. Lens Effects Glow simulates natural effects of light, such as a halo or soft specular highlight.

These effects add depth, definition, contrast, mood, atmosphere, and realism to your scenes. They can also be used to add dazzling special effects.

In this chapter, we will explore how to apply Lens Effects Glow to our scenes. Then we will animate the Lens Effects Glow parameters to create stunning glow effects.

Working with Lens Effects Glow

We learned in the previous chapter that there are limitations in Lens Effects Glow that limit the way it can be used. The limitation we encountered in the last chapter was that when objects overlap one another, it is impossible for Lens Effects Glow to create a clean edge using the Perimeter Alpha filter.

Because we knew we could not successfully apply Lens Effects Glow to our scene at the time it was rendered, we decided we would apply the Glow effect to the scene as a second pass over the rendered frames. This methodology is smart because if the glow was applied successfully but we failed to animate all of the parameters correctly, we would have to re-render the entire scene after the correct changes to the Lens Effects Glow effect were made.

To apply the Lens Effects Glow filter to the rendered images, we will load our scene and hide all the objects except for the logo object. We will then load the rendered frames using Screen mapping as the environment background. Because there are no other objects for the logo object to overlap, the Lens Effects Glow will be applied correctly.

Before adding the Glow effect to our scene, let's explore the several ways in which we can apply the effect.

Exercise 9.1   Preparing the Scene

To conduct our experiment, we will load the logo scene, hide the unnecessary objects, and modify the logo's material properties a bit. Once the scene is configure correctly, we will examine different ways to apply the Glow effect.

1. Load ch08-08.max, the file you created in the previous chapter. We don't need to load ch08-09.max because they are identical files, except that ch08-09.max has a Video Post queue constructed. We will be creating a different Video Post queue to apply the Lens Effects Glow effect.

   We need to hide all the objects except the logo object.

2. To hide all but the logo object, select the Logo object, enter the Display panel, and click Hide Unselected. This will hide all the elements in the scene except the Logo object (see Figure 9.1).

   We need to replace the Environment Map with the rendered images we created in the last chapter. This will allow us to preview exactly how the scene will appear.

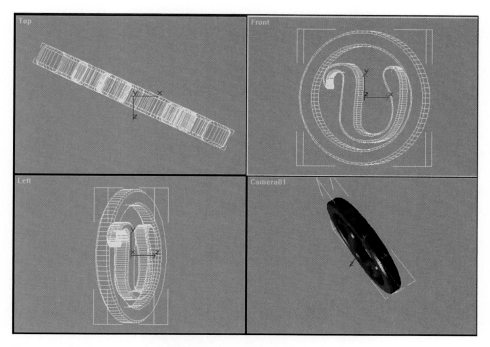

Figure 9.1   Ch08-08.max with only the logo visible in the scene.

3. Choose Rendering, Environment to open the Environment dialog box. To change the Environment Map, click the Environment Map button to open the Material/Map Browser. From the Material/Map Browser, choose Bitmap and click OK to close the browser. In the Select Bitmap Image File dialog box, navigate to your rendered scene images (ch08\images) and choose back0000.tga. Make sure Sequence is checked, click Open to load the image sequence, and then close the dialog box. In the Image File List Control dialog box, click OK to accept the default settings. Close the Environment dialog box.

   Because Lens Effects can use Material Effects Channels to apply the Glow effect, we will add them to the Logo material.

4. Open the Material Editor and activate the Logo material slot. Click the Material 1 button to open the settings for the Logo-Face sub-material. Change its Material Effects Channel to **1.**

   We will now apply a Material Effects Channel to the Logo-Bevel sub-material.

5. Click Go Forward to Sibling to enter the settings for the Logo-Bevel material. Change its Material Effects Channel to **2.** Close the Material Editor.

   As you learned in the last chapter, Lens Effects Glow can also apply the effect using the Object ID of an object. We will assign an object ID to the logo object, allowing Lens Effects Glow to apply the effect.

6. Select the Logo object, and then right-click on the Logo object. From the resulting list, choose Properties to open the Object Properties dialog box. In the G-Buffer group, change Object Channel to **1**. Click OK to close the dialog box.

We are finished making the necessary adjustments to the scene and are ready to begin our experiment.

7. Save your work as **ch09-01.max**.

Exercise 9.2   Setting Up the Video Post Queue

Now that the scene is ready for our experiment, we need to create a Video Post queue to apply the effect.

1. Choose Rendering, Video Post to open the Video Post dialog box (see Figure 9.2).

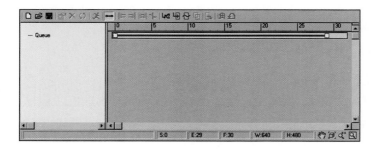

Figure 9.2   The Video Post dialog box.

We need to add a Camera01 Scene Event and then add the Lens Effects Glow Image Filter Event.

2. To add Camera01 to the queue, click Add Scene Event, and in the Add Scene Event dialog box, click OK to accept the default settings (see Figure 9.3).

3. To add the Lens Effects Glow event, click Add Image Filter Event. From the Filter Plug-In group of the Add Image Filter Event dialog box, choose Lens Effects Glow and click OK to close the dialog box.

4. To view the entire queue, click Zoom Extents in the Video Post dialog box. The queue should look like Figure 9.4.

5. Save your work as **ch09-02.max**.

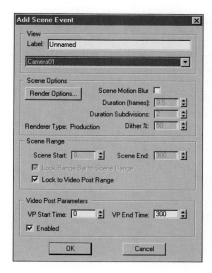

Figure 9.3 The Add Scene Event dialog box.

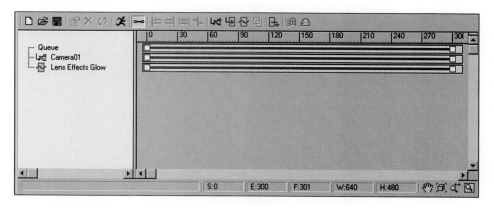

Figure 9.4 The correct Video Post queue.

Experimenting with Lens Effects Properties

The Source and Filters groups in the Properties tab of the Lens Effects Glow dialog box influence how the Glow effect is applied to the rendered scene. It is very important that you understand the purpose of each of these options when applying a Glow effect to your scene.

Exercise 9.3   Opening the Lens Effects Glow Dialog Box

Now we can open the Lens Effects Glow dialog box and begin our experimentation.

1. With ch09-02.max loaded, advance to frame 150, open the Video Post dialog box, and double-click the Lens Effects Glow track name to open the Edit Filter Event dialog box. In the Edit Filter Event dialog box, click Setup to open the Lens Effects Glow dialog box. Activate VP Queue and Preview to preview the scene (see Figure 9.5).

2. Look carefully at the Properties in the Lens Effects Glow dialog box.

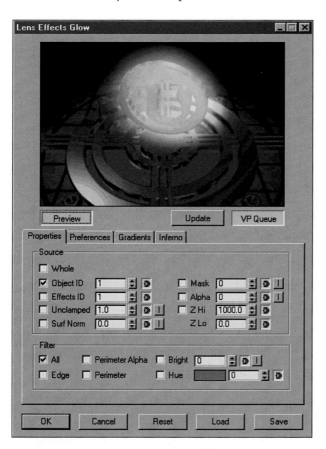

Figure 9.5   The Lens Effects Glow dialog box with VP Queue and Preview activated.

The logo object is a complete glowing mass. This is because the filter is currently being applied to the logo Object ID of 1 we assigned previously. Any positive Object Channel number assigned to an object enables Video Post to access that object when it is applying Video Post filters. In clearer terms, each object in a scene can have a unique Object Channel, which means Video Post can apply a filter to each object individually.

There are two events in the Video Post queue: Camera01 (a scene input event) and Lens Effects Glow (an image filter event). Because we activated the VP Queue button for the Glow preview, Camera01 was rendered as our preview image (the VP queue processes sequentially from top to bottom). This offers us an accurate representation of the results of the VP queue.

In the Lens Effects Glow dialog box, Object ID source is active. Lens Effects examines the scene and locates the pixels of the rendered scene that have an identical numeric match to the Object ID in Lens Effects.

The Source Group

The options in the Source group serve these functions:

- They determine where to apply the effect to the scene.
- They determine which channels of the G-Buffer data the Glow effect is applied to.

Exercise 9.4   Changing the Source

Let's see what happens when we use the Material Effects Channels as the source for the glow.

1. In the Source group of the Lens Effects Glow dialog box, uncheck Object ID and check Effects ID (this is the Material Effects Channel). Examine the preview (see Figure 9.6).

   Doesn't look too different, does it? There is a difference; however, the Glow effect is too large to allow us to see the difference. Let's make it smaller so we can accurately view how it is being applied.

2. Click the Preferences tab and, in the Effect group, change Size to **1** (see Figure 9.7).

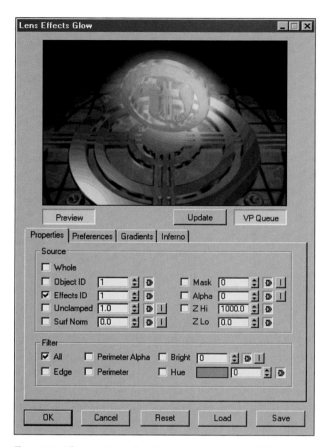

Figure 9.6   The Preview when Source is changed to Effects ID 1.

Now the Glow effect is applied to only the face of the object. This is because we changed the Material Effects Channel of the Logo-Face material to **1**. Since we applied the Material Effects Channel 2 to the Logo-Bevel material, if we change the Effects ID to **2**, we should see the bevel and extruded side of the Logo object glow.

Note

Both the bevel and extruded side of the logo will glow because the Logo-Bevel material is applied to both the Logo's bevel and extruded side.

3. Click the Properties tab and change the Effects ID to **2**. Examine the preview (see Figure 9.8).

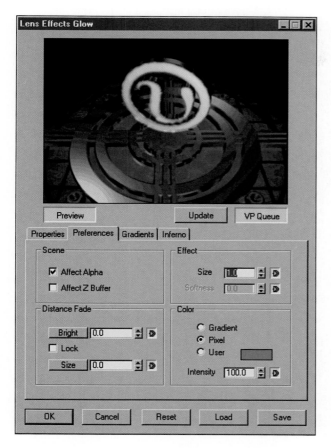

Figure 9.7 The glow preview with Effects ID:1 with a Size of 1.

Experimenting with the Material Effects Channels (or Effect IDs) has provided us with another way to apply Video Post filters to the rendered scene. Effect IDs prove to be more versatile because any object could possess several material IDs. It is important to remember that Material Effects Channels, which are assigned in the Material Editor, can be applied to either the root of a material or sub-material, or the map or sub-map level of a material. The Material Effects Channels certainly provide the most flexibility of all the Source options in the Lens Effects dialog box.

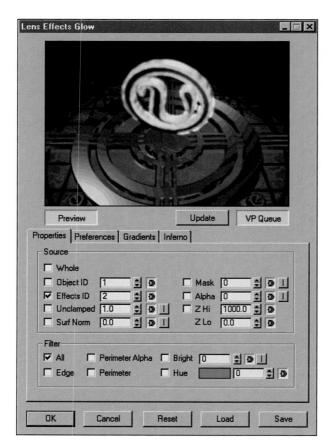

Figure 9.8   The glow preview with Effects ID 2 applied.

The Filter Group

We have just learned how to utilize the Source group to tell Lens Effects Glow *where* to apply the effect. It is time to explore the Filter group, which instructs Lens Effects Glow *how* to apply the effect.

The parameters in the Filter group of Lens Effects determine how the effect is applied to the channel specified in the Source group. The Filter group provides even more flexibility by allowing the user to specify what attribute of the channel to apply the effect to. There are six options in the Filters group: All, Edge, Perimeter Alpha, Perimeter, Bright, and Hue.

To examine the effect each option has on the effect, let's turn our attention to the Lens Effects Glow preview. In the Properties tab, the current filter is All. The All option instructs Lens Effects to apply the Glow effect to every pixel that is designated by the Source channel. The Glow effect spills over the edge of the Source because of the size of the Glow effect.

Exercise 9.5   Experimenting with the Filter Group Options

Let's activate another Filter type and view the result.

1. Check the Edge Filter and view the preview (see Figure 9.9).

Figure 9.9   Filter Edge active.

The Edge option instructs Lens Effects to apply the Glow effect to the boundary edge of the Source channel (in this case, the edges created by Material Effects Channel 2). This is perfect for creating the effect that the source is lighted strongly from behind or for creating a halo around the source.

Let's examine the Perimeter Alpha filter now.

2. Check Perimeter Alpha and uncheck Edge. Examine the preview (see Figure 9.10).

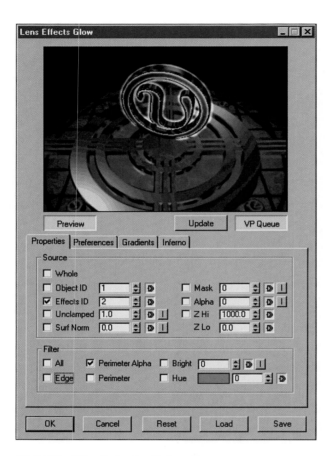

Figure 9.10 Filter Perimeter Alpha active.

The Perimeter Alpha option uses the Alpha Channel of the source and applies a glow outward from its perimeter. The Perimeter Alpha filter keeps the edge where the effect meets the source clean and seamless, except if there is no alpha information to apply the effect to. Notice how beautifully the Glow effect is applied to the outside edge of the logo; then notice how poorly it is applied to the edges that touch the Logo's face. It is applied poorly because there is no alpha information on that edge. This creates an edge that is not anti-aliased.

Let's examine the Perimeter filter. Hopefully, its edges will be cleaner.

3. Check Perimeter and uncheck Perimeter Alpha. Examine the preview (see Figure 9.11).

The Perimeter option applies the Glow effect to the perimeter edge of the source by using Edge inferencing. Using this option eliminates the anti-aliasing problem that resulted from the Perimeter Alpha option, but as you can see in your Preview window, the edge is not accurately positioned.

We will now examine how the Bright filter applies the effect.

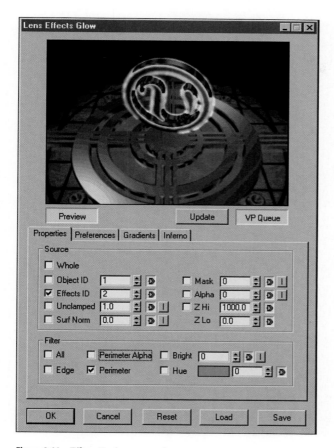

Figure 9.11 Filter Perimeter active.

4. Uncheck Perimeter and check Bright. Enter a Bright value of **90** and view the preview (see Figure 9.12).

   The Bright filter applies the Glow effect to the pixels of the source whose brightness is greater than or equal to the Bright value.

5. Enter higher and lower Bright values and examine the result. A low Bright value will glow more of the dark areas; a high Bright value will glow only the light areas.

   There is only one filter left to explore, Hue. Let's look at that now.

6. Uncheck Bright and check Hue. It seems as though no Glow effect has been applied in the scene.

   The Hue filter applies the Glow effect to pixels that have the same hue as the color assigned in the Hue color swatch. Changing the color swatch to blue should create a glow.

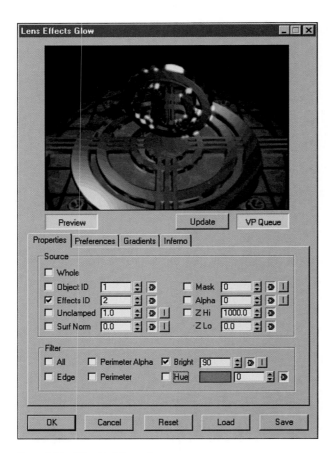

Figure 9.12   Filter Bright active.

7. Click the Hue color swatch to open the Color Selector. Enter RGB (**0,138,255**), click OK to close the color selector, and examine the preview (see Figure 9.13).

   The preview now displays a spotty Glow effect. It is important to remember that the saturation and value of the color do not matter. The Hue filter looks strictly at the hue value of the color swatch and applies the effect to that hue in the scene. The Hue value creates a plus and minus hue range for the effect. A larger number in the Hue value will apply the effect to a wider range of hue in the image.

8. We are finished experimenting, so save your work as **ch09-03.max**.

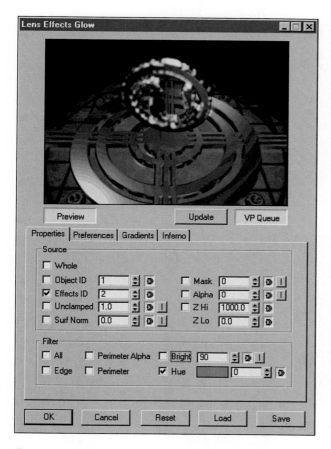

Figure 9.13   Filter Hue with a value of RGB (0,138,255).

Applying a Lens Effects Glow to the Logo Object

Now that we have a broader understanding of how Lens Effects Glow is applied to the scene, we can examine the storyboard to help to determine the best way to apply the Glow effect in the scene. By now you should be quite familiar with the storyboard shown in Figure 9.14.

We should look for two things when examining the storyboard: when the effect appears and how the glow is applied. Comparing the storyboard to our scene (by shuttling through the frames), we decide that the effect should begin to appear at frame 120. Although that may seem a little early, we have to consider the two-second dissolve that will transition the effect on.

Panel 1

Panel 2

Panel 3

Panel 4

Figure 9.14   The storyboard for this project.

Examining how the effect should be applied to the Logo object, we come to the conclusion that the Glow effect does not cover any of the surfaces of the logo. Instead, it is applied from the edge of the logo outward. To duplicate this glow, we know we can use Perimeter Alpha, especially since we don't need to be concerned with the logo overlapping another object.

Exercise 9.6   Applying a Glow to Our Logo

With these two things in mind, we will apply the Glow effect and animate its transition into the scene.

1. With ch09-03.max loaded, advance to frame 150, open the Video Post dialog box, and double-click the Lens Effects Glow track to open the Edit Filter Event dialog box. Click Setup to open the Lens Effects Glow dialog box.

   The changes we made when we were exploring the Source and filter settings should still be active.

   Because we know the Glow effect should appear only around the outside edge of the logo, we will have to use the Object ID Source.

2. In the Source group of the Properties tab, check Object ID:1 to activate it and uncheck Effects ID.

   The Glow effect is now applied to the entire logo, using the Hue filter. For our purposes, however, we need to deactivate Hue and activate Perimeter Alpha.

3. In the Filters group, uncheck Hue and check Perimeter Alpha (see Figure 9.15).

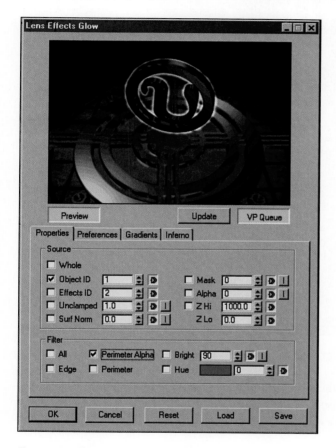

Figure 9.15   Filter Perimeter Alpha active.

The Glow effect is now applied to the Logo object correctly. It looks a little small though. Let's make it bigger.

4. Click the Preferences tab and, in the Effect group, change Size to **3** (see Figure 9.16).

   The size and the application of the Glow effect look perfect. However, the Glow effect is not the correct color. It's blue, and it should be orange. In the Color group of the Preferences tab, the active option is Pixel. This option derives the glow color from the source pixel used to create the glow, resulting in the blue color.

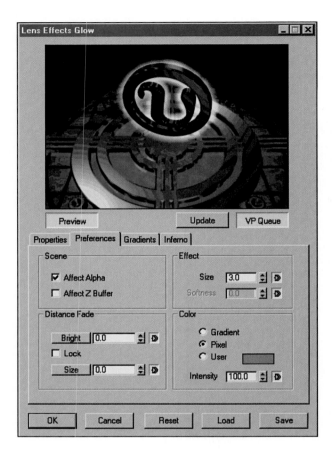

Figure 9.16 Glow with a Size of 3.

But what's that above the Pixel option? Gradient? What does that do? We will find out in the next lesson.

5. Save your work as **ch09-04.max**.

Experimenting with Lens Effects Gradients

You have learned how to apply Lens Effects Glow to your scenes. In this section, we will experiment with the Lens Effects Gradients and will examine the different ways they apply color to the Glow effect. Gradients add versatility and have the potential to create very stunning effects by giving the user plenty of possibilities to apply color and transparency to the Lens Effects.

There are two types of gradients in Lens Effects: Radial and Circular.

- *Radial gradient.* A Radial gradient is a linear gradient that starts at the center of the effect and ends at the outside edge. In Figure 9.17, Radial Gradient 1 has matching start and end flags. Radial Gradient 2 has a white start flag and a darker end flag.

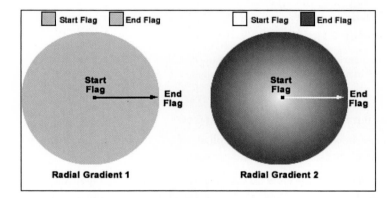

Figure 9.17   Two different Radial gradients.

- *Circular gradient.* A Circular gradient arcs from the 12:00 position and follows the circumference in a clockwise manner, ending where it began (see Figure 9.18).

The combination of these two types of gradients allows the user to create complex effects using Lens Effects.

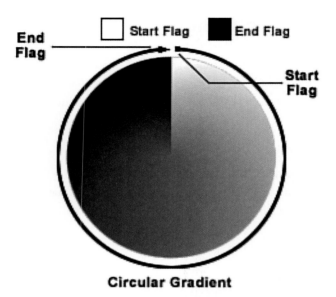

Figure 9.18 A Circular gradient starts at the highest point of the radius of the effect and runs around the circumference in a clockwise manner, ending where it began.

Exercise 9.7   Checking Out the Gradients in Lens Effects Glow

Now that we understand how the gradients are applied, we can explore the gradients in Lens Effects Glow. Put on your safari khakis and get ready!

1. Load TestSphere.max from the ch09 directory of the included CD. Open Video Post and open the Lens Effects Glow dialog box. Make sure the Gradients tab is selected and turn on Preview (see Figure 9.19).

   The first gradient on the Gradients tab is the Radial Color gradient. Notice that the color flag on the left of the gradient is white, and the color flag on the right is blue. It is because of this gradient that the glow has blue on its outside edge. The white color starts at the center of the effect, and the gradient applies linearly to the end of the effect, creating the blue halo.

   Suppose we wanted the glow to be white in the center of the effect, then change to red in the middle of the points, and have blue tips. That's an easy thing to achieve.

2. Click about ¼ of the way from the left of the Radial Color gradient to add a flag. You can then drag the flag to position it accurately; move the flag to Pos=25. Double-click the flag to open the Color Selector and change the color to RGB (**255,0,0**), creating red. The resulting gradient should look like that shown in Figure 9.20.

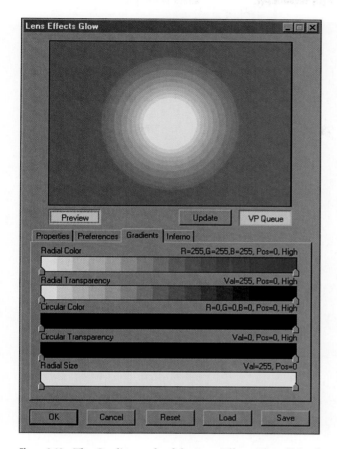

Figure 9.19   The Gradients tab of the Lens Effects Glow dialog box.

The Glow effect should have a white center; as the glow is applied outward, it changes to red; and finally, it finishes with the blue halo. You can clearly see how the Radial Color gradient is applied from the center of the effect and radiates linearly outward to the edge of the Glow effect.

Now that we understand how the Radial Color gradient is applied, we no longer need the red flag. Let's get rid of it.

3. Drag the flag at Pos=25 to either edge of the Radial Color gradient. When the flag moves off the side of the gradient, the pointer points downward to a trash can. Release the mouse button to delete the flag.

The next gradient on the Gradients tab is Radial Transparency. This gradient is applied exactly the same way as the Radial Color gradient. However, this gradient controls the transparency of the effect by using the whiteness level of the gradient; all color information is ignored. The brighter the value, the more visible the effect.

Let's use Radial Transparency to create a transparent core, making the glow appear to be emanating from the center of the effect.

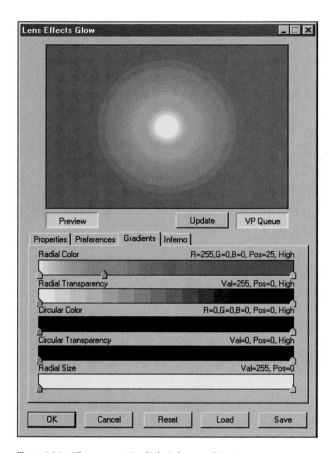

Figure 9.20 The correct Radial Color gradient.

4. Change the value of the flag to the left (the start flag) of the Radial Transparency gradient to RGB (**0,0,0**); then change the value of the flag to the right (the end flag) of the Radial Transparency gradient to RGB (**255,255,255**). This inverts the original gradient. To make the core more transparent, add a flag at Pos=50 and change the value to RGB (**0,0,0**) (see Figure 9.21).

Note

The white dot in the center of the effect is the sphere object, which is the source of the effect.

The Radial Transparency gradient has created the desired effect. The core of the effect is now transparent. The glow still starts at the core of the effect, but the flag we added at Pos=50 (which is black) makes the first 50% of the glow invisible.

The next steps illustrate the use of the Circular Color gradient. Let's set up the Radial Color and Radial Transparency to maximize the viewable result of the Circular Color gradient.

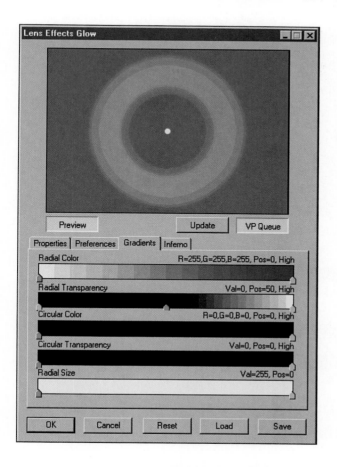

Figure 9.21 The correct Radial Transparency gradient.

5. Change the start and end flags of the Radial Color gradient to RGB (**0,0,0**).
   Change the start and end flags of the Radial Transparency gradient to RGB
   (**255,255,255**) and delete the center flag (see Figure 9.22).

   The Glow effect should be invisible.

   The Lens Effects Glow effect is additive to its background. It multiplies the color
   of the effect over the color of the background. Because the Radial (and Circular)
   color is black (**0,0,0**), the result is an invisible effect. Any number value multi-
   plied by zero is zero, which is why the effect is not visible.

   Now that we understand how Radial gradients work, we can experiment with
   Circular gradients to view their effect on Lens Effects filters. We learned in the
   last step that a Circular gradient is applied starting at the highest point of the
   radius and arcs clockwise around the circumference of the effect. To test this, let's
   create a Circular Color gradient.

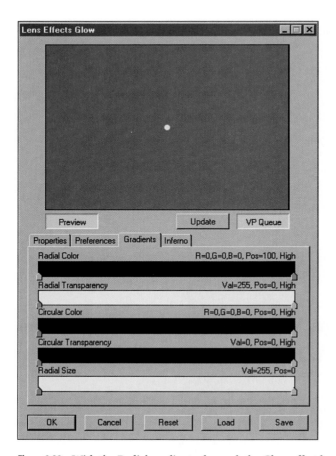

Figure 9.22   With the Radial gradients changed, the Glow effect becomes invisible.

6. Change the start flag of the Circular Color gradient to RGB (**255,0,0**). You will see that at the 12:00 position of the Glow effect, the red color is 100%. As the gradient arcs clockwise around the effect, it becomes transparent when it reaches 12:00 again (see Figure 9.23).

   Let's add more color to the Circular Color gradient to make the effect more visible.

7. Change the end flag of the Circular Color gradient to RGB (**0,0,255**).

   The gradient starts at the color red, then goes to purple (because of its transition to blue), and ends with blue.

   We now have a clear understanding of how Circular gradients are applied. Let's move on to the Circular Transparency gradient. Before we can experiment with Circular Transparency, we need to remove the Radial Transparency, which is now 100%.

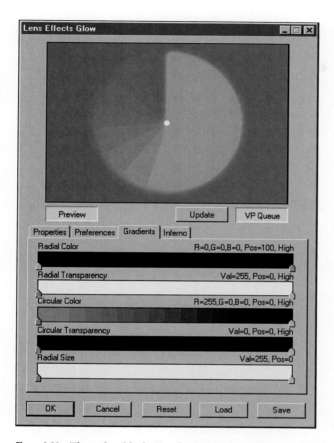

Figure 9.23   The red to black Circular gradient applied to the Glow effect.

8. Change the start and end flags of the Radial Transparency gradient to RGB **(0,0,0)**. This will make the effect invisible again.

   Circular Transparency is applied clockwise, exactly like Circular Color. Much like the Radial Transparency, only the whiteness value of the color is used when determining transparency. The whiter the value, the more visible it becomes. Let's apply a Circular Transparency gradient to the Glow effect.

9. In the Circular Transparency gradient, change the end flag value to RGB **(255,255,255)**. This makes the effect transparent at the 12:00, and as it arcs clockwise back to 12:00, it becomes more visible (see Figure 9.24).

   Let's add another flag to the gradient and view the effect.

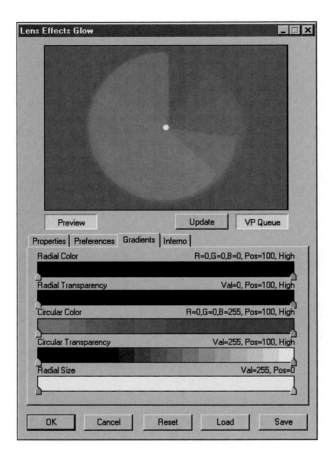

Figure 9.24   The result of the new Circular Transparency gradient.

10. Click in the middle of the Circular Transparency gradient to create a flag. Move it to Pos=50 and change the value to RGB (**0,0,0**) (see Figure 9.25).

As you can see, the Glow effect is now transparent from 12:00 [Pos=0] to 6:00 [Pos=50] and becomes more visible as it arcs from 6:00 to 12:00 [Pos=100].

In the next section, we will experiment with the Radial Size gradient. Let's make the effect completely visible so we can accurately view the results of the Radial Size gradient.

11. In the Circular Transparency gradient, delete the flag at Pos=50, by dragging it off the gradient and releasing the mouse button. Change the start flag of the Circular Transparency gradient to RGB (**255,255,255**) to create a solid white gradient.

We are now ready to experiment with the Radial Size gradient. Notice that the Radial Size gradient is already solid white. This means that the effect is 100% of its possible size (assigned in the Effect group of the Preferences tab).

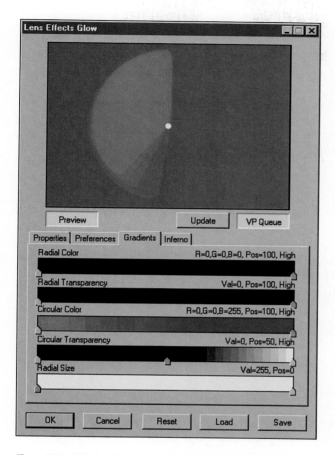

Figure 9.25   Circular Transparency gradient with RGB (0,0,0) flag added at Pos=50.

The Radial Size gradient is applied in a circular gradient fashion, starting at 12:00 and ending at 12:00. The whiteness value of the gradient determines the length of each point. To illustrate this, let's change the gradient.

12. Change the end flag of the Radial Size gradient to RGB (**0,0,0**) (see Figure 9.26).

As you can see, the white value of the start flag has resulted in the 12:00 point at maximum size. As the Radial gradient arcs in a circular gradient fashion, the size of the glow is made gradually smaller as it radiates clockwise; it is so small we can't see it as it returns to 12:00.

You now have an understanding of how the gradients work, and how to use them to maximize the power of the Lens Effects filters in your scenes.

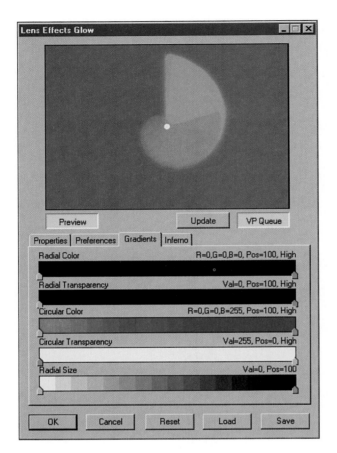

Figure 9.26 Radial gradient with a start flag color value of RGB (255,255,255) and an end flag color value of RGB (0,0,0).

Applying Lens Effects Gradients in the Logo Scene

Now you're ready to add Lens Effects gradients to the Glow effect in the logo scene. Examining the storyboard, it is very obvious that the Glow effect is an orange/red color. Let's open up our scene and make the changes using the skills we have learned.

Exercise 9.8   Adding a Gradient to the Glow Effect

Let's use the Radial Transparency gradient with this scene to make the glow appear to be emanating from the center of the effect.

    1. Load ch09-04.max, advance to frame 120, open Video Post, and open the Lens Effects Glow dialog box. Make sure the VP Queue and Preview buttons are activated.

2. In the Color group of the Preferences tab, activate Gradient. Click the Gradients tab to access its settings.

3. To assign the appropriate colors to the Radial Color gradient, change the start flag color to RGB (**255,160,20**). Click to add a flag at Pos=25 and change its color to RGB (**230,65,15**). Change the end flag's color value to RGB (**230,65,15**) to match the flag at Pos=25 (see Figure 9.27).

Figure 9.27   The Glow effect with the proper Radial Color gradient.

The Radial Transparency gradient needs to be animated, dissolving the effect on between frames 120 and 180.

4. Open the Track View and expand the Video Post\Lens Effects Glow\Radial Transparency\Flag #1\Color track. Select Flag #1's Color title to highlight the track and make it easy to see (see Figure 9.28).

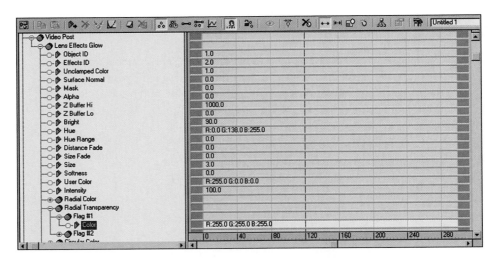

Figure 9.28   Track View with the Video Post\Lens Effects Glow\Radial Transparency\Flag #1\Color track expanded.

5. Click Zoom Horizontal Extents, activate Add Keys, and add keys at frame 120 and frame 180 (see Figure 9.29).

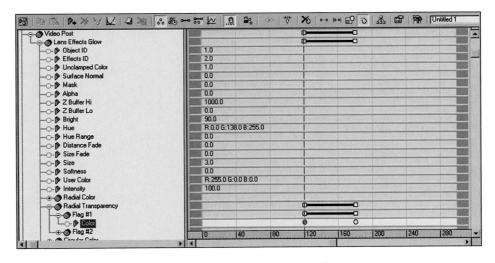

Figure 9.29   Keys added to Flag #1's color track at frames 120 and 180.

We need to change the color of the flag, animating from black at frame 120 to white at 180. Currently both keys contain a value of white.

6. Right-click the key at frame 120 to open the Color dialog box. Change the color to RGB (**0,0,0**) (see Figure 9.30). Then close the Color dialog box.

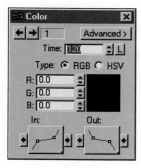

Figure 9.30   The Color dialog box with an RGB setting of (0,0,0) for key 1.

The Glow effect's dissolve transition is complete. The Glow effect will slowly appear between frames 120 and 180 and remain throughout the remainder of the animation.

7. Save your work as **ch09-05.max**.

Exercise 9.9   Adding Pizzazz with Inferno

To add a sense of mystery to the Glow effect as it appears, we will add a gaseous effect to the glow that will surround the Logo object. We will use Inferno to create this effect.

1. Make sure ch09-05.max is loaded. Advance to frame 180 and open the Lens Effects Glow dialog box. Check to ensure the VP Queue and Preview buttons are active. (If you didn't closed the Lens Effects Glow dialog box after you saved your work in the previous exercise, you will need to click the Update button after you advance to frame 180 to re-render the scene.)

2. To set up the Inferno effect, click the Inferno tab to view its settings. Check Red, Green, and Blue to activate the effect (see Figure 9.31).

3. Set Motion to **0**. We don't want the effect to move throughout the scene.

   The Speed value is currently 1. The Speed value refers to the gaseous turbulence of the effect. The default value of 0 is too high.

4. To slow the turbulence down, change Speed to **.35**.

   The Radial Density gradient of the Inferno effect determines how much of the Inferno effect is applied to the glow. A white color will cause the Inferno effect to be applied at 100%; a black color will create an invisible Inferno effect. We will animate the Radial Density gradient to change the intensity of the Inferno effect from 100% at frame 180 to 0% at frame 210. Remember, the Glow effect will be seen only from frames 120 onward.

5. Open the Track View and expand the Video Post\Lens Effects Glow\Inferno Radial Density track. Open the Flag #1 and Flag #2 tracks to display their Color tracks (see Figure 9.32).

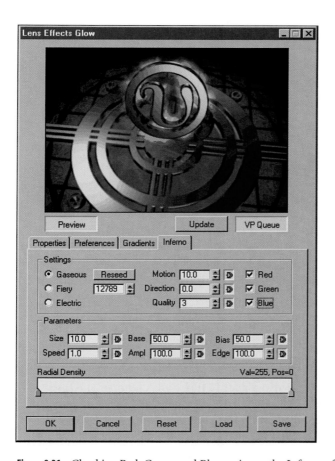

Figure 9.31   Checking Red, Green, and Blue activates the Inferno effect.

6. Click Zoom Horizontal Extents to view the entire length of the animation. Activate Add Keys and create keys at frames 180 and 210 in both color tracks (see Figure 9.33).

The color of all four keys is white—RGB (**255,255,255**). We need to change the color of the keys at frame 210 to black—RGB (**0,0,0**).

7. Right-click each key at frame 210 to open its Color dialog box, and then change the color to RGB (**0,0,0**) (see Figure 9.34).

The color of the Radial Density now changes from white to black between frames 180 and 210. The creation of the Glow effect is complete.

8. Close the Lens Effects Glow dialog box.

Because the Glow effect will be visible only between frames 120 and 300, we will instruct the Video Post queue to calculate Lens Effects Glow between those frames.

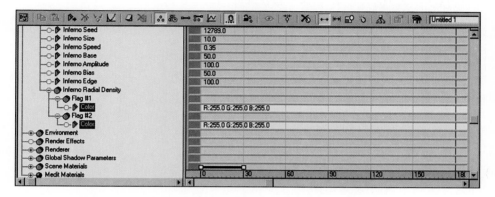

Figure 9.32   The Color tracks for Flag #1 and Flag #2.

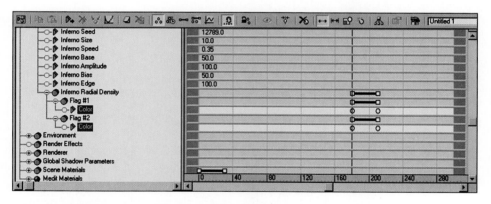

Figure 9.33   The Color tracks with keys added at frames 180 and 210.

9. Double-click the Lens Effects Glow event in the Video Post dialog box to open the Edit Filter Event dialog box. Change the VP Start Time to **120** (see Figure 9.35). Then click OK to exit the dialog box.

10. Save your work as **ch09-06.max**.

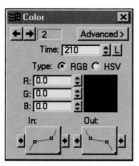

Figure 9.34   The Color dialog box for both keys at frame 210.

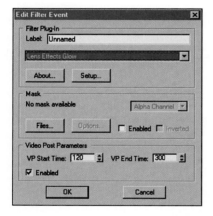

Figure 9.35   The Edit Filter Event dialog box with correct settings.

In Summary

This completes the creation of the Glow effect around the logo. The gaseous Glow effect begins to appear around the logo at frame 120. At frame 180, the Glow effect reaches its full intensity. Between frames 180 and 210, the Inferno gaseous effect disappears, leaving behind a solid Glow effect.

In the next chapter, we will apply the lens flares to the queue and finish the animation. This animation is really coming together.

Chapter 10

Creating the Lens Effects Flare for V

Lens flares are often described as "the most overused effect" in animation. The problem with effects such as lens flares is that most animators don't know how to use these effects appropriately in their scenes.

A flare that stands out like a sore thumb is often the result. If you remember the correct way to apply lens flares, you can create a successful animation. Moderation and subtlety are the keys.

You think to yourself, "I can't wait to see the animated effects to the scene before doing a test render of the entire animation!" Knowing that time is of the essence, you decide to push forward and add the Lens Effects Flare to the scene. You wouldn't want Mr. Boss to stop by only to see you with your feet up on the desk and have to explain you are rendering tests. Looking at the storyboard, you know that adding the Flare effects is going to be a cinch, and it won't be long before you can see the entire animation rendered in all its glory.

Pre-Thinking the Scene and Planning the Effect

Before we jump right in and start adding Lens Effects Flare events to the Video Post queue, we should examine the storyboard and plan the flare effects (see Figure 10.1).

A quick glance at Panel 1 shows us that there are no flare effects during the first frames of the animation. Panel 2 illustrates five separate flare effects. The first is in the center of the logo; the other four represent the light emanating from the beacon objects. Panels 3 and 4 show that the center flare dissipates; however, the beacon objects remain.

Let's think through our scene and analyze when everything is to take place. A breakdown of the scene's animation follows:

- *Frames 0–60:* The camera trucks slowly to the left and remains high above the logo. This is the pre-roll.
- *Frames 60–240:* The camera pedestals down, while continuing its truck leftward. At frame 240, the pedestal motion stops.
- *Frames 240–300:* The camera continues a slow truck leftward at a low angle, adding pad to the animation.

Now let's examine the glow effect around the logo, which we applied in the last chapter:

- *Frames 0–120:* No glow effect appears.
- *Frames 120–180:* The glow effect transitions into the scene. The glow effect remains full strength between frames 180–300.
- *Frames 180–210:* The Inferno effect applied to the glow diminishes, leaving a solid glow effect surrounding the logo.

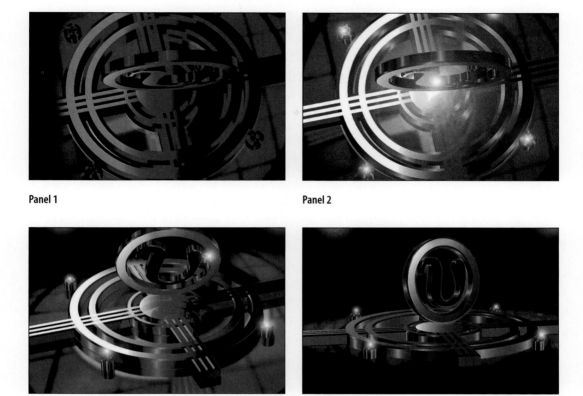

Panel 1

Panel 2

Panel 3

Panel 4

Figure 10.1 The storyboard you've been assigned.

Keeping these vital animation events in mind, we must determine the most logical frames to apply the flare events to, creating overlapping action and interest in the scene. The flare effects need to add interest in the scene, but should not take interest away from the scene.

The Beacon Flares

The flares that appear above the beacon objects should be accents, not primary points of interest in the scene. We must devise a way to disguise their transition into the scene. If we don't successfully conceal their transition, we will actually call the viewer's attention to them; but we want the viewer to be looking at the logo. If the center flare appears first (at frame 30), we will be able to bring the beacon flares on at frame 60, and they will be hidden under cover of the center flare.

The Center Flare

Notice in Panel 2 that the center flare effect is in the middle of the logo object, calling the viewer's attention to the animation and the logo object. The center flare is not an accent; it is a vital event that occurs that tells the viewer "Here comes the animation." The center flare can be compared to the first big firework that is launched on July 4th to say, "Here comes the display!"

We decided that the center flare should appear at frame 30. When should it disappear? By Panel 3, the center flare effect is gone.

Earlier, when we were positioning the highlights on the object in the scene, we learned the importance of overlapping action. So far, our scene has plenty of overlapping action, keeping the animation from going stale. What can we overlap the center flare with to continue the fluidity of the animation?

What if we overlap the end of the center flare with the start of the glow around the logo object? Looking at Panel 3 of the storyboard we can see that neither the glow nor the flare is present. If we did overlap the center flare with the glow around the logo, we wouldn't be sticking to the storyboard. If we decide to breach the storyboard, we'd better have a good explanation in case the issue comes up when the animation is finished.

Overlapping the center flare effect and the glow effect surrounding the logo creates more than overlapping action; it also creates visual contrast. The center flare appears on top of the logo object, and the glow surrounds the logo—creating the illusion that the glow is behind the logo. Overlapping the flare and the glow creates a visual transition for the logo from background to foreground. Overlapping action is one more trick to keep in mind; it helps create the impression that this simple scene is complicated.

Here is how the center flare will be applied to the scene:

- *Frames 30–90:* The center flare effect appears.
- *Frames 90–120:* The center flare appears at full strength.
- *Frames 120–180:* The center flare dissolves out at the same rate the logo glow transitions in, creating a smooth transition and fluid, overlapping action.

Preparing the Scene

Now that we have planned out the timing for the flare effects, we should prepare the scene for the second rendering pass.

Making Adjustments to the Scene

Because we are reaching the end of this project and are almost ready to render the final animation, we should examine our scene and make sure everything is correctly configured.

In the last chapter, we decided we would remove all the objects from our scene (except for the logo object) in order to have clean Alpha Perimeter information for the Lens Effects Glow effect. This means that we need to re-render the logo object over the rendered frames of the scene. This is certainly counter-productive, but it's the only way to create the clean glow effect.

Exercise 10.1   The Logo Object

Because the logo was already rendered in the first pass, we are rendering the logo object again only to obtain its edge information. We can apply a different texture to the logo object, making it transparent over the environment background but still creating the Perimeter Alpha information we need for the glow effect.

1. Load ch09-06.max, the scene you created in the last chapter. Open the Material
    Editor and activate the Logo material preview slot. Click the Type: Multi/Sub-
    Object button to open the Material/Map Browser. Choose Matte/Shadow (see
    Figure 10.2) and click OK to close the Browser.

Figure 10.2   The Material/Map Browser with the Matte/Shadow type selected.

The material preview slot becomes empty, and the Logo object turns white in the shaded Camera01 viewport.

The Matte/Shadow is a material type generally applied to objects that simulate elements of the background image. Matte/Shadow is used to create a matte and shadows for objects that were shot on film and weren't created in the 3D scene. However, we can use the Matte/Shadow material type on the logo because it renders quickly and retains the Perimeter Alpha information of the object in the rendering.

2. Close the Material Editor and save your work as **ch10-01.max**.

Creating the Nodes for the Lens Effects Flare Effect

The Lens Effects Flare needs a node, or source, to know where to apply the flare effects for the four beacons and the center of the logo. A node can be a geometry object, shape, or even a helper object. Because the scene has only the logo object in it, we need to add five nodes into the scene to enable Lens Effects Flare to apply the flare effect.

Exercise 10.2   Creating Nodes for the Beacon Nodes

Because the beacon objects are rendered in the scene we already rendered, we don't want to re-render them. Instead, we will position Point helpers above the beacon objects and hide the beacon objects, leaving the Point helpers visible in the scene. The Point helpers will then be the nodes for the flare effect.

1. Make sure ch10-01.max is loaded. To position the Point helpers, we need to unhide the Beacon objects. From the Display panel, click Unhide by Name to open the Unhide Objects dialog box. Select the four Beacon objects (see Figure 10.3) and click Unhide to close the dialog box and unhide the objects. Click Zoom Extents All to make the beacon objects visible in the viewports.

   Now we will create the Point helpers, which will be the nodes for the beacon flares.

2. Open the Create/Helpers panel, choose Point, and create four Point helpers at these points:

   Point 1: XYZ [**–122,–122,17**]

   Point 2: XYZ [**–122,122,17**]

   Point 3: XYZ [**122,122,17**]

   Point 4: XXZ [**122,–122,17**]

   The Point helpers should be centered to and slightly above the beacon objects.

Note

When we created the first Point helper, the dummy objects that control the camera became visible in the scene. When we finish creating the Point helpers for the beacon objects, we can hide the dummy objects and the beacon objects.

3. Select the four beacon objects and two dummy objects. Then, from the Display panel, click Hide Selected. This leaves only the logo object and point helpers visible in the scene (see Figure 10.4).

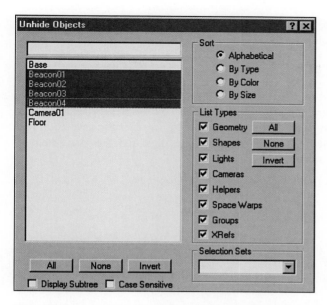

Figure 10.3   The Unhide Objects dialog box with the four beacon objects selected.

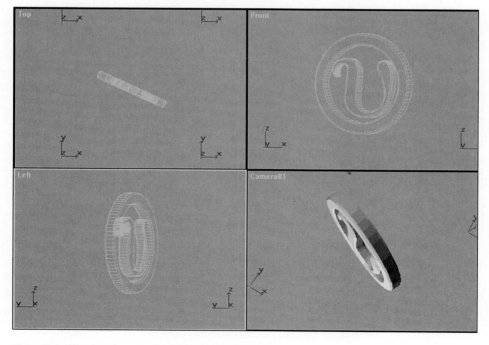

Figure 10.4   The four beacon Point helpers in the scene.

Exercise 10.3   Creating the Center Flare Node

We learned earlier that we could use any object in the 3D scene as a node of the flare effect. In theory, we could use the logo as the node to generate the flare effect; however, we want to precisely position the node.

Looking at Panel 2 of the storyboard, we can see that the flare node should be at the lowest interior curve of the V. If you designed your own logo, you will need to decide where to place the Point helper; make sure it is directly visible throughout the animation and isn't obscured by the logo at any time. If the point becomes obscured, the flare effect will occlude and create an undesirable effect.

1. Create a Point helper in the desired position (see Figure 10.5). Name this Point helper **Point-Logo**.

    The XYZ [**8,–7,70**] position works well in my scene.

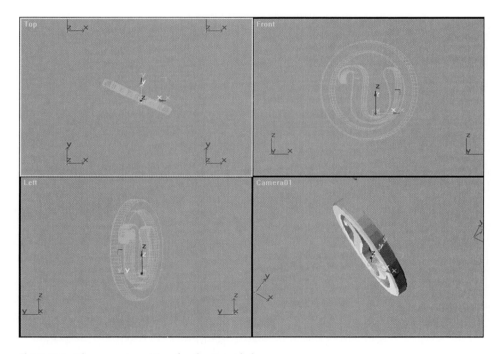

Figure 10.5   The correct position for the Point helper.

2. Shuttle through the animation and make sure the logo object does not obscure the Point helper during the animation. If the object does obscure the Point helper, try a different position until it is visible throughout the animation.

3. Save your work as **ch10-02.max**.

We are finished creating the nodes for the Lens Effects Flare effects in the scene.

Exercise 10.4   Checking the Background Environment

Before we can safely finish the scene, we need to check the settings for the background image that is applied to the scene. Currently, the rendered frames of the scene are loaded using Screen mapping as the background. We should quickly examine its settings to make sure everything is going to render correctly.

1. With ch10-02.max loaded, open the Rendering/Environment dialog box and the Material Editor. Drag the Environment Map button from the Environment dialog box to the first material preview slot in the second row of the Material Editor, replacing the old Env Environment Map. From the Instance (Copy) Map dialog box, choose Instance and click OK to exit. Name the map **Background.**

   In the Coordinates rollout, the Blur value is **1.** A slight blur is being applied to our background image.

2. Change the Blur value to **0.01** to restore the original integrity of the image.

3. Save your work as **ch10-03.max.** Close the Material Editor and the Environment dialog box.

Now we are ready to apply the Lens Effects Flare effects to our scene.

Adding the Beacon Flares

With the scene properly configured, we can begin to add the Lens Effects Flare events to the Video Post queue. Earlier, we determined that the beacon flares would appear at frame 60. Once we create the correct effect, we will need to animate its transition into the scene.

Exercise 10.5   Adding the Flare Event

Because all the beacon objects are the same, we can create one Lens Effects Flare event for all four of them.

1. With ch10-03.max open, open the Video Post dialog box (see Figure 10.6).

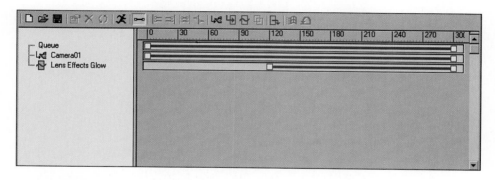

Figure 10.6 The Video Post dialog box.

There are currently two events in the queue: the Camera01 scene input event and the Glow effect that we created in the last chapter. Let's add a Lens Effects Flare track to the queue, creating the beacon flares.

2. Make sure neither track is selected and click the Add Image Filter Event button to open the Add Image Filter Event dialog box. From the Filter Plug-In list, select Lens Effects Flare. The effect is going to start at frame 60, so we can adjust the filter event accordingly. Enter VP Start Time of **60** and name the event **Flare Beacon**, and then click OK to close the dialog box. The Video Post queue should look like Figure 10.7.

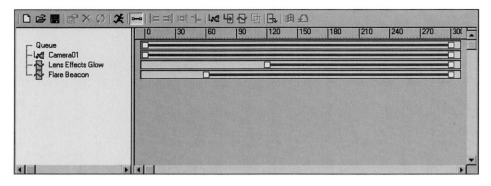

Figure 10.7   The Video Post queue at this point.

3. Advance to frame 150. Double-click the Flare Beacon event title to open the Edit Filter Event dialog box, and click Setup to open the Lens Effects Flare dialog box.

4. Click the Node Sources button to open the Select Flare Objects dialog box, select Point01, Point02, Point03, and Point04, and click OK to close the dialog box.

5. Activate VP Queue and Preview to preview the effect (see Figure 10.8).

That certainly isn't subtle, is it? We will need to change some of the settings to create the desired flare.

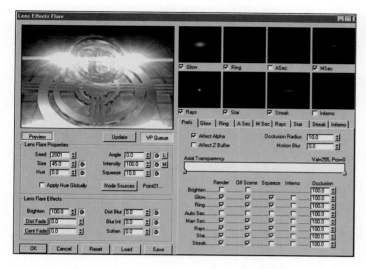

Figure 10.8   The scene preview in the Lens Effects Flare dialog box.

Exercise 10.6   Customizing the Flare Effect

We will need to turn off some of the features of Lens Effects Flare to create the intended effect.

1. In the Prefs tab of the dialog box, uncheck all the Squeeze boxes. Squeeze compresses the circular flare effect, creating an oval.

    Occlusion helps the flare effect disappear when the source node moves behind an object. We don't want that to take place.

2. Set every Occlusion value to **0** (see Figure 10.9).

    Now we will deactivate all the elements of the flare except for Glow. This will allow us to adjust the Glow effect by itself to ensure its quality.

3. In the Render column, uncheck all the flare elements except for Glow (see Figure 10.10).

Note

The Off Scene checkboxes instruct Lens Effects to apply the flare effect to source nodes that do not appear in the camera's view.

We will now adjust the glow's settings in the Glow tab.

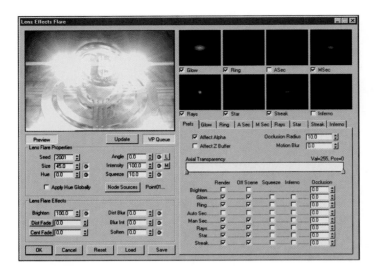

Figure 10.9   The Lens Effects Flare Prefs to this point.

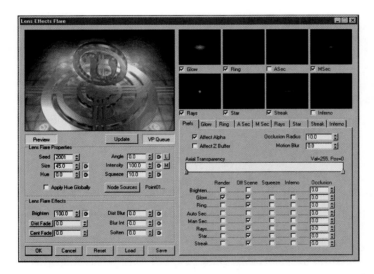

Figure 10.10   The Lens Effects Flare dialog box with only Glow Render checked.

4. Click the Glow tab to view its settings. Because the size of the glow effect is too large, enter a Size value of **60** to make the glow smaller.

    Looking at the storyboard, we can see that the glow should have a white center, and as the glow radiates outward, it should change to a red/orange color.

5. To create the appropriate colors of the glow, enter these values in the Radial Color gradient:

    Flag Pos: 0 RGB (**255,255,255**)

    Flag Pos: 40 RGB (**240,140,5**)

    Flag Pos: 100 RGB (**230,50,25**)

    The glow is too bright. We need to make it less obvious.

6. Enter these values in the Radial Transparency gradient:

    Flag Pos: 0 RGB (**200,200,200**)

    Flag Pos: 60 RGB (**60,60,60**)

    Flag Pos: 100 RGB (**0,0,0**)

    The Glow effect isn't so bright now. If anything, it looks too large; let's make it even smaller.

7. Change Size to **40** (see Figure 10.11).

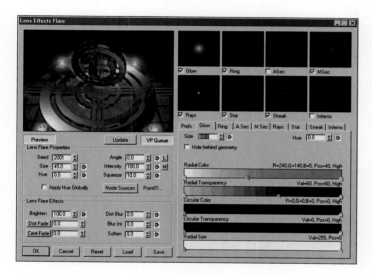

Figure 10.11 The finished Glow effect.

We will now add the Ring effect to the Flare.

8. Open the Prefs tab and check Render for Ring. Click the Ring tab to view its settings.

    The Ring effect is a little hard to see; we need to adjust the Radial Transparency.

9. To make the effect brighter, change the Radial Transparency gradient to these values:

    Flag Pos: 0 RGB (**0,0,0**)

    Flag Pos: 20 RGB (**65,65,65**)

    Flag Pos: 100 RGB (**0,0,0**)

10. Delete one of the flags by dragging it off the gradient and releasing the mouse button. The ring preview should look like Figure 10.12.

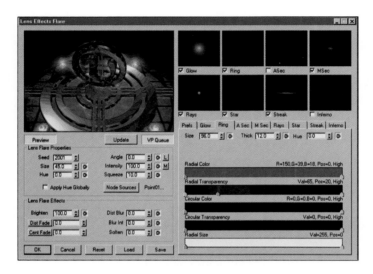

Figure 10.12   The ring effect so far.

11. The rings are still a little too large. To make the rings smaller, change Size to **40**. The rings now match the size of the rings on the storyboard. The preview should now look like Figure 10.13.

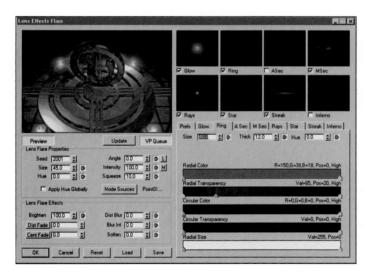

Figure 10.13   The finished Ring effect.

Using Secondaries

Secondaries are effects of light that are created when light passes through the lens of a camera. Think back to those campy 1980s dance programs. Remember those low angle shots of a person dancing with the studio lights visible in the shot? If you weren't too distracted examining the fresh moves the person was busting, you may have noticed the small circles of light formed by the studio lights shining directly into the camera. Those circles of light are called *secondaries*.

Exercise 10.7   Adding Secondaries

Let's apply secondaries now.

1. To activate Manual Secondaries, in the Prefs tab check Render for Man Sec (see Figure 10.14).

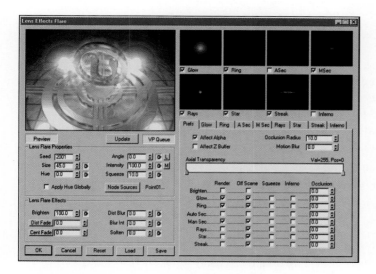

Figure 10.14   Manual Secondaries is checked, which activates them.

The preview becomes "hot" (meaning bright) because of the number, size, and strength of the default manual secondaries. Let's delete the secondaries, leaving only one to work with.

2. Click the M Sec tab to view its settings. Click the arrow pointing to the left (it's next to the text "Man Sec 1") to move to "Man Sec 6." Click the Del button five times to delete Man Secs 6 through 2 (the order progresses backward). The preview looks less bright now (see Figure 10.15).

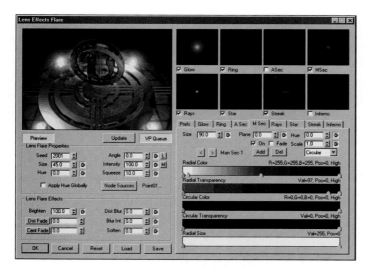

Figure 10.15   The Lens Effect Flare dialog box with only one manual secondary.

We need to adjust the Plane value of the secondary. It is currently 0, which means it is precisely over the node source of the effect. To understand how the Plane value of the secondaries works, imagine a straight line striking through the node source and the exact center of the screen. A positive value will move the secondary towards (or beyond) the center of the screen. A negative Plane value moves the secondary along that line further away from the center of the screen.

3. To adjust the Plane of Man Sec 1, enter a Plane value of **–200**. You will see the faint white glow of the secondary to the outside edge of the nodes.

4. To make the secondary the correct size, color, and shape, enter these values:

    Size: **30**

    Radial Color:

    >   Flag Pos: 0 RGB (**255,0,0**)
    >
    >   Flag Pos: 100 RGB (**255,150,0**)

    Radial Transparency:

    >   Flag Pos: 0 RGB (**0,0,0**)
    >
    >   Flag Pos: 75 RGB (**0,0,0**)
    >
    >   Flag Pos: 90 RGB (**25,25,25**)
    >
    >   Flag Pos: 100 RGB (**0,0,0**)

    The dialog box and preview should look like Figure 10.16.

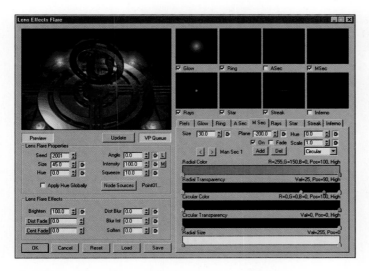

Figure 10.16 The correct settings and preview for Man Sec 1.

We will add one more secondary to the flare.

5. To add another secondary, click the Add button. (The new secondary will be Man Sec 7. However, there are only two secondaries in the effect, not 7. The Add button adds flares sequentially, assuming the first six are still there.)

6. To create the new secondary, enter these values:

   Size: **12**

   Plane: **–350**

   Radial Color:

   > Flag Pos: 0 RGB (**250,160,0**)
   >
   > Flag Pos: 100 RGB (**250,160,0**)

   Radial Transparency

   > Flag Pos: 0 RGB (**0,0,0**)
   >
   > Flag Pos: 70 RGB (**0,0,0**)
   >
   > Flag Pos: 85 RGB (**25,25,25**)
   >
   > Flag Pos: 100 RGB (**0,0,0**)

This creates an almost invisible secondary that is smaller and further away from the source than the previous flare. The dialog box should now look like Figure 10.17.

We have finished creating the flare effect for the beacon objects. Now we must animate it as it transitions from off to on between frames 60 and 120.

7. To animate the transition on for the flare effect, open the Track View, expand the Video Post/Flare Beacon track, and click Zoom Horizontal Extents.

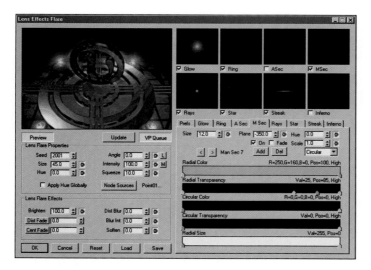

Figure 10.17   The Lens Effects Flare dialog box for Man Sec 7.

8. To add the keys to create the transition, activate Add Keys and click to add two keys in the Intensity track at frames 60 and 120 (see Figure 10.18).

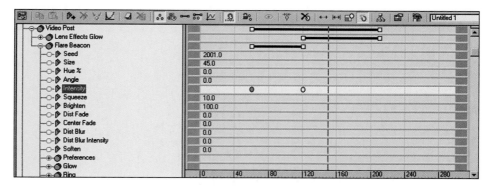

Figure 10.18   Keys have been added at frames 60 and 120 in the Intensity track.

Both keys currently are at 100% Intensity value. We need to change the value for the key at frame 60 so it will create the transition from 0% to 100%.

9. Right-click the key at frame 60 to open the Intensity dialog box and change the Value to **0**. Then close the Intensity dialog box and Track View.

10. Click OK to exit the Lens Effects Flare dialog box and save your work as **ch10-04.max**.

The beacon flares are now complete. In the next section, we will create the center flare effect.

Adding the Center Flare

When we examined the storyboard earlier, we decided the center flare would appear between frames 30 and 90, remain full strength between frames 90 and 120, and finally disappear between frames 120 and 180. The flare will be visible for five seconds, so it better look good.

If we were to apply a flare to the center node as we did with the beacon nodes, we'd have the same uneventful effect. With the beacon nodes, that effect was deliberate. We didn't want the beacon nodes to distract the viewer, so we made them plain and uneventful. The beacon nodes rely on the movement of the camera to obtain subtle manual secondary motion.

However, the center flare is a vital element in the scene; its purpose is to draw the viewer in. We will need to animate it, giving it more action in the scene. What we'll use is a *flare burst*, which means that all the elements of the flare will start in the center of the effect and move outward as the animation continues.

Before we can animate the center flare, however, we need to create it. We have a lot of work ahead of us, so we'd better get moving.

Exercise 10.8   Creating the Center Flare

Now that we have prepared for the center flare effect, we can apply it in the scene. To do so, we will need to add another Lens Effects Flare event to the Video Post queue.

1. Load ch10-04.max, advance to frame 150, and open the Video Post dialog box.

2. Click in a blank area to deselect all the event titles. Click Add Image Filter Event to open the Add Image Filter Event dialog box. Name this event **Flare Center**, choose Lens Effects Flare, enter a VP Start Time of **30** and VP End Time of **180**. Click OK to close the dialog box.

3. Double-click the Flare center event and click Setup to open the Lens Effects Flare dialog box. Click the Node Sources button to open the Select Flare Objects dialog box. Choose Point-Logo and click OK to close the dialog box. Then activate VP Queue and Preview to preview the scene.

   Now we need to deactivate all the elements except for glow, so we can make sense out of the elements. We just did the same thing for the beacon flares, so it will be easy.

4. In the Prefs tab, set all the Occlusion values to **0,** uncheck all the Squeeze boxes, and uncheck all the Render boxes except for Glow (as shown in Figure 10.19).

   We will create the glow first.

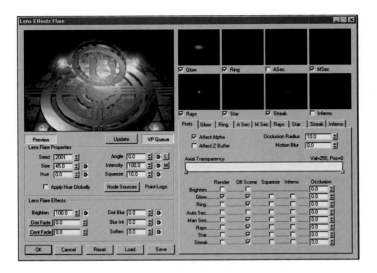

Figure 10.19   The Lens Effects Flare dialog box, displaying the correct Prefs panel.

5. Click the Glow tab to view its settings, and then enter these values:

Size: **75**

Radial Color:

Flag Pos: 0 RGB (**240,230,210**)

Flag Pos: 25 RGB (**235,145,25**)

Flag Pos: 100 RGB (**230,100,30**)

Radial Transparency:

Flag Pos: 0 RGB (**175,175,175**)

Flag Pos: 25 RGB (**150,150,150**)

Flag Pos: 100 RGB (**0,0,0**)

These settings will produce a subtle orange glow with a white core (see Figure 10.20).

Now we will create the Ring.

6. Click the Prefs tab to view its settings and check Render for Ring. Then click the Ring tab to open its settings and enter these values:

Size: **100**

Radial Color:

Flag Pos: 0 RGB (**150,40,20**)

Flag Pos: 75 RGB (**200,110,25**)

Flag Pos: 100 RGB (**150,40,20**)

Radial Transparency:

Flag Pos: 0 RGB (**0,0,0**)

Flag Pos: 75 RGB (**75,75,75**)

Flag Pos: 100 RGB (**0,0,0**)

The result is an orange ring the size of the vertical area of the preview window (see Figure 10.21).

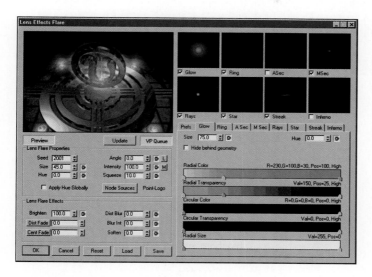

Figure 10.20   The Glow settings for the center flare.

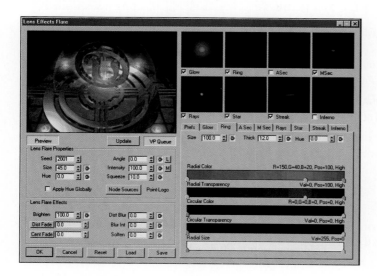

Figure 10.21   The correct settings for Ring.

Because this flare effect is going to be animated, we will create the keys for the elements of the flare as we create the elements themselves; that way we won't forget to animate any of the elements.

The manual secondaries will also be animated throughout the entire animation, so we should offset the animation of the ring to add variance and interest to the flare effect. We will animate the ring in the Track View.

7. Keep the Lens Effects Flare dialog box open, open the Track View, and click Zoom Horizontal Extents. Expand the Video Post/Flare Center/Ring track and locate the Size track (see Figure 10.22).

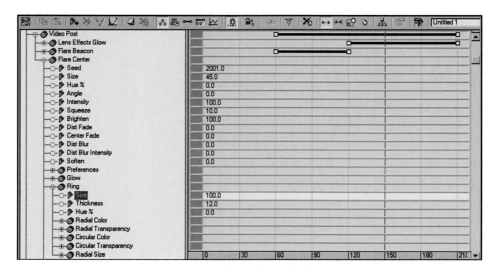

Figure 10.22   Track View with the Video Post/Flare Center track expanded.

Because the manual secondaries will be animated between frames 30 and 180, we will offset the growth of the ring to begin at frame 90 and end at 180.

8. In the Track View, activate Add Keys and click to add keys in the Size track at frames 90 and 180.

The size of the ring is currently 100. This is the maximum size we want it to be. To animate the size of the ring, we need to change only the Size value of the key at frame 90.

9. Right-click the key at frame 90 to open the Size dialog box and enter Value: **0**. Then close the Size dialog box and Track View.

The size of the ring is now animated to grow from 0 at frame 90 to 100 at frame 180. The ring is finished. This is a complex flare effect, so we should save it.

10. In the Lens Effects Flare dialog box, click Save and save your flare as **brst30-180.lzf**.

Now that the flare is finished, you can apply it to any scene by loading it and choosing a Node Source.

Creating Manual Secondaries

We will be adding four animated manual secondaries to the scene. We decided earlier that the flare effect would appear between frames 30 and 180. We will need to keep that in mind when we animate the manual secondaries.

Exercise 10.9   Getting Ready to Create Manual Secondaries

Adding animated manual secondaries to the flare effect will create interest and add action to the scene by creating a "bursting" flare effect. Before we can animate the secondaries, however, we need to create them.

1. In the Lens Effects Flare dialog box, click the Prefs tab and check Render Man Sec. Click the Man Sec tab to open it.

    In the Lens Effects Flare dialog box, the preview monitor has added the manual secondaries. However, the manual secondaries don't seem to be there; instead, the glow in the center got brighter (see Figure 10.23).

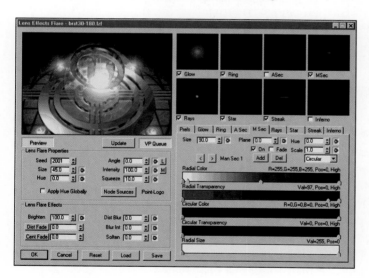

Figure 10.23   The Lens Effect Flare dialog box with manual secondaries active.

To learn why the center of the effect got brighter, instead of placing manual secondaries streaming from the flare, you need to think back to when we were learning about the Plane value. The secondaries are placed on an imaginary line that strikes through the node of the flare and the center of the screen. Because the node is practically in the center of the screen, the secondaries are placed near the node.

Notice the Scale value in the Man Sec panel. This value scales the position of the manual secondaries along the plane, and a larger value moves the secondaries further away. Let's change the Scale value.

2. **Change the Scale value to 5.** Entering the value of 5 increases the scaling of the secondaries along the plane, moving them further away from the source. We can see that the secondaries of the flare are now visible in the preview window (see Figure 10.24).

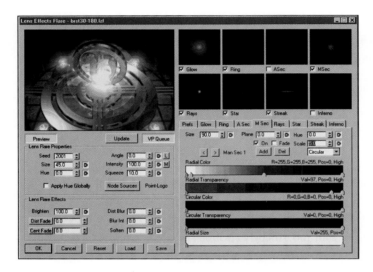

Figure 10.24 The Lens Effects Flare dialog box shows Man Sec with a Scale value of 5.

Exercise 10.10   Manual Secondary 1

Six manual secondaries are in the scene by default. We need only four. Therefore, we will delete 2 through 6 so we have only one to work with. Then we will create the additional ones. If you have time, it's always better to create your own; that way you know exactly what is going to happen.

1. Click the arrow pointing to the left to activate the settings for Man Sec 6. Click the Del button five times to delete Man Sec 6 through Man Sec 2. This leaves Man Sec 1. We will adjust its settings.

2. In the Man Sec panel for Man Sec 1, enter these values:

   Size: **70**

   Plane: **500**

   Radial Color:

   > Flag Pos: 0 RGB (**100,0,0**)
   >
   > Flag Pos: 70 RGB (**100,0,0**)

Flag Pos: 90 RGB (**255,90,0**)

Flag Pos: 100 RGB (**100,0,0**)

Radial Transparency:

Flag Pos: 0 RGB (**0,0,0**)

Flag Pos: 70 RGB (**0,0,0**)

Flag Pos: 90 RGB (**75,75,75**)

Flag Pos: 100 RGB (**0,0,0**)

This creates a large orange secondary below and to the left of the node (see Figure 10.25).

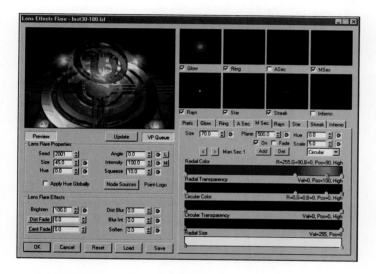

Figure 10.25   The settings for Man Sec 1.

Exercise 10.11   Manual Secondary 2

The second manual secondary we are creating is going to look exactly like the first, except it will have a negative Plane value, which will place it on the opposite side of the node. Although it is not possible to copy and paste manual secondaries in the dialog box, we can copy and paste the gradients, which speeds things up considerably.

1. Right-click the Radial Color gradient of Man Sec 1 and choose Copy.

2. To add another secondary to the dialog box, click the Add button to create Man Sec 7 (which is the second one; remember MAX still assumes there are six originals).

3. Right-click the Radial Color gradient of Man Sec 7 and choose Paste, pasting the Man Sec Radial Color gradient into the slot. Click the arrow pointing to the right to move to Man Sec 1's settings. Right-click the Radial Transparency gradient and choose Copy. Click the button pointing to the right to move to the set-

tings for Man Sec 7. Right-click the Radial Transparency gradient and choose Paste to paste the gradient into the slot. To finish the secondary, enter these values:

Size: **70**

Plane: **–500**

4. Click Save and save the flare effect as **brst30-180.lzf,** replacing the one you saved previously.

We now have identical manual secondaries on the two sides of the node (see Figure 10.26).

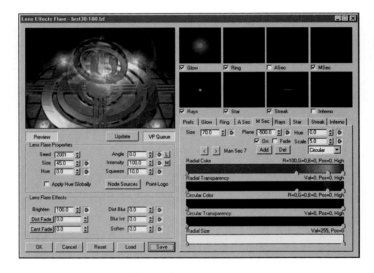

Figure 10.26   The flare effect to this point.

Exercise 10.12   Manual Secondary 3

We still have to create two more manual secondaries to complete the effect. Lens Effects Flare allows the user to create secondaries that are not of a circular shape; we will take advantage of that to create a star-shaped secondary.

1. To add another secondary to the effect, click Add, which adds Man Sec 8. Click the Circular drop-down menu and choose 5 Sides from the list. Enter these settings:

Size: **20**

Plane: **600**

Radial Color:

Flag Pos: 0 RGB (**255,220,40**)

Flag Pos: 10 RGB (**255,120,0**)

> Flag Pos: 85 RGB (**255,60,0**)
>
> Flag Pos: 100 RGB (**255,120,0**)

Radial Transparency:

> Flag Pos: 0 RGB (**120,120,120**)
>
> Flag Pos: 40 RGB (**0,0,0**)
>
> Flag Pos: 85 RGB (**50,50,50**)
>
> Flag Pos: 100 RGB (**0,0,0**)

These settings create a five-sided manual secondary with a bright star-shaped core and a five-sided exterior halo (see Figure 10.27).

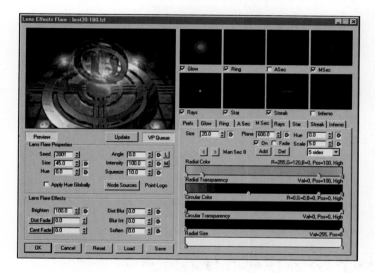

Figure 10.27   The Lens Effects Flare dialog box shows a five-sided secondary.

Exercise 10.13   Manual Secondary 4

We will duplicate manual secondary #3 to create manual secondary #4, except #4 will have a negative Plane value to balance out the effect.

1. Click the Add button to add another manual secondary to the effect. This creates Man Sec 9.

2. Click the left and right arrows to move between Man Sec 8 and 9. Then copy the Radial Color and Transparency gradients from Man Sec 8 and paste them in Man Sec 9. Change the Plane value to **–600** and change the shape to 5 Sides.

   The fourth manual secondary is applied in the upper-right area of the preview (see Figure 10.28).

3. Save the Lens Effects Flare effect as **brst30-180.lzf,** replacing the previous file. Click OK to close the Lens Effects Flare dialog box.

Animating the Manual Secondaries

The settings for the center flare effect are now correct, so we need to animate the settings to create the flare burst. Something interesting to keep in mind is that the Lens Effects Flare dialog box has green buttons next to each animatable parameter. The activated green button means that a particular value will be visible in the Track View. Personally, I do not deactivate any of those buttons because I like to see each parameter that can be animated; it inspires me to animate those parameters, which will hopefully create an exciting effect.

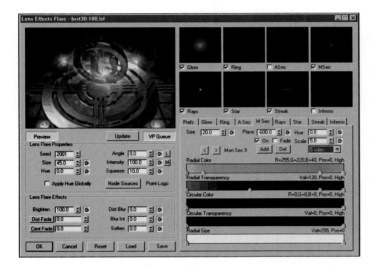

Figure 10.28   The complete flare effect before animation is applied to the secondaries.

Exercise 10.14   Animating Intensity

Earlier we decided that the flare effect would be visible and animated between frames 30 and 180. We need to keep that in mind as we animate the flare's parameters. The Ring is already animated, so all that's left is to animate the Intensity of the flare effect and the settings of the manual secondaries.

1. In the Track View, expand the Video Post/Flare Center track. Activate Add Keys and add keys to the Intensity's track at 30, 90, 120, and 180 (see Figure 10.29).

   We need to adjust the settings of the keys so the key values at 30 and 180 are zero. This is because the flare effect will not be seen before frame 30 or after frame 180.

2. Right-click the key at frame 30 to open the Intensity dialog box. Change the Value to **0.** Click the arrow pointing to the left to move to the key at frame 180 and change its value to **0.** Then close the Intensity dialog box.

   Now the intensity of the overall Lens Effects Flare effect is 0 at frame 30, 100 at frame 90 and frame 120, and 0 at frame 180. That's exactly what we want.

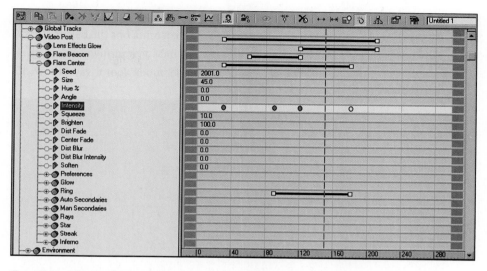

Figure 10.29   The Track View with correct keys added to the Flare Center's Intensity track.

Exercise 10.15   Animating Manual Secondaries 1, 2, 3, and 4

Now we will animate the manual secondaries.

1. Expand the Video Post/Flare Center/Man Secondaries track. From there, expand the Man Sec 1, 7, 8, and 9 tracks. To view all four of the secondaries, you will have to maximize the Track View.

   The secondaries need to be animated so that they are in the center of the effect (on the node) at frame 30 and are at the distance we assigned in the Lens Effects Flare dialog box at frame 180. To achieve this, we will add keys to the Plane track and modify their settings.

2. Activate Add Keys and add keys to each of the Man Secs' Plane tracks at frames 30 and 180 (see Figure 10.30).

   With the keyframes in the correct positions, all we need to do is change each keyframe at 30's value to 0.

3. Right-click each of the four keys you just added to frame 30 separately, and in each of their Plane dialog boxes, change Value to **0**.

   Now each of the manual secondaries is at Plane 0 at frame 30 when the flare effect becomes visible. The values will animate between frames 30 and 180. When the animation reaches frame 180, each manual secondary will be in the position we assigned it in the Lens Effects Flare dialog box.

4. Close the Track View.

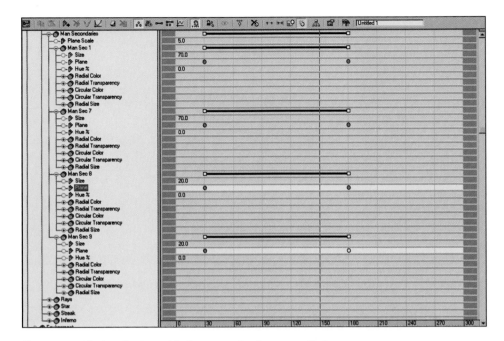

Figure 10.30 The Track View with the correct keyframes applied.

Finishing Up the Scene

Believe it or not, we are finished animating this scene. All that's left is to save the animated flare effect in the Lens Effects Flare dialog box and add an Output Image Event to the Video Post dialog box. Then we can render our scene and revel in the fruits of our labor.

Exercise 10.16   Animating and Rendering the Scene

Let's save the animated Lens Effects Flare and render the scene.

1. Double-click the Flare Center event in the Video Post dialog box and click Setup to open the Lens Effects Flare dialog box. Click Save and save the flare as **brst30-180.lzf**, replacing the previous saves. Click OK to close the Lens Effects Flare dialog box.

   Now we need to add the Output Image Event to the queue, which will save the rendered scene.

2. Make sure no events are selected in the Video Post queue. Click Add Image Output Event to open the Add Image Output Event dialog box. Click the Files button and navigate to your output image directory (ch10\images). Name the file **done.avi** and click Save. Adjust the desired Compression Quality; if you're using Microsoft Video 1 driver, a Compression Quality of **85** will work well (see Figure 10.31). Click OK to close the dialog box, and then click OK to exit the Add Image Output Event dialog box.

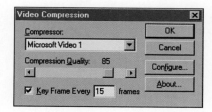

Figure 10.31 The Video Compression dialog box.

3. Save your work as **ch10-05.max**.

4. To render the queue, click Execute Sequence. In the Execute Video Post dialog box, enter the desired Output Size of **320×240** and click Render to render the queue.

That's all, folks. We've finished the project, and now we can sit back and take a long look at what we've accomplished (see Figure 10.32).

Figure 10.32 The completed V.

Real World Case Studies

Chapter 11

Weekend Magazine

Sam Mandragona, the Creative Director, approached me and asked me to start thinking about creating an open animation for *Weekend Magazine*. The animation needed to match the feel of Dateline, because *Weekend Magazine* was to capture the "Best of Dateline" episodes for the week.

Joe Dettmore, the Assistant Creative Director, designed a polished logo and a rough environment for the logo to live in.

Resolving Design and Pre-Production Issues

Together, Sam, Joe, and I started roughing out ideas and color compositions for the animation. We decided that the background environment should consist of a futuristic ring with globes attached at the north, south, east, and west positions. With this in mind, I started roughing out the motion of the animation. I created *stand-in objects* for use in these motion tests. The reason for using stand-in objects is twofold: to make sure the animation will be effective and to avoid wasting time creating the actual objects only to find out the animation isn't effective.

An example of one of these motion tests is included on the CD (ch11\zjoetest1.max). If you load this file into MAX, you will notice that the objects are Standard Primitives: geospheres, boxes, and a tube. This was the very first motion test I created to illustrate my intended motion to Sam and Joe. I asked them to pretend the box in the center of the ring was the NBC peacock, and the two larger boxes that slide in were the two panels the logo appears on. The progression of the animation starts with the camera low and under the ring/globe object. As the camera rises, the peacock rotates to become sandwiched between the large logo boxes (see Figure 11.1). This was created with the intent that the peacock should be the red line separating the two large logo panels.

I created this motion test in a few minutes with Sam and Joe looking over my shoulder. It was enough to know that the objects Joe had envisioned for the animation would work well together. Therefore, I began fine-tuning my tests and creating the production geometry for the animation.

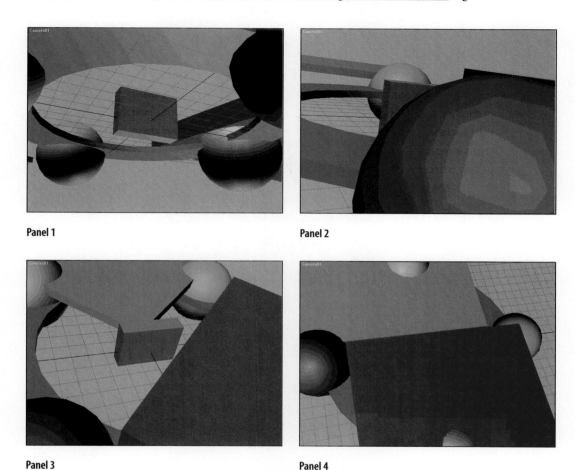

Panel 1

Panel 2

Panel 3

Panel 4

Figure 11.1   The progression of my first motion test.

Creating the Animation

Through the rough tests I created, we knew that everything in the animation was balanced and would create an interesting animation. However, because the look of the animation was not storyboarded or created in color, it was up to me to add color and polish Joe's concept.

As usual, I decided to separate the animation into layers. The first layer would be the background with the ring and globes. The second layer would be the logo elements.

Because I had a strong grasp of what the animation should be, I began to create the objects that would be used in the final animation.

Building the Background

The background layer for the animation consisted of the ring, globes, NBC peacock, and environment. I started building the scene.

The Ring

It took several tries to get the ring object "just right." I started by creating a tube primitive and applying an Edit Mesh modifier. I selected the top and bottom polygons of the tube, extruded them, and scaled the extruded faces to create a bevel. I created several bevels this way to get the correct profile. When I had the correct shape for the object, I selected faces and applied different Material IDs to the faces so I could apply different materials to individual faces without using bitmap textures (see Figure 11.2).

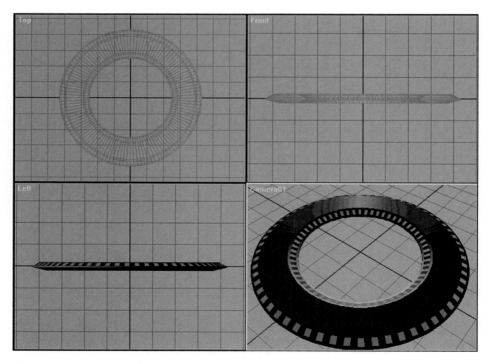

Figure 11.2 The first phase of the ring object.

The next part was the tricky part. Removing the notches for the globes. I created a circle shape and applied a Bevel modifier. The bevel was created in reverse (see Figure 11.3) so I could use a Boolean operation on the tube to remove the notch and create the bevel.

I placed four of these beveled circles in the correct positions to create the notches. Then I converted the tube into a Boolean Compound Object and selected the notch objects, subtracting the notches from the tube (see Figure 11.4).

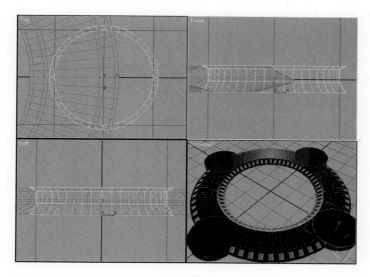

Figure 11.3 The beveled circle shapes that cut the notches from the ring.

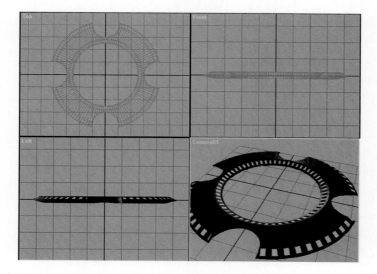

Figure 11.4 The ring object with the notches subtracted.

This took a few attempts to achieve the desired result. Once the ring was precisely the way I wanted it to be, I applied another Edit Mesh modifier, selected the newly created faces from the Boolean subtraction, and applied the appropriate Material IDs to them.

Next, I applied a total of nine sub-materials to the ring object. The shader for all the materials was Metal. The top surface of the ring (the one that faces forward when the animation resolves), is a 75% transparent, metallic dark blue material. The material on the bottom of the ring object (the side of the ring that is visible during the beginning of the animation) is double-sided. The Facing material is a light blue/silver material with a sky bitmap applied as a reflection. The Back material has a dark blue textured surface that is visible through the transparent top face of the ring object. The material on the bevels is a light blue/silver material with the same sky bitmap used as a reflection. The boxes surrounding the ring, which look like windows for a UFO, were created by alternating the Material IDs for every other face. A material was applied to one of the alternating Material IDs, along with self-illumination and a unique Material Effects ID, so that a Lens Effects Glow filter could be applied.

The Globes

The globes were easy. I used a continent object that a friend gave me a few years back. A gold material was created and applied to the continent objects. To create the oceans, I created geospheres slightly smaller than the continent objects. Then I applied a dark blue, heavily textured bitmap to the geosphere objects to create a rustic, yet hi-tech, ocean texture. Finally, I added another sphere primitive with a wireframe texture to create the latitude and longitude lines.

The Ring Burst

The straight lines that "burst" around the ring when the animation resolves were created from a rectangle shape with an Edit Mesh modifier applied to create the geometry. The rectangle object was then rotated and positioned where I wanted it to be on the ring object. I applied UVW Map coordinates to the rectangle object and instanced it around the ring object.

During the animation, the length value of the rectangle shape is animated to bring the lines into the ring object. Because the shape of the object was changing, the UVW Map coordinates also needed to be animated to match up with the size of the rectangle objects at each frame (see Figure 11.5). To accommodate that, I applied a yellow material to the rectangle shapes and applied an animated linear gradient map to make the "streaks" of light.

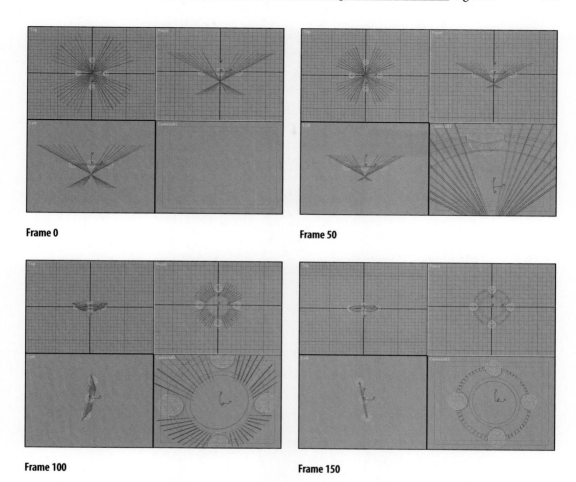

Frame 0

Frame 50

Frame 100

Frame 150

Figure 11.5   The progression of the animation, illustrating the size change of the rectangle burst objects.

The NBC Peacock

To create the NBC peacock, we applied a rounded bevel to two shapes: the outline and the feathers (see Figure 11.6). After creating the object, I applied an Edit Mesh modifier and placed Material IDs on the individual feathers to create the different colors. The material applied to the NBC peacock included a Metal shader and a Raytrace reflection.

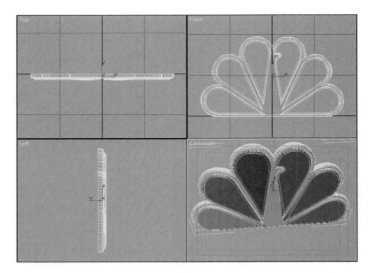

Figure 11.6   The NBC peacock.

The Environment

Creating the background for this project proved to be the most perplexing aspect of the animation. The background design needed to compliment the background and tie the whole mood together. One of the ideas I tried out was making a blue sky background with a grid (simulating TV monitors) as a background. Figure 11.7 shows that background.

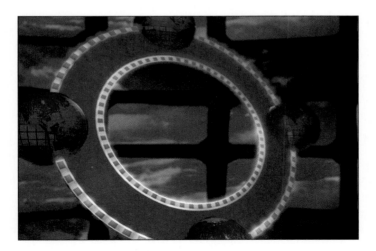

Figure 11.7   Sky/monitor background environment.

Although the background was acceptable because it matched the color and design, it was inappropriate because it took too much attention away from the ring object. I tried several ideas, such as making a grid of smaller spheres surrounding the ring object and making the background a brighter, complimentary color.

Finally, we decided to go with a wireframe grid surrounding the ring object. I created the grid with circle shapes and checked the Renderable option. Then I added an almost-black cloud bitmap as the Background Environment Map (see Figure 11.8).

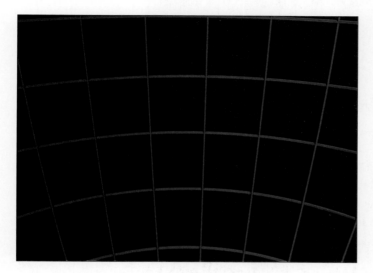

Figure 11.8   The wireframe sphere grid object and black cloud background from the final animation.

The Video Post Queue

The ring, globes, burst, and wireframe sphere grid were animated in the same scene. Before rendering the animation, I created a Video Post queue to add the glows to the "UFO windows" on the ring object and burst objects. A Lens Effect Flare event was then added to the queue to add the lens flare that appears during the beginning of the animation. Finally, the queue was rendered, completing the background for the logo.

Rendering the "Stinger"

Before the logo could be rendered over the background, I had to render the "stinger" burst that occurs as the logo resolves. I created the burst with a box primitive with planar UVW Map coordinates applied. The long box object was then instanced in a circular fashion from the imaginary "emitter" (see Figure 11.9).

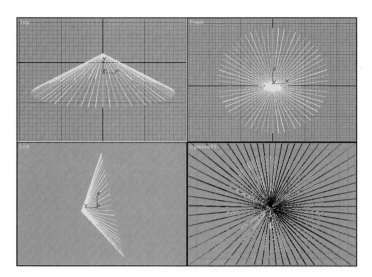

Figure 11.9   The MAX scene of the "stinger" burst.

To create the shooting star effect of the bursts, I added a yellow material with 100% self-illumination to the objects. I applied a linear gradient as an opacity map and unchecked Tiling. To animate the burst, the Offset coordinate value of the gradient was animated between frames 140 and 210. The burst objects were rotated to match the perspective of the ring object, which had already been rendered. This burst was rendered over the background image sequence of the ring and globes.

Creating the *Weekend Magazine* Logo

The background of the animation was complete. Because the logo objects were going to be animated in a separate scene, I needed to ensure the camera motion was exactly the same. I reset MAX and merged the camera into the fresh MAX scene. I then positioned the logo objects in their final position in the scene. When I was satisfied with the placement of the logo, I began to key its animation.

In the following sections, I will describe some of the notable features of the objects in the *Weekend Magazine* logo scene.

The Logo Text

To create the text objects of the logo, I applied a rounded bevel to the shapes of the text and applied an Edit Mesh modifier. I applied three different Material IDs to the face, bevel, and side of the rounded bevel text. Then I applied different sub-materials to those Material IDs to create contrast and interest.

Because the shape of the logo text was so rounded and a rounded bevel was applied, the scene contained too many polygons for me to preview the animation in real-time. If you view ch11\preview.avi on the accompanying CD, you will see that the mesh of the object is very simple and only vaguely resembles the actual rendered logo. Therefore, I applied an Optimize modifier to the text objects of the logo to simplify the mesh in the viewports. Notice in Figure 11.10 that Weekend is optimized.

Figure 11.10   The optimized Weekend mesh.

The Viewports option was set to use the L1 settings. The high Face and Edge Threshold values optimized the mesh to reduce faces in the viewport. The Renderer option was set to use the L2 settings (see Figure 11.11).

The 0 values assigned to the Face and Edge Threshold parameters instructed the Optimize modifier to not apply any optimization to the mesh at rendering time. By using these settings, I was able to work with optimized text objects in the real-time viewports, yet work with rendered unoptimized text objects in the final animation.

Figure 11.11   The unoptimized mesh that resulted from the L2 settings.

The Logo Panels

The panels behind the Weekend Magazine type were created from box primitives. An extruded NBC Peacock was linked as a sibling to the top panel. The stripes on the lower panel were created by applying a striped bitmap as the Glossiness map, using planar UVW Map coordinates.

The red line that "draws on" as the logo resolves was a box primitive with an animated width value.

The Shooters

I created the shooters that streak through the logo as it resolves with box primitives with planar UVW Map coordinates applied. I applied a yellow texture with a linear gradient in the opacity map channel. Then I assigned a unique Object ID to the shooter objects so that a Lens Effects Glow filter could be applied in Video Post.

Creating the Video Post for the Logo Objects

A simple Video Post queue was created for the logo objects. Using the unique Object ID of the shooter objects, a Lens Effects Glow filter was applied. Also, if you look carefully, you'll see large secondary flares in the upper-left corner of the screen after the logo resolves. These were created by a Lens Effects Flare filter in the queue.

A Final Word

The *Weekend Magazine* animation shown in Figure 11.12 was the first animation I created for MSNBC entirely with 3D Studio MAX. I created it over the course of two weeks, as I was juggling other projects that had to be completed. The layer, which included the raytraced NBC peacock object, took the longest to render (almost an hour per frame). *3D Design* magazine awarded the *Weekend Magazine* animation the 1998 Big Kahuna Award in the category of Best Logo/Corporate ID.

Figure 11.12   The completed animation.

Chapter 12

Upfront Tonight

Sam Mandragona, MSNBC Design's Creative Director, approached Vince Diga and myself to create the graphics package for CNBC's nightly news program, Upfront Tonight. Vince was in charge of designing the project, and I was called upon to create the 3D animation for the show's opener.

The feel and the look of the logo were mainly dictated by the *Upfront Tonight* set, which was constructed of metal and glass and has a very futuristic high-tech design (see Figure 12.1). We wanted the logo to reflect that feel, so we designed it to have those elements. Vince quickly began to draft some conceptual logo designs, and I started creating the 3D elements that Vince requested (see Figure 12.2).

Figure 12.1   Concept *Upfront Tonight* set design.

Figure 12.2   One of Vince's preliminary animation designs.

Vince collaborated with me as I created the globe element. The result was the earth in the center of a gyroscope. The earth has a glass outer shell with continents floating above, and in the center of it is a small mechanical metallic core. The colors used are mainly purples, blues, and turquoise to create a nighttime mood. The final look seemed mechanical, but very airy (see Figure 12.3).

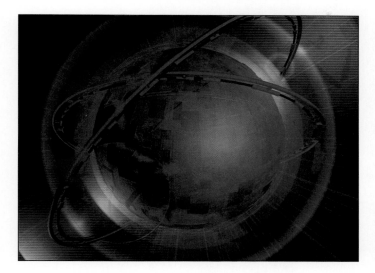

Figure 12.3   The globe exterior used in final production.

Pre-Production

While brainstorming and designing the animation, I was creating objects that helped Vince solidify the look of the animation. Helping Vince along with the design process saved me time because I used this geometry in the final animation. The globe object and gyroscope were completely built before I even started the animation.

The Globe Core

The core object was created from a Sphere primitive with an Edit Mesh modifier. Random polygons were selected, extruded, and assigned different Material IDs. The maps on the core object are a variety of dark blue rectangles of different sizes. Figures 12.4 and 12.5 show different views of the renderings.

Figure 12.4   Rendered globe exterior.

Figure 12.5   The globe object rendered without the hi-tech texture.

The Globe Core Atmosphere

The core's atmosphere was a sphere primitive slightly larger in size than the core sphere. I applied a two-sided material to the atmosphere object. The back material is a transparent glass material to which I applied a star field bitmap as a refraction map. This created the atmosphere for the hi-tech world. The facing material is a transparent material with a raytrace reflection map. This raytrace reflection is not obvious in the previous figures, but it is noticeable later in this section when the metal rings are applied (see Figures 12.6 and 12.7).

Figure 12.6   Only the core atmosphere rendered.

Figure 12.7   The globe core rendered with the atmosphere object.

The Globe Continents

Slightly larger than the atmosphere sphere is another sphere primitive with a continent opacity map. And surrounding the scene is a larger sphere primitive. This sphere creates the larger continents that envelop the scene (see Figures 12.8 and 12.9).

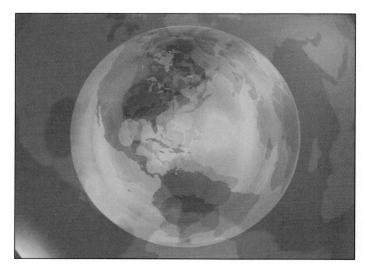

Figure 12.8   Only the globe continents rendered.

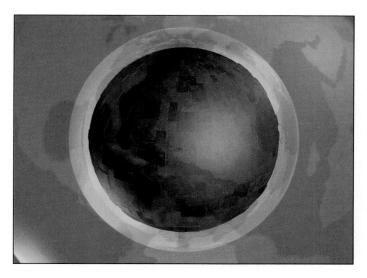

Figure 12.9   The globe continents rendered with the core and core atmosphere.

The Metal Rings

I created the metal rings with standard Torus primitives. I deleted the faces and scaled them to create the larger sections. The materials on the ring objects are red and blue ray-trace materials with a red transparency color applied to each. This red and blue color is obvious in Figures 12.10 and 12.11. However, in the final rendering the red color is not as apparent. That's because the red transparency color of the raytrace material type isn't as obvious over a dark background (see Figure 12.12).

Figure 12.10   Only the metal rings rendered.

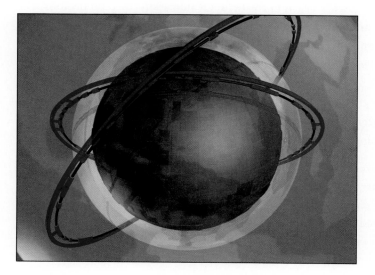

Figure 12.11   The metal rings rendered with the globe objects.

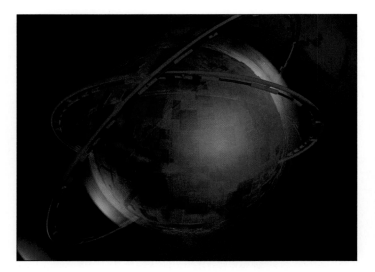

Figure 12.12   The metal rings rendered over the black background.

With these objects complete, I had the majority of the animation finished before I even started. These objects were rendered in a test animation called upfront02.avi. When you view this animation, an over-exaggerated particle trail is quite obvious in the scene. This particle trail was added to help producers visualize our idea for the animation.

Creating the Animation

Once a final logo was chosen, I began to create rough animation based on the logo. The purpose for creating this animation was to get approval for motion, look, and style. I created a rough animation with a production-quality logo. To the producers, the logo is the most important element in the animation. The rest of the animation included a rough model of the earth and gyroscope. (If you want to see the animation, view ch12\upfront3.avi on the accompanying CD.) This preview animation was sent out for approval. The producers liked the movement and how the whole look of the graphics package was progressing, so Vince and I proceeded from there.

With approval to move on with the animation, I started to plan. The peacock and camera were inside the mechanical core during the beginning of the animation (upfront3.avi), and the camera moved to the exterior of the core by the end of the animation. This presented the first problem. If you view upfront3.avi again, you will see a very noticeable jump when the camera moves to the outside of the globe and the shaded globe exterior appears. Because of this, it was clear that the animation needed to be rendered as two separate animations and then dissolved between frames 85 and 120 to transition from the globe interior to its exterior. The two animations were created with essentially the same geometry and the exact same camera motion.

Interior Animation

The interior animation is 120 frames long, making the interior appear through the end of the dissolve. At frame 89, the camera passes through the globe element. This is perfectly clear when you view upfront3.avi. The peacock object needed to be inside of this globe during frames 0–120 without the exterior of the globe ever being seen. To hide the exterior of the globe object, I had to modify it and render it separately from the peacock.

Layer 1

I loaded the core object that I built for Vince while he was designing the logo. Remember the steps I took to create the core object: I created a sphere primitive, applied an Edit Mesh modifier, and extruded random faces to create dimension. In Figure 12.13, you can see that I deleted half of the core and flipped the normals of its faces so they would face inward. I did this to allow the camera to view the interior of the core object. Because half the core is deleted, the camera can't see the exterior of the core as the camera moves outward.

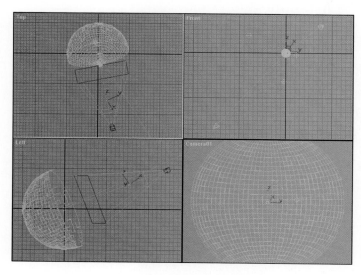

Figure 12.13   The scene that creates the background.

The 120 frames of this background scene were rendered in Video Post with a Lens Effects Focus filter to defocus the rendering (see Figure 12.14).

Figure 12.14   The rendered background with Lens Effects Focus applied.

Layer 2

After the 120-frame interior core animation was rendered, I was ready to add the peacock and interior elements. I built the scene to fit into the globe object (see Figure 12.15). Figure 12.16 shows the rendered scene.

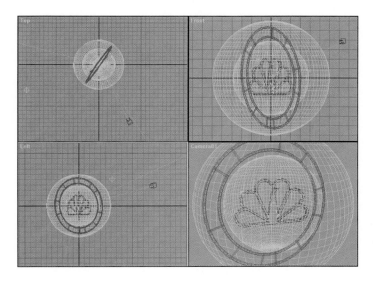

Figure 12.15   The globe interior peacock scene.

Figure 12.16 The rendered globe interior peacock scene.

The Peacock Outline

I created the peacock outline object by applying a very thick rounded bevel to the outline shape. The luminous quality of the material is the result of the Opacity Falloff Out and Opacity Type Additive filter parameter values set in the Extended Parameters of the material. Figure 12.17 shows the peacock object.

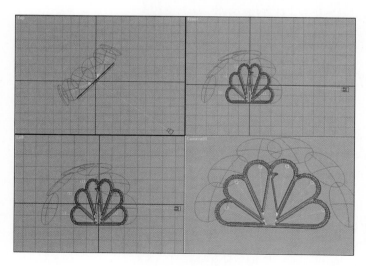

Figure 12.17 The peacock object with spotlights that generate its color.

The Peacock Feather Color

Using volumetric spotlights, I created the color in the feathers of the peacock. To create the streaks of light, I rendered six loopable noise animations, one for each color. I created these noise animations by loading a blank session of MAX, creating a camera, and applying a noise map type as the Environment Background Map. The phase of the noise map was animated to create the turbulence. I used six spotlights, starting at the center of the base of the peacock and emanating outward along each peacock feather (see Figure 12.18). I then applied the turbulent noise image sequence to each spotlight as a projection map.

Figure 12.18   The spotlights that generate the peacock feather color.

The Metal Rings

The metal rings are standard Torus objects with cylinder primitives connecting the two rings. I created the material with a Metal shader configured to make a dull specular highlight. The metal rings also have a blurred raytrace reflection type applied.

The Continents

The interior scene has two continent spheres. The first, and most obvious, is teal and is directly inside of the metal rings. The less obvious sphere is purple and is on the direct outside the metal rings. Both materials have a spherical opacity map to remove the "oceans" from the sphere. The mystical look of the continents is caused by the Additive Opacity.

The Rendered Interior Animation

After I created, lit, and animated the scene, I added the background layer to the scene as a Background Environment Map and rendered the 120-frame animation (see Figure 12.19). Oh, by the way, it took about 24 hours to render those 120 frames on three computers.

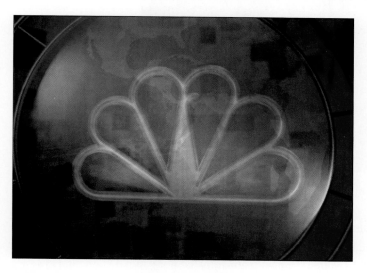

Figure 12.19   The complete interior animation.

With the interior animation complete, it was time to create the second half—the exterior animation.

Exterior Animation

Frames 0–120 of the interior animation were already created. The exterior animation consisted of frames 85–600, finishing the 20-second animation. Remember that the dissolve from interior to exterior was to occur during frames 85–120. I created many layers and composites to build the final exterior animation. Figure 12.20 shows just one frame.

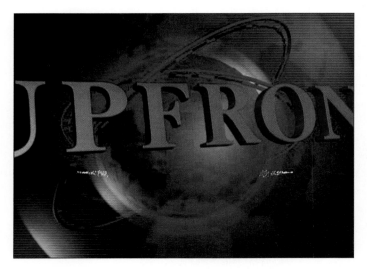

Figure 12.20   A frame from the complete exterior animation.

Layer 1: The Background

I created the background layer (shown in Figure 12.21) in much the same way we created the background for Hidden Eyes: with an animated noise radial gradient. However,
in this case, I used two animated noise gradients, one for each corner. I adjusted the U
and V offsets to place the center of the gradient in a corner. Then, by masking the radial
gradients with a Mask map type and a striped bitmap, I created the horizontal stripes in
the background.

Figure 12.21   The background layer.

Layer 2: The Background Flare

After rendering the striped background shown in Figure 12.22, I applied it into a blank MAX scene as a Background Environment Map. I created a camera and Omni lights to provide node source information for the flare effect (see Figure 12.23).

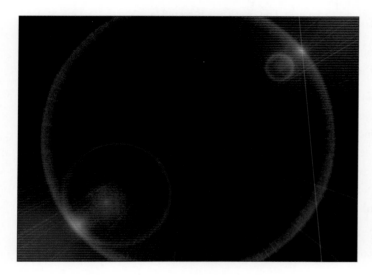

Figure 12.22   The Background flare layer.

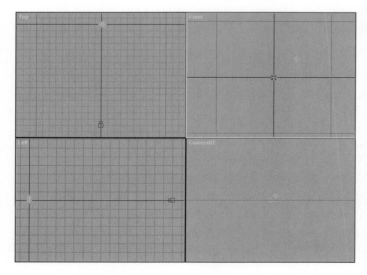

Figure 12.23   The Background flare scene.

Pay particular attention to the two Omni lights in the scene: One is in the center of the camera viewport, and one is slightly offset upward and to the right of the center Omni light. Although these lights do not illuminate anything in the scene, they are used as the node sources for the flare effects.

There are two flare effects in the scene. The first Lens Effects Flare Video Post event uses the Omni light that is centered in the Camera01 viewport. This event creates the large ring and rays applied on the background. The Omni light that is offset in the Camera01 viewport was used as the source for the secondary flares.

You might be asking yourself, "Why didn't you just use the node source in the center for the ring, rays, and secondary flares?" The answer is simple. If you recall, when we were working on the V project, we had a node source near the center of the screen. When the node source is in the center of the screen, the Scale value of the secondaries has to be increased to move the secondaries further away from the node source. Offsetting a second node source further from the center of the image not only allows me to move the secondaries further from the source without scaling, but it also allows me to align their orientation accurately.

After animating and configuring the Lens Effects Flare filters, I rendered this layer of the animation.

Layer 3: The Exterior Globe

The background was finished. It was time to create the exterior core/globe layer shown in Figure 12.24.

This was a relatively easy layer to create because I had built most of the geometry when we were designing the animation. I used the globe core, the atmosphere, the metal rings, and the continent spheres I had created during the design phase of this project. The only thing to be finalized was the particle effects.

Although there appear to be two particle trails in the final animation, there are actually four. Two particle effects create the wide trail behind the globe object, and two more create the narrower foreground particle trails. The material on the particles is a face-mapped radial gradient to which I applied noise to create a sparkling effect. The particle trails had to be carefully timed to the music track so the effect would make sense. When I finished creating this layer, it was rendered. The background was complete (see Figure 12.25).

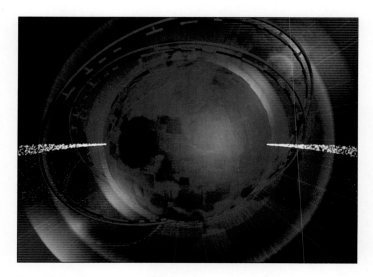

Figure 12.24   The exterior globe layer.

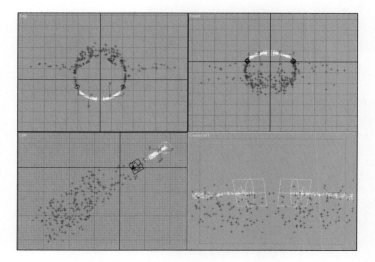

Figure 12.25   The particle effects scene.

Layer 4: The Text

The background was now complete and rendered, as shown in Figure 12.26. That meant the project is ready for the text, shown in Figure 12.27. I created the shape of the text and the horizon line in Adobe Illustrator and imported them into MAX. After adjusting the vertices of the shape, I added a rounded bevel to the logo object using Bevel Profile.

Then I applied an Edit Mesh modifier to the text and applied different Material IDs to the face, bevel, and extruded side of the logo. The materials of the logo are all two-sided to allow the interior of the logo object to be viewed through the transparent face of the logo object.

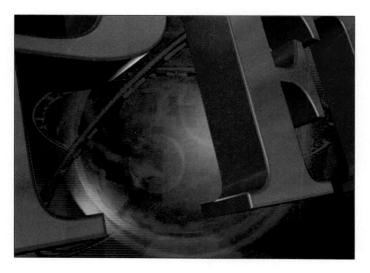

Figure 12.26   The rendered text from the animation.

Figure 12.27   The text layer.

I detached the word *Upfront* from the object to create a separate object. Then I detached each letter of *Tonight* so they could be individually animated. Also, I assigned each letter of *Tonight* a different Object ID value so I could create a unique Lens Effects Glow event for each letter.

I detached and cloned the red horizon line, creating two identical horizon objects. I applied to each of these horizon objects a unique Slice modifier to create the "write on" effect that follows the particles.

After animating the scene, I created a Video Post queue to add the glows to the individual letters of *Tonight* as they rotated. To do this, I created one Lens Effects Glow effect, saved it, and loaded it for each of the individual letters. Then I opened Track View and animated the intensity of each glow effect to cue with each letter's rotation. I rendered the queue, and the fourth layer was complete.

Layer 5: The Logo Flare

To complete the exterior animation, I needed to create the flare effects for the tips of the particle trails, as shown in Figure 12.28. I created two point helpers and bound them to a circle shape with a path motion controller (see Figure 12.29).

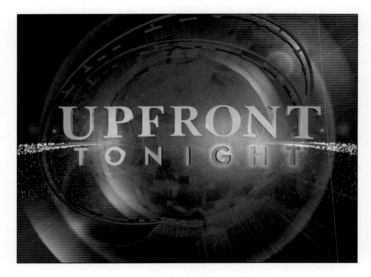

Figure 12.28   The logo flare layer.

The point helpers precisely match the motion of the particle effects. These point helpers function as the node source for the Lens Effects Flare in Video Post. The point helper that is visible in the center of the scene creates the final flare that flashes when the particle effects "crash" together.

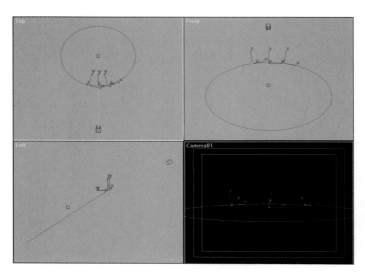

Figure 12.29 The logo flare scene.

Creating the Transition from Interior to Exterior

With the interior and exterior animations complete, I created a Video Post queue with a Cross Fade Transition to achieve the dissolve between frames 85 and 120. To help hide the dissolve, I created another Lens Effects Flare event to add secondaries over the transition (see Figure 12.30).

Figure 12.30 The dissolve transition.

You can view the finished animation by viewing ch12\upfront1.avi.

A Final Word

As an animator, I found this project to be very challenging and fun to work on. It was the first project of this size and complexity that I developed and animated entirely inside 3D Studio MAX. The combination of transparency, raytrace materials, and raytrace reflections boosted rendering times up to 45 minutes per frame for the complex layers, such as the globe with continents (see Figure 12.31). It took more than two days of rendering time rendering on a quad 200MHz Pentium Pro and two dual 300 Pentium Pros across a network. When I finished rendering the animation, it did not require any color correction or external compositing; it airs exactly the way it was rendered from 3D Studio MAX.

Figure 12.31   The completed animation.

Chapter 13

NBC News— Decision 98

A few months before the 1998 elections, the Creative Director, Sam Mandragona, approached me and asked me to start thinking about creating the election package. We envisioned the entire package being designed using the elements from the interior of the United States Capitol rotunda.

It didn't take long for me to realize that an opening animation actually taking place inside of the rotunda would create a stunning animation. It also didn't take me long to realize that it would be an overwhelming task to create such a complicated animation, which would undoubtedly have an incredible polygon count and many complex objects choreographed in a very tight space.

Building the U.S. Capitol Rotunda

After talking with Sam about the Decision 98 animation, I realized the amount of work that was in store for me. We still had a few months before the animation needed to be complete. Because we were busy with other projects, the production of the animation wasn't slated to begin for weeks. The same week, my father called me and asked if I would be interested in going to a museum exhibit in Washington DC. I accepted his invitation and told him we would need to go to the U.S. Capitol to take a few pictures of the interior.

My father and I went to the U.S. Capitol late in the day on a Saturday. It was overcast that day, and when we got inside we realized that it was far too dark to take pictures of any quality. We decided to come back Sunday morning. It was a perfect day, and the lighting inside was ideal. Between the two of us, we shot three rolls of film, photographing every visible square inch of the rotunda interior.

When the pictures were developed, I scanned them in to create textures and taped the pictures together to create a panoramic view of the rotunda. I hung up the taped pictures on my wall as an instant reference of the interior. Figure 13.1 shows the rendered interior of the rotunda, and Figure 13.2 shows the wireframe interior.

Creating the Textures

Because I wasn't officially slated to start this project, I secretly worked on it at home. I knew much of the success of the illusion of being inside the capitol was going to depend on the quality of the textures. I wanted to keep the polygon count of the rotunda low, so I decided to create detailed textures that could be applied to simple objects, which would serve as a canvas for the textures to be applied. I knew if I tried to model the details of the rotunda, the file would be huge and complicated to animate.

Figure 13.1   The rendered interior of the Capitol rotunda.

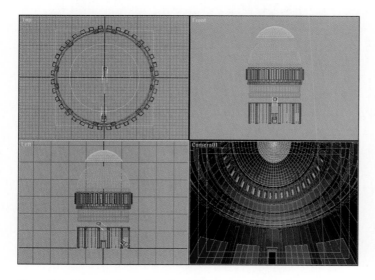

Figure 13.2   The wireframe interior of the Capitol rotunda.

The photographs of the interior of the capitol rotunda were not immediately usable. The walls in the photographs were curved and viewed from a low angle. I needed to make them square and tilable in order to use them as textures in MAX. Therefore, I loaded the scans into Photoshop and broke sections into layers. I then used the Distort transform on the texture to straighten the images. I didn't place too much importance on color correcting; I only wanted some temporary textures to see if I could create the illusion of being inside the rotunda with textures. Figure 13.3 shows three of the resulting textures.

Dome texture   **Pillar texture**   **Door texture**

Figure 13.3   Textures used to create the rotunda.

The texture used to create the rounded dome is tilable right to left. The texture used for the front of the pillars is really three textures I created so that the repetition wouldn't be visible.

Creating the Model

When I had created enough textures, I started to construct the interior of the rotunda from the bottom up. I used an architectural drawing of the rotunda interior as a reference for scale and position.

The Pillars

I created the basic shape of the pillar with a box primitive and an Edit Mesh modifier to extrude faces. When the pillar mesh was complete, I applied UVW Map modifiers to the front, left, and right sides of the pillar (see Figure 13.4).

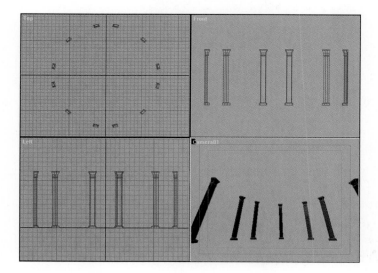

Figure 13.4 The pillar objects.

The Walls

To build the wall sections, I started with a cylinder primitive object. I carefully ensured that there were face edges behind all the pillars so I could break the cylinder into pieces for texturing purposes. The seams created at the meeting of two wall sections would be hidden behind pillars. Notice in Figure 13.5 that the edges of the wall objects are hidden behind pillars.

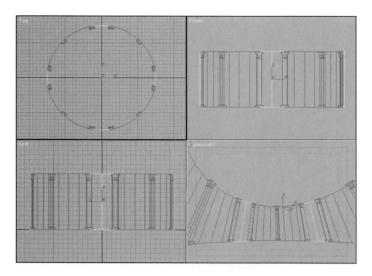

Figure 13.5 The "seams" of the wall objects are hidden behind pillars.

The wall sections that contain doors (the selected objects) were short sections of wall between two closely positioned pillars (see Figure 13.6). The main wall objects are longer, and the length of each joins two door wall sections.

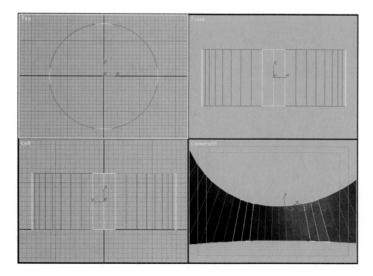

Figure 13.6 The wall objects; the door sections are selected.

When the objects were complete, I applied planar UVW Map coordinates to each wall so I could apply the brick wall texture.

The Doors and Paintings

I created the doors with a square upside-down U shape that was extruded and box modeled to create the top of the door. When the door object was complete, I added planar UVW Map coordinates for the front and sides of the object (see Figure 13.7).

The paintings are simply curved box primitives with planar UVW Map coordinates.

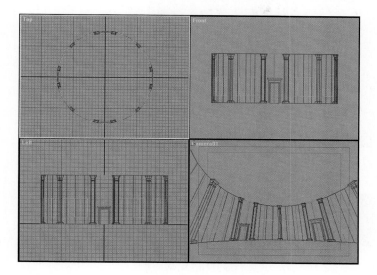

Figure 13.7   Doors and paintings are added to the scene.

The Frieze Area

The entire frieze area of the rotunda was created with tube primitive objects (see Figure 13.8). I applied an Edit Mesh modifier to each tube object, and I extruded and scaled the top polygons of the tube to create the correct profile. I applied different Material IDs to each "ring" of faces and applied cylindrical UVW Map coordinates to the objects.

The maps that were placed on the frieze objects were created to tile right to left (see Figure 13.9).

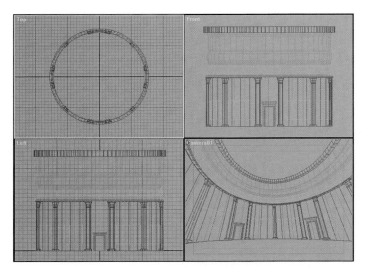

Figure 13.8   The frieze area is added to the scene.

Figure 13.9   The wreath texture for the frieze area of the rotunda.

The Windows

I created the windows from an extruded window shape and created the panes with renderable shapes. Actually, I created only one window object and instanced it around the interior of the rotunda. I then created a pillar from a box primitive and instanced it around the rotunda interior to separate the windows (see Figure 13.10).

The Dome

The dome, shown in Figure 13.11, was the simplest object to create. For each dome, I used a sphere primitive, applied an Edit Mesh modifier, and deleted the unnecessary faces. On the lower, larger dome, I applied spherical UVW Map coordinates to accept the tilable dome texture. On the higher and smaller dome cap object, I applied planar UVW Map coordinates to place the painting on the ceiling.

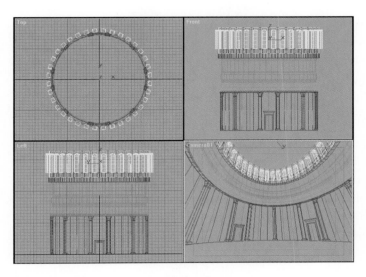

Figure 13.10   The windows are added to the scene.

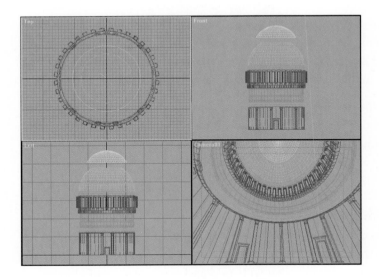

Figure 13.11   The dome objects are added to the scene.

The Floor

The floor is simply a square shape with an Edit Mesh modifier applied (to change it into a mesh) and with planar UVW Map coordinates.

Bringing the Scene to Life

It took about two weekends to texture and model the interior of the capitol rotunda. The first weekend, I built and textured everything up to and including the frieze objects. Test renders proved to be quite successful, and I couldn't wait to finish the model so I could view it in its entirety. The second weekend, I sneaked into work to build the windows and dome areas of the rotunda. When the model was finished, I was ready to create my first test render.

I used an image of a bright blue sky as the Environment Background Map using Spherical Environment coordinates. I also added a unique Material Effects ID to the Environment Background Map so I could apply a Lens Effects Glow effect to the sky. This created a soft glow of light around the windows, adding realism to the scene. I added a point helper outside the rotunda to act as the source for a Lens Effects Flare filter that would represent the sun.

I added a camera to the scene and animated it. The Video Post queue was then rendered overnight. When I came into work the following Monday, I viewed the very first test animation (ch13\capitol.avi). I called Sam into the 3D room to look at the test animation. After explaining to him when the animation was built, we agreed that the animation should, undoubtedly, take place inside the U.S. Capitol rotunda. I was relieved to see that my temporary test textures were more than enough to pull off the effect.

Sam asked Victor Newman to design the animation. Victor, in turn, approached me, and we discussed the animation. He asked for particular shots of the rotunda so he could begin to storyboard the animation. I rendered out the frames, and Victor began designing the animation.

Creating the Animation

Victor's storyboard was designed and approved well before I needed to start the animation. I had plenty of time to think through the production and creative issues in the storyboard. Victor created a very elaborate animation with an unbelievable number of objects and complicated motion choreography. It was clear by looking at the storyboard that the animation would have to be created in three sections, otherwise the camera would have to move too drastically to maintain the integrity of his idea.

When I received the music for the animation, Sam and I dissected the music into three sections, one for each part of the animation. Each section had to be separated from the others so the transitions would occur naturally. After breaking the music into sections, I animated three separate rotunda interior scenes, one for each section of music. The three sections were then edited into one animation with music. We carefully viewed the animation of the empty capitol rotunda and listened to the music to make sure the transitions fell into place in the best possible areas of the animation.

After deciding on the best places for the transitions, I began to create the animation.

Section One

To create such a complex animation, Sam and I decided it would be best to create the animation in layers. These layers would be composited by Francine Izzo in the Quantel Hal Express. The Hal Express is a proprietary 2D-animation/compositing machine. This allowed the two of us to work simultaneously. I created the scenes and rendered them; Fran color-corrected, composited, and added subtle effects.

The Rotunda Background

The rotunda background animation was animated and rendered as .tga files with Alpha Split so Fran could create a separate key signal to composite the time lapse clouds in the windows. Fran also color-corrected the rotunda rendering, saturating it with color and adding more contrast to the overall image. When Fran finished the composite, she sent the file back to me for the next layer (see Figure 13.12 and ch13\shota-01.avi on the accompanying CD).

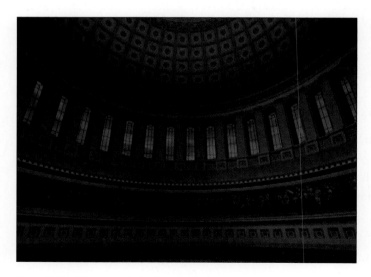

Figure 13.12   The rotunda background.

98 with Shooters

This layer of the animation contains the glass 98—the 98 outline with particles and the patriotic shooters (see Figure 13.13). Fran's background composite was returned to me so I could render this scene over it.

Figure 13.13   The 98 with shooters.

The Glass 98 and Particle Outline

Next, I added a rounded bevel to the 98 shape, creating the glass 98. The material on the glass 98 was the result of a Metal shader with a relatively strong specular highlight. I applied a colorful reflection bitmap to the glass 98 to create the splashes of color that appear on its surface. I also added colored lights in the scene to add more color to the glass object. Figure 13.14 shows the wireframe.

The outline that emanates from the 98 is a copy of the 98 shape. The 98 shape has Renderable checked, so the shape would render as a thin outline object. The material applied to the outline is similar to the glass 98 material, except the Additive Opacity Type is active to create its bright appearance.

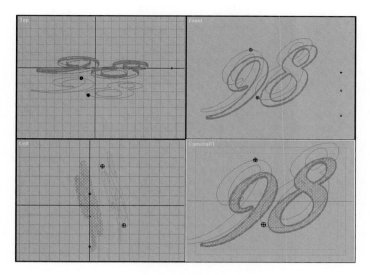

Figure 13.14   The wireframe for glass 98 and particle outline.

The particles that travel along the 98 outline are Particle Cloud particle systems. A low speed value and 10% motion inheritance is applied to the particles. As the emitter moves, the particles not only travel their low speed value but also inherit the motion of the emitter. The particle type is facing, and the material applied to the particles is a bright orange color with a radial gradient opacity map. The radial gradient creates a hot particle core and a soft falloff around the edge of the particle. Each particle cloud emitter was assigned a different Path motion controller. One path was created for the 9 and another for the 8.

The Patriotic Shooters

The shooters, shown in Figure 13.15, are Torus primitives with an animated slice to make them "write on." Each shooter is actually two Torus primitives; the circumference of one is slightly smaller than that of the other, but the radius they travel is the same. This creates a glow effect.

This is how this method creates a glow effect: The material on the shooters is a 50 percent transparent two-sided material, and a 100 percent Falloff Out amount is applied in the Extended Parameters of the material. Also, Additive Opacity Type is active. The Falloff Out instructs the material to fade around the edges, creating a more solid core. The Additive Opacity Type makes the material brighter as it overlaps itself and the background.

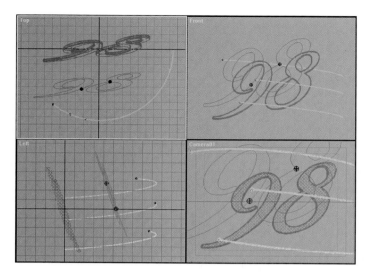

Figure 13.15   The wireframe for the patriotic shooters.

The smaller Torus in the center of the effect creates a bright effect because, at that point, there are four additive layers (material double-sided). The larger Torus, because of the opacity falloff, creates the glow effect. To add dimension to the shooters, a screen-mapped linear gradient was used as an opacity map. The gradient went from left to right and was black on the sides of the screen and white in the middle. This made the shooters more transparent on the sides of the image and brighter in the center.

A particle cloud emitter was animated to follow the "tips" of the shooters. To animate the particle cloud to follow the tip of each shooter, the particle cloud was positioned at its start point, and the pivot for the emitter was positioned in the center of shooter circles. This enabled the emitter to be rotated on its local axis and travel in a circle. The particles had very little speed and 10 percent motion inheritance, which simulated the spark effect perfectly.

This scene was rendered and given to Fran for color correction (ch13\shota-02.avi).

The State Names

Usually when I create text, someone traces the text out in Adobe Illustrator and sends me the outlines. You may recall importing an .ai file when we were working on the Hidden Eyes logo; if so, you know what a pain it could be to fix all the shapes and vertices. I wasn't looking forward to adjusting 50 states worth of shape names. Therefore, instead of getting all the state names as one huge file, I got all the letters of the alphabet so I would only have to adjust each letter once. In turn, I had to spell out each state name individually in MAX (see Figure 13.16).

Figure 13.16 The state names.

I created one big shape of all of the state names and applied a bevel modifier (a rounded bevel would have added way too many polygons to the scene). After beveling the text, I assigned a different Material ID to the face, bevel, and side of the object. I then detached the five rows of text into separate objects, scaled them to different sizes, and applied a Bend modifier to arch the rows of text. I applied a gold transparent material to the face and sides of the state names and a silver bevel. I matched the arc of the state names to the shooters by using the shooter animation as a background and adjusting the camera (see Figure 13.17).

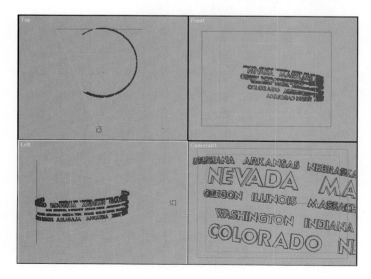

Figure 13.17 The wireframe state names.

This layer was rendered and sent to Fran for color correction and enhancement. Along with the Alpha Split key info, I used the three different Material IDs on the state name object to give Fran a matte for the face, bevel, and sides of the objects. Fran used these mattes to punch up the color and add more color to areas of the state names that needed work. The resulting animation was then ready for its final layer (ch13\shota-03.avi).

NBC News and Stars

Creating this layer was much like creating the previous layer. I created and beveled shapes for the stars and NBC News text. I applied unique Material IDs to the face, bevel, and side of the beveled objects and then applied materials. The image on the stars is simply a diffuse map. When the objects were complete, I applied a Bend modifier to the object to create an arch to match the state names. The scene was then rendered and sent to Fran for color correction and final effects.

When Fran finished this layer, we decided we should apply a Lens Effects Flare effect to the 98. I created an animated lens flare, much like the one we created during the V project. Fran rendered it over a gold background and composited it over the animation. The first section of the animation was complete (see Figure 13.18 and ch13\shota-04.avi on the accompanying CD).

Figure 13.18   NBC News and stars.

Section Two

Section one was complete, and it looked great. This was the first time we attempted a 3D-compositing project of this scale, and the result was great. Fran and I were getting a knack for working together, raiding one another's CD collections for music to keep us going while we were working those long days.

It was time to create the second section of the animation. It turned out to be a very tricky endeavor. Everything had to appear as though it was exactly the same as the first shot so that when the camera transitioned, it wouldn't look as though any time had passed from section one to section two. It had to look live, as though it was all taking place then and there, and the whole event was so huge that multiple cameras were needed to capture it all.

The Rotunda Background

This background was much like the background for section one. I created a camera to look directly downward at the rotunda floor and animated the camera to slowly rise higher in the rotunda. Fran used the Alpha Split animation to composite the clouds in the windows. We thought this was very funny because you would certainly not be seeing clouds if you were in the top of the rotunda looking down through the windows. If you were looking down through the windows you would see the top of the Capitol building, a parking lot, or the ground. But because the clouds looked so cool in the windows, we collectively agreed to take the "If you don't tell, I won't tell" approach, and we left the clouds in. Fran also added a slight blur to the center of the image, which created a deep-focus effect (see Figure 13.19 and ch13\shotb-01.avi on the accompanying CD).

Figure 13.19 The rotunda background.

The Patriotic Shooters

The next layer to be rendered over the rotunda background was the patriotic shooters. The shooters had to appear to be continuing from the previous shot, so I created them using an animated slice Torus object in the beginning of the animation. I created a second set of shooters and animated them to cue with a musical accent. This layer was rendered and sent to Fran for color correction (see Figure 13.20 and ch13\shotb-02.avi on the accompanying CD).

Figure 13.20   The patriotic shooters.

The Stars

The stars in this shot ended up being very tricky. It was complicated to make the motion of the stars look natural and fluid. I created these stars by beveling a star shape and assigning different Material IDs to the face, bevel, and side. I applied a Bend modifier to give the stars a slight bend. Then, to control the animation of the stars, I added dummy objects to the scene (see Figures 13.21 and 13.22).

I created a dummy in the center of the scene for each star. The dummy was used to animate the lift of the star objects individually. The local X axis of the star objects was used to rotate the stars to face the camera.

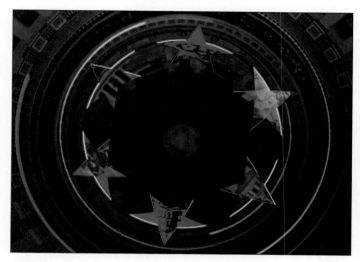

Figure 13.21   The stars.

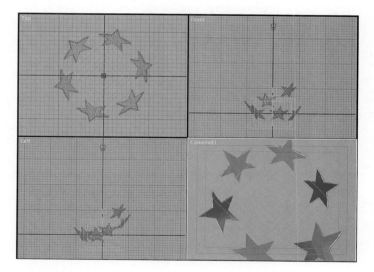

Figure 13.22   The star scene.

In the .avi for this layer (ch13\shotb-03.avi), you will notice that there are vertical stripes in the stars as they rotate toward the camera. That is the reflection of the rotunda windows on the star. Because the stars were not actually in the rotunda, I had to use a Reflect/Refract map of the rotunda. I created the Reflect/Refract map by opening the rotunda scene and creating a point helper in the center of its area. In the Material Editor, I chose a Reflect/Refract map type and chose the point helper to create and save the map. Doing so created six images: top, bottom, right, left, front, and back (see Figure 13.23). These images are seamless to one another and create a cube map that will surround the star objects.

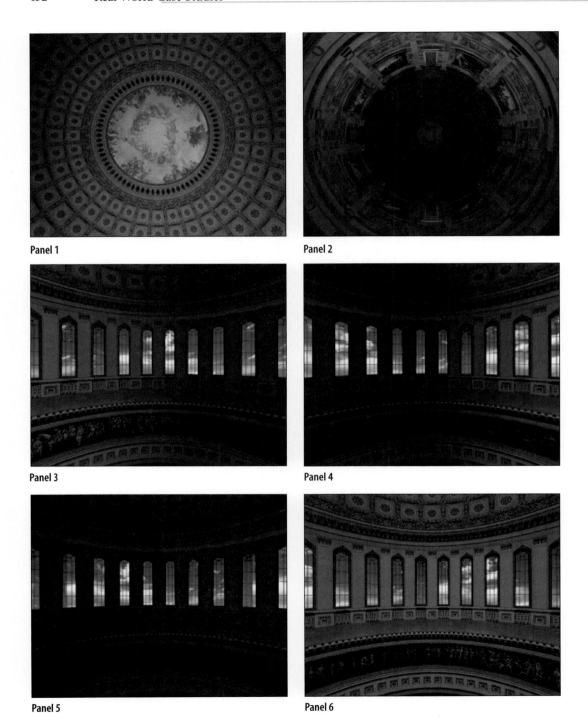

Panel 1

Panel 2

Panel 3

Panel 4

Panel 5

Panel 6

Figure 13.23   The Reflection/Refraction images for the star.

You might notice that the sky in the Reflect/Refract images is blue, and not purple as it appears in the final render. Shhhh! If you don't tell, I won't tell. You will see the Reflect/Refract map on many of the objects in the animation.

This layer was rendered and sent to Fran for composite and color correction. When she finished, she sent it back to me to add the next layer.

The NBC News—Decision 98 Logo Build

Figure 13.24 shows a critical layer in the scene. It illustrates the formation of the NBC News—Decision 98 logo in the animation. I created it in two separate layers to give to Fran for composite.

Figure 13.24   The NBC News—Decision 98 logo build.

The NBC Peacock

The peacock was the first layer I completed (see Figure 13.25). It had to be a separate layer so Fran could transition it in and out as needed. To create the peacock, I applied a rounded bevel to a peacock shape. When animating the peacock, I carefully positioned lights to create highlights as it rotated with the NBC chimes in the music.

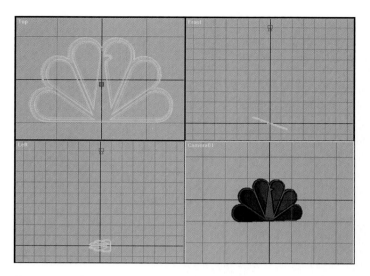

Figure 13.25   The NBC peacock scene.

The NBC News—Decision 98 Logo Build

Every object needed its own unique motion and rotation, but they all had to act like one unit. Therefore, I had to create a complex hierarchy for the logo objects (see Figures 13.26 and 13.27).

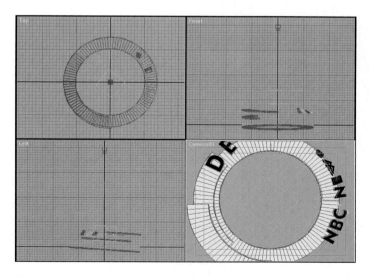

Figure 13.26   The NBC News—Decision 98 viewport at this point.

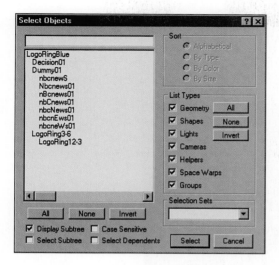

Figure 13.27   The hierarchy of the logo objects.

The blue logo ring was the parent object of the hierarchy; this ring would slowly rotate top forward during the animation, rotating the sibling logo object with it. The Decision text was positioned next, and its pivot was centered to the logo so the text could be slowly rotated around the circumference of the blue ring.

The NBC NEWS text was trickier to animate. It had to rotate around the circumference of the blue ring, but each letter was to rotate on its individual local axis to lay down on the logo. To achieve this effect, I detached each letter and made it a unique object. I centered the pivot to each logo, rotated to its start position, and linked each letter to the parent dummy helper. The parent dummy helper rotates the NBC NEWS letters around the circumference of the logo ring, but each letter's local axis was used to lay the letter down individually.

The LogoRing3-6 and LogoRing12-3 objects are the teal and orange one-quarter rings that appear at 12 to 3 o'clock and 3 to 6 o'clock on the finished logo. For each ring, I moved its pivot to the center of the logo. When the LogoRing3-6 object rotates, the LogoRing12-3 moves with it and with its very subtle rotation.

This Decision 98 logo and the Peacock layers were sent to Fran for compositing. She applied the logo object first and then dissolved the peacock in and out of the scene. Fran also created and applied the soft orange glow in the center of the logo (ch13\shotb-04.avi).

98 and Lens Flares

This section was essentially complete. All that was left was to render out another 98 and create some lens flares to add punch and continuity to the scene, as shown in Figure 13.28.

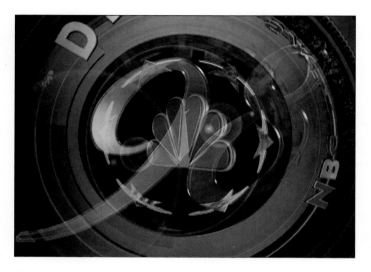

Figure 13.28   The 98 and lens flares.

The 98

The 98 was simple: I loaded it from the previous section and saved it with a unique name. I deleted the particle systems and created and rendered a new camera animation.

The Lens Flares

For this, I created a camera and positioned two point helpers in the scene to act as the node sources for the two flares in this section. The first flare is the quick flare that transitions the peacock into the scene. The flare was created much like the Lens Flare we created in the V project. The intensity was animated to transition the flare in and out of the scene. The plane of each secondary was animated to "burst" the secondaries from the source. There is also an animated ring element in the flare.

The second flare is the lingering flare that appears with the musical accent of the harp in the music. The flare was created in the same way as the previous one, by animating the intensity of the flare and the plane of the secondaries. Once again, an animated ring was added to the flare to help the burst effect.

The 98 and flares were sent to Fran for compositing (ch13\shotb-05.avi). This completed the second section of the animation.

Section Three

As with everything, time is of the essence. Unfortunately, time wasn't on our side. I began section three of the animation only two days before the entire animation was to be completed. That didn't leave too much time for experimentation or error. The good thing was that most of the complicated animation was already complete, and all that was left was to finish the logo build.

The Rotunda Background

The rotunda background animations were complete for all three shots before we even started the rest of the animation. We thought it would be cool if we could see the Washington, D.C. skyline through the windows of the rotunda. I found a fairly accurate shot of what might be seen from the rotunda windows, created the skyline, and gave it to Fran to help her create the night sky background. She took the skyline, added it to the time lapse clouds, and composited the rotunda interior over it. When you view the animation, you will see the Washington Monument through a window to the left of the scene (see Figure 13.29 and ch13\shotc-01.avi on the accompanying CD). Unfortunately, in the finished animation, most of the skyline is covered by the logo and is not visible.

Figure 13.29   The rotunda background.

The Logo Stars

We decided the star objects should appear from the bottom of the screen and arc upward to form the ring of stars around the logo. Because we were extremely tight on time, I started thinking about the easiest and fastest way to create the effect. I thought about using a path follow and created some tests. However, each star following the same path shape would require animating each star individually and entering in different start and end percent of path values to have the stars end in the correct positions. There had to be an easier way than that.

I created one star object, moved its pivot to the virtual center of the logo, and used that pivot point to rotate and instance the remaining stars. Each star was now an individual object that could be animated separately. The pivot was in the same place in 3D space for each star object. If I selected all the stars and rotated them about their local axis, they would all rotate in unison around the circumference of the logo (see Figure 13.30).

Figure 13.30   The logo stars.

I moved and rotated all the stars, in unison, to the start position. I advanced to frame 90 and activated the Animate button. Then I rotated and moved all the stars, in unison, to their finish position. The stars all moved and rotated to the finish position in unison. Finally, I opened the Track View and offset each individual star's track to make each star animate independently of the others (see Figure 13.31).

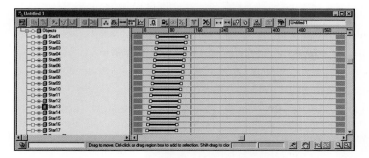

Figure 13.31   The Track View for the star objects.

You can view the result of the animation in all four viewports by viewing ch13\
shotc-02w.avi.

By mere accident, some of the stars appear on the right side of the screen as they travel
downward to reappear from the bottom center of the screen. Because they did travel off
the screen before they reappeared at the bottom, I knew Fran could fix it in composite,
so I left it that way. I sent the layers to Fran, and the resulting composite was complete
(ch13\shotc-02.avi).

Notice in the bottom right corner of the screen that the stars are still traveling downward
and off the screen, only to reappear as they travel upward. This was because of a mis-
communication between Fran and me. She did remove some of the stars that appeared
higher on the right side, but not the lower ones. She will fix that when she composites
the next layer. When you examine the next composite, you will see that the stars in the
lower right are removed.

The NBC News—Decision 98 Logo Build

Now we were really crashing for time. We had about a day and a half to finish the animation in its entirety. I still needed to finish the logo build. Because I didn't have much
time, I loaded the logo elements from the previous section and used them as my elements. Fran created the flag animation that was placed on the disc in the center of the
logo. I animated the logo and started rendering test frames to make sure everything
looked fine. The NBC NEWS type needed to be changed to black, so I made that quick
material adjustment. However, the test renders of the black letters on the ring looked flat
and unacceptable. I asked Fran if there was anything she could do to give the NBC NEWS
text a little punch in the composite, and we agreed that she should put a slight glow
around it.

I rendered the scene, and when it was finished, I rendered a second pass of only the NBC NEWS type so she could add a glow to it using the Alpha Split animation. Fran composited the logo elements and added the light blue glow to the NBC NEWS type. She also added a gold glow around the stars and the logo object during the composite using the Alpha Split of the layers. When she finished the composite (see Figure 13.32 and ch13\shotc-03.avi on the accompanying CD), she sent it back to me for the next layer.

Figure 13.32   The NBC News—Decision 98 logo after Fran finished the composite.

The 98

All that was left was to animate the 98 for the logo. I simply loaded the previous 98 from the other sections and animated it to join with the logo. In this section, the glass 98 needed to transform into a chrome 98. Because we were so tight for time, we decided that Fran would create the transformation in the Hal Express. I rendered the entire animation with a glass 98, and then I rendered the entire animation with a chrome 98. This way Fran had complete control over the transition, and she could more easily make changes to the timing. Fran created the drop shadow on the logo disc by using the Alpha Split animation of the 98 (see Figure 13.33 and ch13\shotc-04.avi on the accompanying CD).

Figure 13.33   The 98.

Final Effects

We were in the last day of production for the animation when we reached this phase. Tension was certainly high, and we knew that we had to finish the animation.

The 98 Outline

To tie the end of the animation in with the beginning, we decided to bring back the 98 outline with the particle highlights. Because of the short time window, I loaded the outline and particle cloud elements from the first section and adjusted their keyframes to match the motion of the logo build in the third section. I rendered the outline and particles and gave the animation to Fran for composite.

The Lens Flares

While Fran was compositing the 98 outline into the scene, I quickly created the two lens flares for the scene. I didn't concern myself with the timing of the flares, because I knew Fran could composite them in during the appropriate frames in the animation. I started with a new scene and created a camera and node sources in the correct positions. I loaded the flares that I created previously for the other sections and adjusted their parameters to create the necessary lens flares.

Fran took these elements into the Hal and created the final composite (see Figure 13.34 and ch13\shotc-05.avi on the accompanying CD).

Figure 13.34 Final effects.

A Final Word

When the three sections were complete, my job was finished. I sat with Fran as she attached the three sections with dissolves. She added the music, and we watched the animation. It looked great (see Figure 13.35, and ch13\done.avi on the accompanying CD). All of the planning and hard work really paid off. It was remarkable how fantastic all the elements that I carefully cued to music meshed together, creating a very moving and interesting animation. This was our first attempt at an animation of this scale, and it was a success. To this day, we can play the animation with no audio and hum the music with perfect cadence.

This animation, in its entirety, aired only one day. However, the interior of the U.S. Capitol rotunda was used throughout the package (I built those animations while working on this project), and Fran manipulated the layers of this animation to create shorter versions of the animation that were aired several days following the election.

Figure 13.35   The completed animation.

Index

O

Q-R